1985

Communication and Group Process

Consulting Editor, Michael Burgoon

Communication and Group Process

Techniques for Improving the Quality of Small-Group Communication

Third Edition

Halbert E. Gulley
Northern Illinois University

Dale G. Leathers
University of Georgia

Holt, Rinehart and Winston
New York   Chicago   San Francisco   Atlanta
Dallas   Montreal   Toronto   London   Sydney

Library of Congress Cataloging in Publication Data

Gulley, Halbert E
Communication and group process.

First and second editions published in 1960 and 1968 under title: Discussion, conference, and group process. Includes bibliographies and index.
1. Interpersonal communication.   2. Small groups.
I. Leathers, Dale G., 1938-   joint author.
II. Title.
BF637.C45G84   1977   301.15'54   76-44532
ISBN 0-03-089406-9

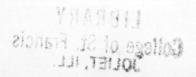

Preface

This book presents a new and distinctive approach to the study of small-group communication. Although the first edition, *Discussion, Conference, and Group Process,* appeared in 1960, this third edition, *Communication and Group Process,* develops an original perspective unlike that in any other book on small-group communication.

Although we believe that this conceptual perspective will prove to be very valuable, we have not forsaken those subject areas that made earlier editions of this book so popular. For example, Part 2 provides the type of knowledge that is essential for one to be an intelligent and productive member of a small group.

Truly amazing changes have come about in our society and our attitudes about how we should relate to each other. The changes are at least equally large in approaches to small-group communication.

There is today less emphasis on controlled laboratory research as a means of discovering how individuals and small groups operate to bring about consensus and more interest in field studies and observations in "real" situations. There is much more concern with individual awareness, fulfillment, and authenticity and with sensitivity to the group's impact. Even labels have changed. *Discussion* was the name most often given earlier to decision-making interaction in the small group. Although we still use the word *discussion* today, we prefer *small-group communication* as the label for our approach to the study of interaction because it suggests more adequately the many complexities involved.

In this third edition, there are two authors where formerly there was one, and this change, too, reflects the growing complexity of this area of study.

Despite the changes in scope and interest, our two central goals in offering this book remain unchanged. We propose to help students to understand better how groups function and to what ends and especially to gain insight into the functions and operation of *communication* in small groups. Secondly, we aim to help students become better group members and especially to be more effective communicators and listeners in small-group situations. Our primary focus will be on small group decision making.

Almost everyone receives frequent practice in group interaction. The family is often a discussion group. Participation in decision making, long characteristic of democracy, has in recent years become important in businesses, labor unions, churches, colleges, and virtually all organizations where people work together or socialize. Increasing interdependence in a complex society means more reliance on group decisions and fewer instances where individuals can go their isolated ways. Increasingly, also, group interaction is being used to achieve self-understanding and therapy.

Discussion looks easy because it is a common experience, largely unstructured and informal; but much of the interaction occurring in small groups is of poor quality. Because interaction involves complex relationships, reaching good decisions is not easy, and communication skill in group situations does not develop by accident. Thoughtful group members do not underestimate the need for study of small group communication.

Some people feel that able individuals naturally possess the capacity to talk with others or that such aptitude develops through exposure and casual experience. Although natural ability, intelligence, and experience contribute to effectiveness, study and directed practice are essential.

This book can, of course, be used to satisfy a great variety of instructional and individual needs. Where there is flexibility as to the way an individual studies the small group, we would suggest that the individual actually be given the experience of working in a group. The most realistic and valuable experience in groups typically comes outside of the classroom. Thus we would draw your attention to the "group project" assignment set out at the end of Chapter 1. We have found that this assignment provides a stimulating learning experience that allows the group members to apply many of the concepts in this book. This assignment focuses attention on the relationship between quality of group communication and product.

Our efforts as the authors of this book were truly interdependent. From the time of our first meeting until we read the last page proofs, we have had numerous in-depth discussions. Because we stress the importance of self-disclosure in this book, we candidly admit that we experienced conflict along the way. Certainly, our vigorous and sometimes heated exchanges did not suffer from the debilitating effects of a consensus environment. We are pleased to report that a positive interpersonal outcome has resulted from our many meetings. We will be even more pleased if you agree that we have produced a high quality product.

It is a pleasure to acknowledge the contributions and help of many persons in the preparation of the third edition. Our indebtedness is great to those colleagues who have generously given constructive criticism. Editor Roth Wilkofsky exhibited commendable interpersonal skills. We also wish to express our gratitude to Nadine Gulley for able editorial assistance and to Virgene Martin for expert typing as well as editorial improvement. Finally, we wish to express gratitude to Nancy and Stephen Leathers for their nonmanipulative and trusting behavior.

H. E. G.
DeKalb, Illinois

D. G. L.
Athens, Georgia

June 9, 1976

Contents

Communication and Group Process

Part 1
THE NATURE
OF SMALL-GROUP
COMMUNICATION

Executive conference room of the Royal Crown Bottling Company; printed with permission.

1 An Approach to Small-Group Communication

Small-group communication is a distinctive phenomenon. It is distinctive because groups possess the
potential to produce complex, high-quality outcomes
not associated with any other type of human communication. It is distinctive because the members will encounter a set of forces that do not operate in any other environment; these forces may either be exploited or
exploitative. It is distinctive, finally, because those intragroup forces interact with the communication skills and personal qualities of the discussants
in ways that can promote or impede the attainment of the personal and
professional goals of group members.

The complexity of small-group communication is undeniable. It can be
either a source of satisfaction or frustration. Such complexity makes small-
group communication uniquely challenging. Effective communication in
the small group demands constant vigilance and continuous concentration.

Consider for the moment the picture opposite this page. The photograph
features the conference table of a major corporation in the United States.
The discussions held around this conference table have affected the lives
of many individuals. These discussions have frequently taxed the communication skills of the conferees to the limit. We, of course, cannot
possibly know all the factors that interacted to shape the communication
and the decisions that resulted. We can, however, imagine how we might
function were we seated at this table.

As an effective communicator, we would have to be aware of all those
factors that might affect communicative interaction. What do you believe

4

these factors would be? Which ones would you consider desirable and which undesirable?

Did you consider the following factors: the impact of seating arrangement on the perceived status of the participants, the relative inability of the discussants seated at the ends of the table to make effective use of the nonverbal cues of the other conferees, the question of whether this group is using an agenda, the possibility that the group is too large for balanced and vigorous interaction, the possibility that this group lacks effective leadership, and the probability that group members did not make full use of the corrective potential of available feedback?

This is just a beginning. Many other factors may have a significant impact on the quality of communication in this group. Individually and collectively, these factors may function to create serious communication problems. This is a sobering realization when we consider that few groups deal effectively with the communication problems that they encounter. In fact, most groups have a limited capacity to deal with such communication problems because members neither recognize the communication problems when they occur nor have the knowledge of the techniques needed to deal satisfactorily with the problems when they do arise.

Major Approaches to the Study of the Small Group

"A democratic society derives its strength from the effective functioning of the multitude of groups that it contains. Its most valuable resources are the groups of people found in its homes, communities, schools, churches, business concerns, union halls, and various branches of government. Now, more than ever before, it is recognized that these units must perform their functions well if the larger systems are to work successfully." [1]

We can recognize the general validity of this observation and still have some reservations about it. To study small groups realistically is to recognize that *there is often a major gap between our idealized picture of what a group ought to be and what it actually is.* Too frequently, we believe, authors of books such as this one are inclined to substitute an idealistic picture of the perfect group for the more realistic picture of a group that typically encounters serious problems.

There is a danger in uncritically accepting popular misconceptions about the small group. Our own study of the small group is apt to be more realistic if we are on the alert for such misconceptions. The follow-

[1] D. Cartwright and A. Zander, eds., *Group Dynamics: Research and Theory,* Third Edition (New York: Harper and Row, 1968), p. vii.

ing are merely suggestive of a great number of misconceptions that have persisted over time: (1) groups are basically democratic in nature, (2) groups usually have well-defined objectives and goals, (3) groups usually become more important to their members than their individual needs, (4) groups engage in discussion but not debate, and (5) groups must be free from dissension and conflict to be effective.

Such reservations do not suggest any disillusionment or disenchantment with the small group. They simply suggest that we must work in groups under conditions as we find them. These conditions are rarely utopian and frequently far different from what we would prefer.

Our study of the small group is further complicated by the fact that groups serve a wide variety of functions and purposes. Clearly, a panel discussion, an encounter group, and a work group vary not only with regard to basic function but with regard to the conceptual perspective from which they may most fruitfully be studied. Thus the psychologist often uses the group as a way of releasing the inhibitions of the members and, ultimately, identifying their emotional problems. The sociologist studies the small group to discover hidden forces that may be working in larger societal units. Finally, the communicologist studies the group with the aim of understanding the dynamics of interaction that determine the quality of communication.

To achieve their disparate objectives, researchers have necessarily used strikingly different approaches in their study of the small group. The following approaches seem particularly important for the reader of this book: (1) the human potential approach, (2) the rhetorical approach, (3) the group dynamics approach, and (4) the systems approach.

THE HUMAN POTENTIAL APPROACH

To a large extent, the human potential movement is a response to a change in our cultural values:

> The rapid technological change we have been experiencing for the past several decades has resulted in rapid cultural change within our society. Our culture seems to be changing from an emphasis on achievement to an emphasis upon self-actualization, from self-control to self-expression, from independence to interdependence, from endurance of stress to capacity for joy, from full employment to full lives.[2]

Nonetheless, many individuals reject the human potential movement and the approach to groups that it represents. This rejection seems to be based on two factors: (1) a belief that the human potential approach symbolizes a rejection of the work ethic and our traditional preoccupa-

[2] D. W. Johnson, *Reaching Out: Interpersonal Effectiveness and Self-Actualization* (Englewood Cliffs, N.J.: Prentice-Hall, 1972), p. 2.

6   tion with a group's productivity and (2) a belief that the human potential approach is the result of fuzzy thinking and impressionistic research.

Make no mistake about it. Many people still believe that problem solving is the only legitimate purpose for which a group should be used. They assert somewhat smugly that with sufficient "problem pressure" even highly incompatible members will get the job done. This fixation on group productivity has tended to polarize thinking. If you express concern for the interpersonal needs of group members, you are apt to be dismissed as a "fun and games" type.

In addition, some reject the human potential approach on methodological grounds. Opponents of the approach claim that it emphasizes the visceral response at the expense of the logical response; they claim that it is based on the subjective interpretation of nonempirical research. Indeed they note derisively that today it's "astrology, tomorrow yoga, biofeedback on Tuesday, encounter groups on Thursday. From the occult solution to the touchy-feely solution and back again we wind our desperate way. Or you can take your choice among Billy Graham, the Jesus Freaks, or the latest guru from India." [3]

We contend that such beliefs are errant because they are based only partially on fact. Johnson notes perceptively that such beliefs are geared to the dubious assumption that "a person's interpersonal effectiveness increases as his behavior becomes more rational, logical, and objective. To the contrary, a person's interpersonal effectiveness increases as all the relevant information (including feeling) becomes conscious, discussable, and controllable." [4]

Thus the main value of the human potential approach may be traced to the assumption that effective communication requires a sensitive reading of and response to the feelings of those with whom we communicate. To do less is to invite serious communication problems, is to risk the inaccurate perception of events and information, and ultimately is to risk the positive interpersonal relationships that are a major part of high quality communication. [5]

In broadest perspective we should recognize that the conceptual territory of the human potential movement has not been clearly defined. This problem and the excesses of some proponents of the approach should not obscure the insights that the movement has provided, however. Indeed, the unifying goal of heightening personal and interpersonal awareness seems commendable. This goal is pursued from a variety of specific perspectives. These perspectives might be put on a continuum that ranges from a concentration on personal awareness to interpersonal awareness— biofeedback, transcendental meditation, body and sensory awareness,

[3] S. L. Tubbs and J. W. Baird, *The Open Person: Self-Disclosure and Personal Growth* (Columbus, Ohio: Charles E. Merrill, 1976), p. 6.

[4] Johnson, *Reaching Out*, pp. 89–90.

[5] Ibid., p. 90.

gestalt therapy, transactional analysis, general semantics, and encounter groups.[6]

The human potential approach uses the group not as a vehicle for developing products but as a means for gaining greater insight into the personal and interpersonal behavior that takes place in the group. Although this approach is very different from the systems approach used in this book, it provides useful concepts and techniques that are selectively integrated into the conceptual framework of this book.

THE RHETORICAL APPROACH

The rhetorical approach to the small group is the oldest but by no means the least useful. Rhetoric and its counterpart, dialectic, draw attention to the vitally important functions of the verbal communication system. Aristotle and Plato both took an interest in these two subjects and it was Socrates, of course, who used skillful questioning as a means of clarifying thought and eliciting precise answers during speculative discussions. Through the intervening centuries, rhetoric—the study of persuasion and the complex interrelationships among communicator, message, and the responses of receivers—has enjoyed more consistent favor. Rhetoric has been tarnished in some periods, however, through misuse by the sophists of early Greece and through distortion by the elocutionists of the nineteenth century in Britain and the United States. It has received emphasis in the twentieth century, being newly championed within departments of speech communication in America. Recently, it has been revived as a respectable study within many departments of English in its full-bodied sense rather than as only a truncated course satisfying the freshman composition requirement.

Departments of speech communication not only have sponsored courses in classical rhetoric but also have offered courses in persuasive speaking and have promoted extracurricular debating activities where rhetorical principles again assumed importance. The rediscovery of dialectic has been slower and less direct.

The Greek sophists damaged the reputation of dialectic as well as rhetoric. Aristotle thought dialectic useful in developing skill in reasoning, defining, and in asking and answering questions; it offers a "process of criticism wherein lies the path to the principles of all inquiries." For Plato, dialectic was even more valuable, being a disciplined path to truth including all of logic. Where the sophists used the method for logical hairsplitting and verbal gymnastics, Socrates employed it for serious inquiry. In Plato's *Republic,* Socrates advocates postponing the study of dialectic until the age of thirty because youngsters "when they first get the taste in their mouths, argue for amusement" and "like puppy-dogs, they rejoice in pull-

---

[6] Tubbs and Baird, *The Open Person,* p. 4

ing and tearing at all who come near them. . . . But when a man begins to get older, he will no longer be guilty of such insanity; he will imitate the dialectician who is seeking for truth, and not the sophist, who is contradicting for the sake of amusement."

The respectability of dialectic was not helped at all by the scholars of the Middle Ages, who had more time on their hands than facts with which to speculate about the realm of the spirit and the number of angels who could dance on the head of a pin. Neither has the word recovered from its use by Karl Marx in his conception of dialectical materialism.

Nevertheless, contemporary interest in group discussion has some of its roots in dialectic, for the method has been used by some persons in the past as a serious and orderly process of inquiry: "It is concerned with every phase of thought: with the establishment of definitions; the examination of hypotheses in the light of their presuppositions or consequences; the formulation of inferences and proofs; the resolution of dilemmas arising from opposition in thought."[7] The same departments of speech communication that gave a new birth to rhetoric began in the 1930s to introduce courses in discussion. At the University of Illinois in 1936, L. S. Judson produced a paperback, *Manual of Group Discussion*, and in 1939 from the School of Speech, Northwestern University, came a textbook published nationally for use in college courses.

The rhetorical approach emphasizes the development of critical thinking skills. Critical thinking skills "include both dialectical and investigative abilities: those *attitudes* useful to the exercise of critical intelligence; the *knowledge* of techniques of reasoning necessary to effective critical thinking; and the skills of discourse needed in the analysis of evidence and reasoning and the communication of reasoned opinion."[8]

Critical thinking skills are emphasized in Chapters 4, 5, and 6 of this book; they are the type of skills that can be developed only by diligent study and hard work. In some quarters it has become fashionable to dismiss such skills as old hat. If you are truly concerned about the quality of group outcomes, however, the neglect of your critical thinking skills is a luxury you cannot afford.

THE GROUP DYNAMICS APPROACH

The group dynamics approach continues to provide the student of the small group with much valuable knowledge. It differs from the human potential approach in the requirement that conclusions about the small group must be supported by carefully conducted empirical research.

[7] "Dialectic," *The Great Ideas: A Syntopicon of Great Books of the World* (Chicago: Encyclopaedia Britannica, 1952), p. 347.

[8] W. S. Howell and D. K. Smith, *Discussion* (New York: Macmillan, 1956), p. 28. Howell and Smith treat the subject of critical thinking skills in great detail and with unusual insight.

It differs from the rhetorical approach with its sharp focus on *group* interaction.

The group dynamics approach has at least four identifying characteristics: (1) emphasis on theoretically significant empirical research, (2) interest in the interdependent factors that shape interaction in the small group, (3) emphasis on the interdisciplinary relevance of small group research, and (4) emphasis on the potential applicability of findings to real problems that group members must confront. In broadest perspective, therefore, group dynamics "refers to a field of inquiry dedicated to achieving knowledge about the nature of groups, the laws of their development, and their interrelations with individuals, other groups, and larger institutions." [9]

As the definition of group dynamics suggests, this approach focuses on the impact of forces generated within the small group that affect interaction. It examines the impact of such intragroup forces as social facilitation, cohesiveness, uniformity pressures, group standards, and the structural properties of groups on individual and collective behavior.

Although knowledge of such intragroup forces is a necessary requirement for a complete understanding of communicative interaction in the small group, it is not a sufficient requirement. The group dynamics approach rarely features the nature of small-group communication as such and tells us little about how group members may develop their comunication capacities to exert a positive influence on group outcomes.

THE SYSTEMS APPROACH

The three approaches to the study of the small group described to this point all have demonstrable strengths. Each approach provides insights that are incorporated into this book. None of these approaches will provide a complete understanding of the nature and functions of small-group communication, however.

We believe that the systems approach has the most potential for providing such understanding. We must recognize that

the student of human communication is interested in identifying and defining the nature of those factors which materially affect the quality of communicative interaction. Once this objective is accomplished, the larger goals of explaining and predicting the quality of subsequent communicative interaction under given conditions are within reach. Maximum power of explanation and prediction is dependent on our ability to understand *relationships* between commu-

---

[9] Cartwright and Zander, *Group Dynamics*, p. 4. M. E. Shaw, *Group Dynamics: The Psychology of Small Group Behavior* (New York: McGraw-Hill, 1971), p. 357, contends that group dynamics has exhibited some weaknesses: (1) an overemphasis on laboratory research with a consequent neglect of field research, (2) an overemphasis on ad hoc groups without appropriate emphasis on traditioned groups, (3) a failure to apply research findings to current social problems, and (4) a failure to develop integrative theories.

nication variables. The most illuminating frame of reference for viewing and analyzing such relationships seems to be general systems theory.[10]

The systems approach has already been used to study noncommunicative behavior in the small group and communication behavior outside of the small group.[11] It has not been used for a comprehensive analysis of those factors that make up and affect *small-group communication,* however. We believe, therefore, that our detailed and specialized treatment of the small-group communication system is unique.

A systems approach that did not focus on communication behavior would be of limited value. Our focus is on communication behavior and embraces most, but not all, of the assumptions made by those doing research on small-group communication.[12]

Our application of the systems approach to small-group communication differs from the typical approach of communication scholars in at least two ways. First, we are not primarily interested in how the *average group* functions. Second, we are not satisfied with a *description* of communication in the small group. To concentrate on how the average group does function tells us little about how it should function. To describe but not to evaluate such communication has limited value. Without evaluation and measurement of the quality of small-group communication, we cannot really know whether we must work to improve that communication.

Our application of the systems approach emphasizes those components of the small group communication system that are most apt to affect quality of communication. Thus we give particular attention to the codability of messages, channel capacity, and the corrective potential of available feedback.

Most individuals have a vested interest not only in discovering how the individual and his group are functioning communicatively but also in discovering what steps can be taken to attain maximum communicative effectiveness and efficiency. This book has been designed to help the reader achieve that overriding objective.

More specifically our own efforts have focused on the following objectives: (1) *defining and describing those forces that can vitally affect the small-group communication system,* (2) *identifying and illustrating the effects of those variables that can either raise or lower the quality of small-group communication,* (3) *providing practical tools for measuring the quality of small-group communication,* and (4) *developing a set of techniques that can be used to deal effectively with communication problems in the small group.*

[10] D. G. Leathers, *Nonverbal Communication Systems* (Boston: Allyn and Bacon, 1976), pp. 12–13.

[11] Ibid., pp. 225–249.

[12] A. A. Goldberg and C. E. Larson, *Group Communication: Discussion Processes and Applications* (Englewood Cliffs, N.J.: Prentice-Hall, 1975), pp. 54–58.

Achieving such objectives is not an easy task. It requires the use and synthesis of two distinctive types of knowledge—theoretical and applied. In one sense, this book emphasizes theoretical knowledge. It is theoretical in the sense that the concepts presented and the conclusions reached are compatible with, and may help to develop, communication theory. It is also theoretical in the sense that we employ a systems perspective that is designed to illuminate all of the major *relationships* that affect quality of small-group communication. Although Chapter 2 is the most theoretical chapter in the book, all chapters have been based on the same theoretical perspective.

At the same time, we have no desire to cultivate the role of the intellectual dilettante. We do not provide theoretical knowledge as an end in itself but as a means to increase your potential to communicate effectively in the small group. In that sense, we believe that almost all of the knowledge in this book has applied value.

We recognize that contemporary society makes increasing demands on our time. As a form of self-protection, we must try to use that time efficiently to produce positive results. In deciding what book to read and what knowledge we want to acquire, many of us are forced to ask the same question: what is in it for me?

There should be much applied knowledge in this book that is for you. We do not offer a ten-step plan that will assure communicative effectiveness, nor do we offer any easy or foolproof formulas. We do offer a set of concepts and techniques that have already been carefully tested. They provide you with the potential for becoming a more effective communicator. Whether you actually become more effective will depend to a large extent on the diligence with which you apply the knowledge in this book.

As you read this book, we suggest that you keep our central thesis in mind: *quality of small-group communication is a major determinant of quality of group outcomes.* Frequently, the quality of small-group communication appears to be *the* major determinant of quality of group outcomes.

The implication of this thesis is obvious. Our own success in groups is typically defined by the quality of the outcomes that our groups produce. We should, therefore, be motivated to acquire the type of knowledge that gives us a maximum chance of being successful. It is that type of knowledge that helps to answer the question that we have raised—what is in it for me?

We believe that this book provides a comprehensive and satisfying answer to that question. You, of course, will provide the final answer to the question.

As we begin, we draw your attention to three concepts of major importance in this book: (1) quality of communication, (2) quality of group outcomes, and (3) techniques for improving communication quality.

The quality of small-group communication is a measure of the effectiveness with which meanings are exchanged among group members. A great variety of factors function to disrupt the small-group communication or to impair the effective exchange of meanings.

A decrease in the quality of small-group communication can have disastrous consequences; the most disastrous consequence is often a marked drop in the quality of group outcomes. Groups are capable of producing both *interpersonal* and *task* outcomes. The first type of outcome is associated with interpersonal behaviors that materially raise or lower the level of member satisfaction. The second type of outcome refers to the relative excellence or inferiority of the group's product when judged against a set of criterion measures (for example, is a proposed solution effective and feasible?).

It is difficult, if not impossible, to *assure* high-quality communication. It is possible, however, to improve significantly the quality of communicative interaction in the small group. The techniques presented in this book were developed for the express purpose of helping you attain that goal. As you will discover, this book contains many useful communication techniques. We ask that you pay particular attention to three new techniques: (1) the Techniques Test for Resolving Communication Problems in the Small Group, (2) the Visual Test of Nonverbal Cues in the Small Group, and (3) the Leadership Communication Behavior Test.

These tests were developed for a simple yet compelling reason. Our students have consistently asked what to do when confronted with small-group communication problems, how to make effective use of the nonverbal communication systems, and what types of leadership communication behavior are most desirable.

The techniques in this book represent our answers to the questions raised above. They are designed to serve the twofold purpose of measuring your current communication capacity and improving your future communication performance.

Organizational Format

The organizational format of this book lends itself to a great variety of uses. For workshops and seminars on small-group communication, the student might be asked to concentrate on only two or three of the five parts of this book. For a course that lasts a quarter or a semester, the sequence of parts and chapters presented in the Contents has proved to be very useful.

In one sense, each of the five parts of this book is a self-contained unit. As such, the order in which the parts are read may be varied to suit the requirements of a particular course (we do not recommend, however, that the chapters that comprise a part be separated).

The organizational format of this book, therefore, allows considerable flexibility in the instructional approach to small-group communication. For example, some instructors might prefer to begin a course with the mechanics of planning and researching a discussion before moving to the more theoretical question of what approach should be used for studying the subject. In this instance, Part 2 should be assigned *before* Part 1.

Similarly, a logical case can be made for beginning with a focus on the outcomes that result from communicative interaction (Part 4) before studying the communicative interaction that shapes such outcomes (Part 3).

Finally, many students of the small group feel that leadership must be considered before anything else. Certainly, successful groups should choose a suitable leadership style and use communication effectively to perform essential leadership functions. If leadership is to be given first consideration, the student should begin by reading Part 5.

Whatever the sequence the reader chooses to follow, it is wise to begin by studying the Contents. The Contents should give you a more comprehensive idea of what this book is designed to do. In the eleven chapters that follow, we attempt to direct your attention to all of the major types of problems and responsibilities with which you will have to deal in the small group. We also attempt to spell out the relative advantages and disadvantages of the responses you are apt to make to such problems.

SUPPLEMENTARY READING

Applbaum, R. L.; Bodaken, E.; Sereno, K.; and Anatol, K. *The Process of Group Communication*. Palo Alto, Calif.: Science Research Associates, 1974. Chapter 1.

Bormann, E. G. *Discussion and Group Methods*. Second Edition. New York: Harper and Row, 1975. Chapters 1, 2, and 13.

Goldberg, A. A., and Larson, C. E. *Group Communication: Discussion Process and Applications*. Englewood Cliffs, N.J.: Prentice-Hall, 1975. Chapters 1, 2, and 3.

Gouran, D. S., "Group Communication: Perspectives and Priorities for Future Research." *Quarterly Journal of Speech* 59 (1973): 22–29.

Larson, C. E. "Speech Communication Research on Small Groups." *Speech Teacher* 20 (1971): 89–107.

Leathers, D. G. *Nonverbal Communication Systems*. Boston: Allyn and Bacon, 1976. Chapters 1 and 10.

———. "Quality of Group Communication as a Determinant of Group Product." *Speech Monographs* 39 (1972): 166–173.

Steiner, I. D. *Group Process and Productivity*. New York: Academic Press, 1972. Chapter 7.

QUESTIONS AND EXERCISES

1. What are the basic differences between the human potential approach and the group dynamics approach to the small group? Choose the approach you prefer, and defend your choice.
2. Are you more concerned about how the "average" group functions or about how the "ideal" group functions? Why?
3. We maintain that there is a direct relationship between the quality of small-group communication and the quality of the group product. What are the implications of this finding for a member of a small group?
4. On the basis of your previous experience in small groups, identify what you believe to be your own strengths and weaknesses as a communicator. Indicate *why* you believe they are strengths and weaknesses.
5. If you were in charge of selecting the members for your group, what procedure(s) would you use? Why?
6. Your task as a group is to choose a socially significant project that you can complete in seven weeks—previous groups have prepared brochures on available housing, entertainment outlets, and food services in their community. One group made a film on rape prevention and treatment, a second group became a performing jazz combo, and a third group did a live radio program on sexual behavior at the university. Two hours of class time each week should be used for group meetings on the project; each meeting is to be tape-recorded. At the end of seven weeks, your group is to turn in a written committee report describing and analyzing the product your group turned out. Your group should spend the last four weeks of class analyzing and evaluating the group's communication that was tape-recorded. During the final week of class, your group should present a one-hour analysis of the communicative interaction in your group.
7. Before you read further, please take the Techniques Test for Resolving Communication Problems in the Small Group (Chapter 7), the Visual Test of Nonverbal Cues in the Small Group (Chapter 8), and the Leadership Communication Behavior Test (Chapter 12). *Make sure that you do not look at the answers to the tests either before or after you take them.* Keep your test results until you have a chance to read and study Chapters 7, 8, and 12. At this point, take each of the tests again. Then compare results to see if your performance improved after exposure to the concepts that were described and analyzed in this book.

2 The Small-Group Communication System

The small group is a social system. Unlike some of the lower-order insects and animals, group members are not dependent on one another for their physical survival. Their interdependency is no less real or compelling, however. The form of the interdependency is less tangible but infinitely more complex. Group members are bound together because of the distinctive nature of the process by which they interact. It is this process that generates and shapes forces that make the group more than the sum of its parts; this process makes individuals responsive to forces that are not a simple function of individual choice.

Steiner captures the essence of such forces when he writes that "process is not merely a prerequisite to productivity; it is also the adhesive by which the members of a group are bonded to one another. Without process, the whole would be nothing but the sum of its parts, and the group could be relegated to the realm of metaphor or illusion. However, the group is an active enterprise in which members reciprocally shape one another's actions. Collective process transforms an assortment of individuals into a social system." [1]

The reader should consider this statement very carefully. It suggests that

---

[1] I. D. Steiner, *Group Process and Productivity* (New York: Academic Press, 1972), p. 165. See J. P. van Gigch, *Applied General Systems Theory* (New York: Harper and Row, 1974), pp. 32–56, for a description and definition of the components that comprise a system.

16   there are important, substantive differences in the behavior of individuals and groups. It implies that there are certain forces operating in a group that make small-group communication different from other types of communication. Indeed there is now evidence to suggest that "when a person functions as a member of a group, his behavioral predispositions are likely to be less critical than the demands of the social system." [2] The demands of this system are such that an individual's behavior undergoes measurable change by virtue of the fact that he has become a group member.[3]

Elements of the System That Shape Small-Group Communication

Simply asserting that group behavior differs from individual behavior is not enough. In isolation that assertion is about as profound as George Allen's repeated assertion that his football team is giving 110 percent. The fundamental question is, What are the demands of the group as a social system that shape and modify the behavior of the individual members?

More specifically, we are concerned with those intragroup forces that can significantly affect the quality of communication in the small group. Identifying such forces is a difficult task.[4] Nonetheless, the following forces stand out as particularly important because of their potential for affecting the quality of small-group communication: (1) *cohesiveness,* (2) *social influence,* (3) *interdependency,* (4) *compatibility,* (5) *uniformity pressures,* (6) *power,* (7) *size,* and (8) *leadership.*

[2] Ibid., p. 170. We can think of the operating discussion group as a social system in which (1) certain inputs (2) are modified by a number of dynamic interactional processes (3) leading to particular outputs. Potential input variables in small groups are almost limitless in number. They range from discussants' intelligence to their credibility. In this book we attempt to concentrate our attention on those input variables that have a *major impact* on interactional processes *within the* small group—ascribed status and closed-mindedness (both discussed in detail in Chapter 8) are good examples of important input variables. Although we do treat major input variables selectively, the emphasis is on those factors that shape the quality of communicative interaction in the small group (Part 3) and, therefore, are major determinants of the quality of interpersonal and task outcomes (Part 4).

[3] Ibid., p. 168.

[4] The set of intragroup forces identified here is not necessarily exhaustive but represents those forces that are particularly important. J. E. McGrath and I. Altman, *Small Group Research: A Synthesis and Critique of the Field* (New York: Holt, Rinehart and Winston, 1966), pp. 103–189, have made perhaps the most exhaustive attempt to identify and classify variables that affect interaction in the small group. They focus on many variables such as the personalities, abilities, and attitudes of group members, which are of only incidental concern to us because such variables can also operate outside of the group context. In a doctoral dissertation under our direction at UCLA, Raymond Zeuschner, Jr., "Measurement of Communication Variables in the Small Group: Models, Instrument, and Theory" (1973), examined the interrelationships of the major variables that affect interaction generally and communication specifically in the small group.

Group cohesiveness is the aggregate of those forces that make the group attractive to an individual and impel him to stay in it. Groups may gain or lose cohesiveness. Individuals may not. The level of cohesiveness in a group may have a powerful impact on group behavior. "Members of high-cohesive groups are cooperative, friendly, and generally behave in ways designed to promote group integration, whereas low-cohesive group members behave much more independently, with little concern for others in the group.[5]

The reader might easily view cohesiveness as a type of interpersonal behavior. Although cohesiveness may affect interpersonal relationships, it is different from the interpersonal behaviors described in Chapter 9. Cohesiveness is a matter of the attractiveness of the group for the individual, whereas interpersonal relationships involve feelings of members for each other as persons. These concepts are related, nonetheless, and all contribute to the social climate and the individual's relationships with the others as persons.

There can be little doubt that as the level of cohesiveness rises, the needs of the individual members become less important, and the goals of the group as a social system become more important. As a group becomes more cohesive, members tend to subordinate their own needs to general concerns of the group. This behavioral modification is reflected in both a quantitative and a qualitative change in the nature of communication.

There is *more* communication in high-cohesive groups. Moreover, the content of that communication takes on a very positive tone. Members tend to be very friendly, cooperative, and satisfied. There is a substantial amount of positive reinforcement in the high-cohesive group.[6]

Attractiveness of the group depends on its goals, programs, and the assessment that outsiders make of the group. These factors all help determine the degree to which a group can satisfy the individual's need for affiliation, recognition, and so on. Highly cohesive groups display more "we" feeling, more friendliness, greater loyalty, less friction, fewer disruptions, and, in a business organization, less worker absenteeism and turnover.

Clearly, most people like to be members of cohesive groups. High cohesiveness is not an unmixed blessing, however. It can negatively affect communication. Many of the author's own laboratory studies demonstrate that the positive reinforcement characteristic of cohesive groups consistently results in very digressive and, consequently, inefficient communication. Moreover, uniformity pressures in a group often increase significantly as cohesiveness increases. As we shall see in Chapter 7, cohesiveness is a necessary condition for the insidious development of "group-think."

[5] M. E. Shaw, *Group Dynamics: The Psychology of Small Group Behavior* (New York: McGraw-Hill, 1971), p. 197.
[6] Ibid., pp. 197–201.

18

Social influence is the force exerted on group members' behavior by virtue of the fact that they are aware that other members are observing them and their behavior. Some individuals do not react well to being observed in groups. Thus Zajonc writes that "he would advise the student to study all alone, preferably in an isolated cubicle, and to arrange to take his examinations in the company of many other students, on stage, and in the presence of a large audience."[7]

Certainly, most individuals get "up" to some degree, either subconsciously or consciously, when in the presence of others. In some cases, this stimulates useful communication; in others, it stimulates useless drivel. We know that some individuals perform more efficiently while being observed by others whereas some become distracted or resentful. It is the emotional climate in the small group that is most affected by the social influence of being observed by others and interacting with them. This climate is examined in detail in Chapter 9.

Interdependency is a vital and omnipresent force in the small group. Steiner notes that "members are functionally interdependent when the goal activity of one cannot succeed without the assistance of others. The most capable member of a group cannot provide the solution to a disjunctive task unless his associates are willing to let him do so, and when tasks are divisible, behavioral interdependence is almost inevitable."[8] Indeed the interdependency that is characteristic of the small group is a force that highly motivated and intelligent members often find quite stifling.

Recently, a very attractive blonde student walked into her instructor's office, sobbing. She was soon to graduate as a member of Phi Beta Kappa. Her sobbing had nothing to do with personal problems or her faithful attendance at, and attention to, the lectures. As she told it, she had always been a very successful person, highly independent and self-sufficient. She felt great frustration and insecurity as a member of one of the groups in her discussion class because she would not trust the group to do what she thought she could do better. Subconsciously, however, she knew that she could not accomplish the group task alone. Because she and all group members were receiving a grade based on the quality of the group product she knew that others shared her fate and that members of her group were functionally interdependent. By the end of the quarter this student had become an enthusiastic and smoothly functioning member of the group. She also recognized that the force of interdependency in the small group shaped her behavior in ways that she did not fully understand and could not fully control.

Compatibility exists when *group members can interact without generating serious problems in their interpersonal relationships*. Level of com-

---

[7] R. B. Zajonc, "Social Facilitation," in D. Cartwright and A. Zander, eds., *Group Dynamics: Research and Theory*, Third Edition (New York: Harper and Row, 1968), p. 71.

[8] Steiner, *Group Process and Productivity*, p. 171.

patibility among group members can be measured with William Schutz's FIRO-B (fundamental interpersonal orientations). Rosenfeld and Jessen find that compatible groups use significantly more "lines" of communication and that fewer clique groups form.[9] Moreover, as compatibility decreases, anxiety, tension, and amount of member dissatisfaction increase.

Compatible groups tend to produce satisfying interpersonal outcomes for the members. Compatibility is not simply a function of passivity, pliability, and docility, however. As we shall point out in Chapter 9, discussants must frequently be assertive, critical, and disclosing. However the discussant behaves, he* must do so with full cognizance of the fact that group compatibility tends to increase as the perceived attractiveness of the individual members increases.

Interpersonal attraction is related to the way each individual estimates his own and others' attitudes, status, and power as these are affected by interaction in the discussion situation. Some group discussions are more satisfying, rewarding, and productive than others; hence attractiveness of the other individuals present will be altered. Persons who are pleasant, help the group, or have power to reward others are attractive. In turn, these attractive individuals respond by liking those who obviously like them. These interpersonal relationships have a reciprocal, circular quality leading toward and reinforcing compatibility among group members.

Interaction is easier among persons who are attracted to each other. Communication rate increases in the group when interpersonal relationships are harmonious. When members talk with accepting and approving persons, they tend to exhibit less defensiveness and aggressiveness and, in turn, are more attentive when others talk.

When interpersonal relations are compatible, members report higher satisfaction with the discussion and perceive the groups as more successful and productive. Again, this development is reciprocal. Seeing the groups as successful often leads to better relationships and makes a high-quality, acceptable outcome more likely. However, these interactions are not yet clearly confirmed in the experimental literature. Congenial, harmonious groups are not always more productive. The variables accounting for the effects of different interpersonal behaviors have not yet been identified fully or specifically enough to explain all the variation occurring.

On the negative side, we do know that some interpersonal behaviors are particularly undesirable. They consistently reduce the level of compatibility in the group and are associated with unsatisfying interpersonal outcomes. In particular, we know that nonassertive, manipulative, nondisclosing, and trust-destroying behaviors have a very negative impact on

---

[9] L. B. Rosenfeld and P. A. Jessen, "Compatibility and Interaction in the Small Group: Validation of Schutz's FIRO-B Using a Modified Version of Lashbrook's PROANA5," *Western Speech* 36 (1972): 38.

* The use of *he, him,* and *his* to refer to indefinite sex or to groups of both sexes is for convenience and should not be thought of as a sign of sexism.

interpersonal relationships in the small group. They function to lower the level of compatibility. Both individually and collectively, they can function as an intragroup force that effective groups must confront and work to control.

Uniformity pressure is identified with the *need individual members feel to modify their opinions or behaviors when they are different from the majority of the group.* We have all felt pressure to conform at some time. I can recall a number of times when I sat drinking beer with friends while realizing that I really dislike beer. Of course, we do not always conform to the collective expectations of other human beings. Often they conform to ours. This fall I rented a good-sized tractor, aerator, and other equipment to work on my lawn. Two days later I beheld neighbors on each side of me proudly driving around their lawns on good-sized tractors pulling aerators.

In small groups, uniformity pressure often takes on much less humorous and more negative forms. We do know that group members who are exposed to a unanimous but incorrect majority opinion will more often change their opinion to agree with the group's opinion than individuals who do not experience such pressure. Moreover, the greater the degree of uniformity pressure, the more individuals are apt to change their opinions. Finally, members who sense a low level of personal acceptance in the group are much more apt to modify their opinion so that it is consistent with the group consensus.[10]

Power is a force that can be exerted only in the presence of others. When exercised in groups, it often works to modify or block the instinctive behavioral predispositions of individual members. Clearly, a given individual may bring a great deal of power to a group because of personal achievements or organizational position. In addition, the individual may generate power by virtue of his or her performance in the group. In either case, we contend that the person exercising *power* in a small group at any given moment is the *individual who controls rewards.*[11]

Powerful group members often have a disproportionate impact on communicative interaction and, ultimately, the group outcomes that result from such interaction.

Influence attempts may be direct, or power may operate indirectly. The basis for influence may be the attractiveness of the person or the fact that he or she is liked, respected, and esteemed. The influencer may have power because of expert knowledge or because he or she has authority over members and can give or withhold rewards. Power relationships are the lines or networks of influence within the group during the discussion. These may also be referred to as the power structures. There may be sev-

[10] Shaw, *Group Dynamics*, pp. 251–252.
[11] Ibid., p. 260. Shaw defines power as the *control of reinforcers.*

eral different grids of attraction, expert power, authority, and other kinds of influence operating at the same time.

One kind of indirect influence is behavior contagion, which occurs when an individual's behavior is imitated by others without any conscious intent on his or her part to lead the others to copy him or her. When a popular girl adopts a new hair style, other girls may soon appear with the same style. In discussion, one person's suggestion may be taken up by the group spontaneously.

Another kind of indirect influence comes from the individual's position within a set of hierarchies recognized by the group. Examples are numerous. The holder of a particular title or job will have status with some groups and may use this status as a source of power. He or she may be chairman of the board of directors or president of the student body. Such an individual may be a professor meeting with a student group or the quarterback on the football team. He or she may be the mayor with a city council or the prime minister in a summit meeting. Seniority is another type of positional power. A person may have power within an industrial group if he or she has been with the company since it was founded. Upperclassmen typically control important appointive positions on campus; the elders on a church board have power there. The person of wealth may have power in some groups either as the member of the board of directors who owns the largest bloc of stock in the company or as the member of the YMCA board whose grandfather owned the land, built the building, and endowed the institution and who is the wealthiest supporter and the best potential source of financial aid. Still another source of positional power comes from social standing. In some groups a person of influence may be the girl who lives "in a big house on the hill" with family ties to those who have social prestige in the community or the member of a student committee who represents the best—that is, the most prestigious—fraternity on the campus.

A position may give its holder high influence if he or she has authority over others. The boss has legitimate power over employees and influences them because he or she can confer or withhold rewards. An assignment as designated leader within a group itself may be a source of positional power.

A member can *earn* influence with a particular group by his or her behavior in the past or during the discussion, when he or she earns a reputation for having certain abilities. This kind of power is particularly important in continuing groups. For example, individuals may have status because they are educated or competent, or they may earn a reputation for being honest and frank. Other individuals may have prestige because of their ability to restate and clarify complex points. Still other individuals may consistently contribute proposals for action that later prove sound. In other ways, they may gain in influence because of past successes in or out of the group. Other members may exercise power because they have helpful insights and contribute ideas that lead to breakthroughs. Again, others may have influence because of friendship ties. In many situations, of course, power due to competence or knowledge of the problem will be tied to the problem. Those who are influential may thus shift from time to time within a discussion and from meeting to meeting of continuing groups.

Whether a member makes direct influence attempts or affects others through contagion, the extent to which the group follows may depend, among other things, on the initiator's positional or earned power within the group. Of course, different groups will react to power figures in different ways.

Nonetheless, group members react to high-power members in rather predictable ways. There is empirical evidence to support the conclusion that high-power members are typically better liked than low-power group members; are the objects of more deferential, approval-seeking behavior; and, as you might expect, have more influence upon the group.[12]

Size refers simply to the *number of individuals who make up a small group.* It is often a vitally important force in shaping the quality of communication in the small group. At first glance, one might assume that an increase in group membership is desirable. After all, such an increase means that more resources and minds are brought to bear on a problem. The relationship between group size and, ultimately, group productivity is far from a simple one, however. As Steiner writes, "an increase in group size may augment potential productivity without creating a corresponding increase in actual productivity. Too many cooks may spoil the broth because they get in one another's way, or because each insists on adding his own favorite seasoning. This can happen even if, collectively, many cooks know more about brewing broth than do few cooks. Although superior resources often permit large groups to have a higher level of potential productivity than smaller groups, size also tends to complicate the procedures by which resources must be used if maximum efficiency is to be attained."[13]

Up to a point, group productivity clearly increases as group size increases. However, productivity tends to increase at an increasingly slower rate. For the decision-making small group, the optimum size would seem to be between five and six members. Anything smaller places severe limitations on available resources and the ability of group members to specialize and use division of labor. Anything significantly larger can have highly undesirable effects on communication within the group.

Large groups that were originally designed to be small groups rarely

[12] Ibid., p. 285.
[13] Steiner, *Group Process and Productivity,* p. 78.

function effectively. As members are added, the potential for extended interaction between and among all members becomes more limited. Because balanced and vigorous interaction is hard to attain even in groups of ideal size, the oversized group is often dominated by one or two individuals. Obviously, each additional member further limits the "potential communication time" available to other group members. In groups experiencing interpersonal problems the sense of feeling rushed is particularly serious; it may often be attributed to group size. In short, from a standpoint of task accomplishment, an increase in group size will typically result in increased productivity that is not proportionate to the increase in size. From the perspective of interpersonal relationships in the group, an increase beyond five or six members often creates more problems than it solves.

Leadership is the *exercise of influence in the small group*. The individual who is exerting the dominant influence at any moment is leader. Leadership is a concept of relevance to any type of collective behavior. It is a particularly important force that affects group members. Like cohesiveness, interdependency, or uniformity pressures, leadership becomes operational when individuals are in each other's presence. After all, influence cannot be exerted in a vacuum: the chief of staff cannot be chief without a staff.

Frequently, leadership is exercised in such a way that group members will subordinate or suppress their individual needs in an attempt to achieve group goals. Few factors are more influential in modifying the individual behavioral predispositions of group members than effective leadership. For the successful leader, we often sacrifice some or all of our own objectives for the overriding goals of the group.

Leadership may, of course, affect group behavior in many ways. Usually, studies are geared to examine the impact of leadership on either the group's task behavior or its interpersonal behavior. Stogdill concludes that task-oriented leadership results in increased group productivity when role differentiation is maintained and followers are clearly informed of the leader's expectations. Furthermore, followers are more satisfied with task-oriented leadership when the leader's expectations are carefully structured. Interpersonally oriented leadership does not seem to be consistently related to increased productivity but does increase satisfaction of group members. Interpersonally oriented leaders who provide freedom of member participation in group activities and exhibit concern for the followers' welfare and comfort are consistently successful in raising the level of cohesiveness in the group.[14]

[14] R. M. Stogdill, *Handbook of Leadership: A Survey of Theory and Research* (New York: The Free Press, 1974), p. 419. Leadership behavior is clearly an important intragroup force that can affect the quality of both interpersonal and task outcomes. There are a great

The Small-Group Communication System

It is clear that the small group functions as a social system. It is also clear that the eight major forces just described interact within that system in ways that have a major impact on the quality of small-group communication. Important as cohesiveness, social influence, interdependency, and the other intragroup forces are, however, they are not communication variables per se. *They act upon the small-group communication process but are not among the central components that make up that process.*

In short, when we write of the small-group system, we are writing from the general perspective of all behaviors that shape interaction in the small group. When we write of the *small-group communication system,* we are writing *only* about those *behaviors that group members use to exchange meanings. The small-group communication system is comprised of a set of interlocking and interacting systems that are used in the attempt to exchange consensually shared meanings.*

The effectiveness and efficiency with which the small-group communication system functions differ substantially from group to group. As members of a small group, we should be concerned with optimum effectiveness and efficiency. To attain optimum communicative effectiveness and efficiency, we must (1) understand the *nature* and *functions* of the *individual communication systems* (or subsystems) that make up the larger system, (2) understand how the *central components of a system* function to exchange meanings, and (3) understand how to *record* and *measure* both the *quantitative and qualitative dimensions of communicative interaction* within the larger system.

COMMUNICATION FUNCTIONS OF THE SYSTEM(S)

Small-group communication consists of four interlocking and interacting systems: (1) the verbal communication system, (2) the visual communication system, (3) the auditory communication system, and (4) the invisible communication system.[15] Although all systems serve identifiable communication functions in the small group, the verbal and visual communication systems are particularly important. Chapters 7 and 8 examine the distinctive functions and potential of these two communication systems.

---

variety of leadership behaviors, however. We maintain that "leadership communication behavior" is particularly important. In Chapter 12 we examine the relationship(s) between the quality of leadership communication behavior and the quality of interpersonal and task outcomes.

[15] D. G. Leathers, *Nonverbal Communication Systems* (Boston: Allyn and Bacon, 1976), pp. 11–14 and 225–249.

The verbal communication system clearly has great functional significance in our society. At the same time, we must recognize that individuals frequently use the great potential of the verbal communication system in an attempt to attain rather unsavory ends. Verbal communication is susceptible to unethical uses because it is often the product of careful and extended thought. Ironically, such extended thought can result in verbal messages that are intended to confuse, mislead, or deceive.

The abuses of verbal communication are not hard to identify. Such abuses are multiple, but three common types may help make the point: (1) the use of doublespeak to conceal the communicator's true intentions and motivations, (2) the use of language to convey sexist bias, and (3) the use of emotively charged words to obscure or circumvent reasoned discourse.

Doublespeak is the use of language to mask one's intent with seemingly innocuous and emotively neutral circumlocutions.[16] During the Nixon administration, the president's men became some of the most visible proponents of doublespeak. As the Watergate controversy reached its peak, press secretary Ron Ziegler was asked whether the Watergate tapes were still intact. He replied:

> I would feel that most of the conversations that took place in those areas of the White House that did have the recording system would in almost their entirety be in existence but the special prosecutor, the court, and I think, the American people are sufficiently familiar with the recording system to know where the recording devices existed and to know the situation in terms of the recording process but I feel, although the process has not been undertaken yet in the preparation of material to abide by the court decision, really, what the answer to the question is.

Ron Ziegler was hardly the sole offender. During the Vietnam war, the Department of Defense and many public officials specialized in the use of doublespeak. *Pacification center* was substituted for *concentration camp, termination* for *killing, incursion* for *invasion, selective ordnance* for *napalm,* and *incontinent ordnance* for *off-target bombing* in the official lexicon.[17]

Understandably, such perverted use of language bred more than a little distrust and suspicion of both the written and spoken word. Doublespeak probably reached its height—or depth—during the Watergate hearings. However, the phenomenon seems to have permeated a wide variety of organizations and groups in our society. Professors are now preoccupied with "viable" ideas, not "good" ideas. Engineers are concerned with "interfacing" with other individuals and divisions in the corporation, not with "relating." At times, doublespeak becomes the theater of the absurd. How

---

[16] H. Kahane, *Logic and Contemporary Rhetoric: The Use of Reason in Everyday Life* (Belmont, Calif.: Wadsworth, 1976), p. 104.

[17] Ibid., pp. 101–102.

26   else can we explain the numbing spectacle of intelligent individuals referring to a shovel used by the military as a combat emplacement evacuator,
a parachute as an aerodynamic personnel accelerator, insurance against
an early death as life insurance, or illegal eavesdropping as intelligence
gathering? [18]

If the use of doublespeak to mislead or deceive is a function of the communicator's faulty judgment, the use of language to transmit sexist bias is
as much an inherent weakness of the English language as a function of
communicator bias. Kahane emphasizes that a number of features of the
English language make it difficult to avoid making undesired references
that seem to express sexist attitudes. For example, *masculine* singular pronouns are typically employed when singular pronouns are used, many pro-
fessions employ male terminology (for example, congressman, statesman,
chairman), and many nouns take female endings as in usherette, countess,
and aviatrix. To be scrupulously fair about the last problem, we would
have to refer to male counterparts as usherer or counter.[19]

Finally, emotively charged words are often used. They may be substituted for reasoned discourse or have the effect of blocking reasoned reactions; they stimulate the viscera rather than the mind. Thus a *New York
Daily News* editorial on a campaign bill was entitled "A Snare and a Delusion." It featured such emotive expressions as the bill's *"ogreish* feature"
and *"saddling* the taxpayers with the cost of the campaigns" and also
referred to a "well-disciplined *band of zealouts.*" [20]

Clearly, verbal communication can be abused by the unwholesomely
motivated. At the same time, we must remember that verbal communication is more typically used to serve vitally important functions. Most scholars view language "as fundamentally a system of symbols, and meaning as
a matter of symbols representing or naming objects, ideas, or behavioral
responses." [21] As such, we may use language to serve a referential, ideational, or behavioral function; many times it is used to serve all three
functions.

The ability to name and label persons and events accurately is not easy.
To do so with sufficient precision so that intelligent consumers will reach
consensual agreement on the meaning of such persons and events is a
necessary condition for effective human communication. To use symbols
to describe concepts and ideas accurately is essential to the higher-order
thought processes characteristic of effective communication. Finally, the
ability to use symbols in such a way as to formulate messages that trigger
at least somewhat predictable responses from receivers is necessary if communication is to be both reasonably effective and efficient.

[18] Ibid., p. 102.

[19] Ibid., pp. 107–108.

[20] Ibid., p. 98.

[21] J. Stewart, "Concepts of Language and Meaning: A Comparative Study," *Quarterly
Journal of Speech* 58 (1971): 124.

"While language is not the only manifestation of man's capacity for symbolic behavior, it is a very important medium for transmitting symbols." [22]
As we shall point out in Chapter 8, nonverbal communication also serves
many symbolic functions. Nonetheless, verbal communication has unparal-
leled potential for the exchange of *ideas*.

The functional capacity of the verbal communication system is high-
lighted in the following attributes of the system: (1) the capacity to use
words propositionally—this is the ability to use basic linguistic units such
as words to form more complex linguistic units such as sentences; (2) the
capacity to use words meaningfully—words become a really effective force
in controlling behavior when we move from the signal to semantic levels;
(3) the capacity to use words to bind time—through language we gain the
capacity to describe other places and times that neither sender nor receiver
has observed personally; and (4) the capacity to use words to transmit purpose and understanding—a man without language would indeed be a communicator ill-equipped to deal with the modern world.[23]

Although the general importance of verbal communication is undeniable, we should not assume that all types of communication or all
communication situations require verbal communication that is defined by
identical or even similar qualities. Indeed the verbal communication characteristic of the small group is particularly challenging because of its unique
qualities and the consequent set of communication skills that are necessary to use the verbal communication system effectively.

In many ways, the small group provides an ideal environment for the
operation of the verbal communication system. Participants are in close
physical proximity so that the physiological demands of oral communication should be manageable. In theory, at least, feedback is unrestricted,
unlimited, and immediate so that the communicator should have a wealth
of reactive input to modify his or her message to make it more effective.
Finally, the informal and intimate atmosphere characteristic of the small
group should promote rather than impede effective verbalization.

On closer inspection, however, it becomes obvious that the nature of
linguistic interaction in the small group is such that it is difficult to use the
verbal communication system effectively. In particular, verbal communication in the small group is difficult for the following reasons: (1) *language
is used nonpropositionally*, (2) *language is used arbitrarily*, (3) *language is
used discontinuously*, (4) *language is used nonfluently*, (5) *language is used
redundantly*, and (6) *language is used restrictively*.

The language of discussion is frequently nonpropositional. Verbal communication in the small group rarely conforms to a syllogistic pattern. How
often have you heard a discussant make a statement like the follow-

---

[22] J. E. Goggin, "An Evolutionary Analysis and Theoretical Account of the Discontinuous
Nature of Human Language," *Journal of Communication* 23 (1973): 175–176.
[23] Ibid., p. 176.

ing? "People like Ralph Nader who attack our major corporations are un-American. You just attacked General Motors. Therefore, you are un-American." Should a member of your group use such propositional language, you would probably be incredulous. The deviation from the linguistic norm would be so great that you might think him demented. As the example suggests, the language of discussion is rarely propositional. This is so because of the spontaneous, interactive nature of discussion. Discussants rarely have the time to develop a propositional argument fully; they frequently leave unstated one or more of the propositions central to a complete unit of reasoned discourse.

Secondly, the language of discussion has an arbitrary quality in that the linguistic units used to exchange meaning(s) are variable rather than fixed. In one instance, a discussant may express a single meaning with a single word; in another instance, with a sentence fragment; and in still another, with a rambling monologue of fifteen minutes' length. Meaning is an elusive concept for those receiving verbal messages in the small group. Such receivers cannot rely on the uniformity of linguistic units that is characteristic of written discourse. In a well-organized book, for example, meaning is associated with the key words of a carefully crafted sentence, which, in turn, is designed to express the central meaning of a paragraph. Because of the almost ruleless nature of linguistic interaction in the small group, paragraphs are nonexistent, key words are often difficult to find, and a complete sentence is an oddity to be treasured by the language purist.

Thirdly, language in the small group is used discontinuously. One's attempts to communicate verbally are frequently interrupted. Nonverbal communication in the form of facial expressions and gestures sometimes takes precedence over the use of language or is substituted for language. Then, too, silence is one of the most eloquent forms of communication in the small group. The discussant who can sustain his verbal output to enunciate a set of conceptually related ideas is the exception rather than the rule.

Fourth, language in small groups is used nonfluently. This is a matter of degree, of course. Discussions are not typically characterized by unending gibberish, trough noises, and stuttering. On the other hand, the frequency of nonfluent behaviors in the small group is apt to far exceed those in a public speech, a briefing session, or even an interview. Nonfluencies are sounds, words, or phrases in verbal behavior that are unnecessary for understanding the meaning of an oral message.[24] Anyone who has studied the transcripts of group discussions recognizes that such nonfluencies as word repetitions, sentence incompletions, stuttering, the omission of all or parts of words, and intruding, incoherent sounds appear frequently. The

[24] D. S. Prentice, "The Effect of Trust-Destroying Communication on Verbal Fluency in the Small Group," *Speech Monographs* 42 (1975): 265.

recently popular "You know" and "I mean" phenomena are also present with disturbing regularity.

Fifth, language is used redundantly in the small group. Perhaps this is so, in part, because sensitive listeners in the small group are rare; discussants are often wrapped up in the profundity of the comment they are *about* to make rather than listening to the comment currently being made. Hence we often repeat an idea a number of times just to make sure that someone heard it. Furthermore, oral discourse in the small group does not have the same built-in safeguards against redundancy as written discourse. Most of us recognize a redundant piece of prose when we read it. Redundancy is much more difficult to monitor in the continuing orality of the small group. Individual verbosity is not too difficult to detect, but group verbosity is another matter. At best, we may have only an intuitive feeling that the entire group is sinking in a sea of words.

Finally, the language of discussion is used restrictively. The linguistic code typically employed is restricted.[25] Frequently, experts are brought in, and they can effectively use only that limited lexicon that is meaningful to *all* group members. Furthermore (and this is particularly true in zero-history groups), the apparent risk of self-disclosure and task pressures are such that members are reluctant to reveal much about the unique perspective that they bring to the group. As a result, they tend to use a restricted linguistic code that forces other members to guess about their values and beliefs as well as the overall perspective from which they operate.

Whereas ideas are exchanged primarily by verbal means, the emotional content of a discussion is shaped primarily by the nonverbal communication systems. The functional importance of the nonverbal communication systems is hard to exaggerate. Group members must place a high priority on their ability to convey and perceive accurately a subtle difference in feelings and emotions. They must be able to separate sincere and trustworthy discussants from those who are insincere and self-serving. They must be able to detect role expectations of other members and communicate their own expectations. They must be able to detect cues to behavioral predispositions of other discussants and modify their own behavior accordingly. They must be able to exert some control over interaction and be able to

[25] G. C. Whiting, "Code Restrictedness and Opportunities for Change in Developing Countries," *Journal of Communication* 21 (1971): 42, writes that restricted "code users make use of less of the language's syntactic possibilities and are more redundant in their syntax. Since syntactic complexity may hide poverty of thought this is not an unmitigated evil. But syntactic complexity may also function to convey more precisely complex thought; therefore the limitation of using relatively few syntactic strategies may be damaging." For other interesting perspectives on linguistic behavior, see T. S. Frentz, "Toward a Resolution of the Generative Semantics/Classical Theory Controversy: A Psycholinguistic Analysis of Metaphor," *Quarterly Journal of Speech* 60 (1974): 125–133, and S. Worth and L. Gross, "Symbolic Strategies," *Journal of Communication* 24 (1974): 27–39.

recognize the efforts of others to exert such control. Finally, they must be concerned with their ability to attain or retain a positive image in the group. These are all vitally important communicative functions in the small group. Significantly, these functions are typically performed most effectively and efficiently by the nonverbal communication systems.

Of the various nonverbal communication systems, the visual communication system is most important in the small group. It is so named because it functions to convey meanings that are decoded by sight. The face is the most important source of meaning in this system; the face is an *affect display system*. As such, it functions as a dependable source of information as to the emotional tone and content of the discussion. Significantly, discussants vary considerably as to their capacity to convey meanings by facial expression and to perceive accurately meanings that are being transmitted.

Gesture and posture are closely related forms of visual communication. Gestures serve the primary communicative functions of controlling the flow and frequency of contributions as well as providing cues to discussants' behavioral predispositions. In contrast, posture functions to communicate role expectations and the nature of the perceived relationships among group members.

Although visual communication is not confined to facial expression, gestures, and postures, these three methods of communicating meaning are particularly important in the small group. In Chapter 8 the functions and potential of all applicable nonverbal communication systems are examined in depth.

MAJOR COMPONENTS OF THE SYSTEM(S)

By now we probably all can agree that small-group communication is a very distinctive phenomenon. It is made up of four interacting communication systems, which are, in turn, comprised of their subsystems. We know, furthermore, that these systems perform different communicative functions and transmit different types of meanings with varying degrees of effectiveness.

Although the functions of the communication systems differ, all systems share the same basic components.[26] In the small group, the system com-

---

[26] R. V. Harnack and T. B. Fest, *Group Discussion: Theory and Technique* (New York: Appleton-Century-Crofts, 1964), pp. 399–424, have done a uniquely useful job of identifying and analyzing the basic components or parts that make up the small-group communication process. They emphasize the central components of the source-encoder, message, channels of transmission, decoder-receiver, and feedback. Because message, channel, and feedback components are probably more affected by intragroup forces than source-encoder or decoder-receiver variables, they are treated first in this chapter. The other components are analyzed from a different perspective in Chapter 7. See B. A. Fisher and L. C. Hawes, "An Interact System Model: Generating a Grounded Theory of Small Groups," *Quarterly Journal of Speech* 57 (1971): 444–453, for a stimulating but abstract application of systems theory to small-group communication.

ponents of most practical importance are the message, the channel, and feedback. The skill with which group members use each of these components to achieve individual or group objectives tends to vary substantially.

Codability of Message   Clarity of expression is particularly important in the small group. This is so for two reasons. First, the level of tolerance for ambiguous messages is often unacceptably high. Secondly, the group's willingness to deal effectively and efficiently with ambiguous messages is often unacceptably low. Theoretically, any group member who receives an ambiguous message should move immediately to seek clarification. In practice, however, members often exhibit a strong reluctance to seek clarification of ambiguous messages. In seeking such clarification, one runs the risk of being perceived as uninformed or unintelligent because one cannot be sure that other members view a given message as ambiguous. Because most members are anxious to attain or retain the image of the well-informed participant with well-developed powers of comprehension, they are often reluctant to seek clarification of the ambiguous message. I have often observed laboratory groups with fascination as highly intelligent group members consistently allowed other members to make highly ambiguous contributions while they made no attempt to seek clarification.

Messages that express specific meanings clearly because they have easily identifiable referents are said to have high codability. The concept of codability comes from linguistic research. This research has focused on a communicator's ability to choose a label that identifies the precise color he or she is observing at the moment. Farb describes the concept of codability in graphic terms:

> The English speaker finds himself totally unable to name many colors by any of the categories available to him; he is forced to make up his own term or to use a comparison, such as *It looks like the color of swamp water*. The ease with which verbal labels can be attached to colors is known as "codability." The color that a speaker of English unhesitatingly describes as green has high codability for him, and it also evokes a quick response from speakers of his language, who immediately know what hues fall into that category. Similarly, when a Shona says *citema,* a high-codability color, other members of his speech community immediately know that he refers to "greenish-blue." In contrast, the color that a speaker describes as *like swamp water* has low codability, which means that other speakers cannot be certain exactly what color is intended.[27]

The forces operative within the small group are such that high codability of message is a necessary attribute of high quality communication. For example, a contribution that refers to the Fifth Amendment of the U.S. Constitution has high codability; all well-informed discussants should know exactly what the Fifth Amendment refers to. In contrast, if I refer to the circumscribed sovereignty of a given government, my contribution has low

[27] P. Farb, *Word Play: What Happens When People Talk* (New York: Bantam, 1975), p. 198.

codability because the referents of circumscribed sovereignty are unclear. Group members would have to guess as to the meaning of the term, and, as we have already seen, many group members are reluctant to seek clarification of the low-codability contributions because of the unique pressures that they are experiencing in the small group.

Group members who do not use messages with high codability will not effectively convey their intended meaning(s). In addition, low-codability messages frequently contribute to inefficient communication because those receiving the messages must take an inordinate amount of time and energy in attempting to determine the meaning of the message. Because group members often tolerate and thus tacitly encourage ambiguous messages, high codability of messages is particularly important in the small group.

Channel Capacity   Messages may be transmitted through many different channels. Indeed each of the communication systems described previously in this chapter has a separate channel. For example, facial expression, gesture, and postures are each associated with separate channels.

Many discussants seem to assume, however, that they transmit messages only through the verbal channel. They fail to recognize that a number of channels may be conveying messages at any given moment and that the capacity of these channels varies significantly.

Recently, I (Leathers) presented a week of communication workshops to engineers and executives in Los Angeles. One of the most impressive participants was a man we shall call Edward Mellon. Ed was highly intelligent and held a top managerial position in a major corporation. From a verbal standpoint, Ed was a model discussant. His use of the verbal channel was highly functional. He expressed himself clearly, concisely, and directly. Invariably, his comments focused directly on the objectives of his group.

His use of the nonverbal channels of communication was very dysfunctional, however. Unintentionally, he conveyed many nonverbal messages that tended to delay and obstruct the attainment of his own objectives. For example, by his subtle but perceptible facial expressions, he constantly communicated displeasure with other group members who resisted his ideas. By his strong and forceful hand gestures, Ed repeatedly attempted to cut off the verbal expressions of his fellow discussants. With his imperial demeanor and posture, he conveyed a type of condescension and superior status that visibly irritated other group members and caused them to resist his leadership moves.

Ed Mellon was astonished when my analysis of his videotaped communication revealed all the nonverbal messages he was conveying. In effect, the ideational content of Ed's messages was commendable in the sense that it was geared directly to accomplishing the group's task objectives. The emotional content in the form of nonverbal messages was dysfunctional in that it revealed feelings and attitudes about other discussants that they found unacceptable.

Ed clearly did not recognize that communication channels differ with re-gard to the effectiveness and efficiency with which they handle different types of information. Indeed channels vary with regard to (1) the *speed* with which they can *transmit signals,* (2) the *ability* of the *channel to separate its own signals* from those of other channels, (3) how *accurately meanings* are *communicated* through the channel, (4) the *effectiveness* with which the *channel communicates emotional information,* and (5) the *effectiveness* with which the channel *communicates factual information.* Taken collectively, these five channel attributes make up the channel capacity of any given channel. The rated capacity of the different interpersonal channels of com-munication is recorded in Table 2.1. In making these ratings, I have used a

TABLE 2.1

Communication System	Channel Capacity
Facial	Speed = 5 Channel Separation = 5 Accuracy = 4 Emot. Information = 5 Fact. Information = 2
Gestural	Speed = 5 Channel Separation = 3 Accuracy = 4 Emot. Information = 4 Fact. Information = 3
Postural	Speed = 2 Channel Separation = 2 Accuracy = 2 Emot. Information = 3 Fact. Information = 1
Proxemic	Speed = 3 Channel Separation = 2 Accuracy = 3 Emot. Information = 4 Fact. Information = 1
Artifactual	Speed = 1 Channel Separation = 4 Accuracy = 4 Emot. Information = 4 Fact. Information = 3
Vocalic	Speed = 5 Channel Separation = 2 Accuracy = 3 Emot. Information = 4 Fact. Information = 1

TABLE 2.1 (Cont.)

Communication System	Channel Capacity
Tactile	Speed = 1 Channel Separation = 2 Accuracy = 3 Emot. Information = 4 Fact. Information = 1
Olfactory	Speed = 1 Channel Separation = 5 Accuracy = 3 Emot. Information = 4 Fact. Information = 1
Verbal	Speed = 2 Channel Separation = 3 Accuracy = 4 Emot. Information = 2 Fact. Information = 5

five-point scale, where 5 = very good, 4 = good, 3 = average, 2 = poor, and 1 = very poor.

Look, for example, at the rated channel capacity of facial communication. Because the face can change instantly from one expression to another and hence from one potential meaning to another, the face is rated 5 or very good as to speed of transmission. Similarly, the face is highly visible, so that one is not apt to confuse meanings conveyed by facial expression and touch. Because facial expressions are clearly separated from other nonverbal cues and verbal cues, channel separation is rated 5. The face also handles emotional information very well (rated 5) but factual information with limited effectiveness (rated 2).

By contrast, the verbal channel is rated only 2 in speed of transmission. Verbal discourse by its very nature tends to be an inefficient medium of communication. Our language seems to feature redundancy, digression, and ambiguity. Channel separation for verbal messages is rated only 3 because it is often difficult to separate the meanings of verbal signals from other sources of meanings. Accuracy is rated 4 because discussants have the ability to transmit verbal messages of very high codability. Finally, the ratings of the verbal channel on emotional information (2) and factual information (5) reflect the fact that the verbal messages can be used to exchange ideas very effectively but that words are an ineffective medium for the exchange of feelings and emotions.

Table 2.1 should have much practical value for the member of the small group. In the first place, it should make him consciously aware that he is conveying messages through many different channels. When these messages convey conflicting messages, the discussant may be perceived as insincere or inept or both. Secondly, the discussant who places a premium on expressing his or her feelings honestly and directly should take pains to see that he or she is making maximum use of channels such as facial expression, which have the greatest capacity for conveying emotional information. Finally, whenever the discussant is not communicating high-codability messages via one channel (let us say, verbal), he or she should make an added effort to increase the codability of his or her message by the more effective use of one or more nonverbal channels that will provide supplemental and clarifying meanings.

At this point, the reader may say, "I understand the importance of messages and channels as components of the small-group communication system, but how do I know that I am making effective use of these components?" Your best guide to communicative effectiveness is the kind and intensity of feedback you receive.

Feedback Feedback is perhaps the single most important component of the small-group communication system. Without feedback we have no precise measure of how well the members are functioning as a communication system or how well the members are functioning individually. Both positive and negative feedback can provide group members with valuable information as to the current, qualitative state of communication in the group.

Positive feedback and negative feedback provide group members with very different types of information. Generally, positive feedback will increase the magnitude and frequency of the communication behavior it follows. Obviously, positive feedback can have very beneficial effects when it follows desirable communication. Thus the group member who receives positive feedback when expressing himself or herself directly and concisely is apt to continue to express himself or herself directly and concisely *and* to do so with greater frequency. Conversely, positive feedback that follows undesirable communication behavior can have very undesirable effects on the quality of communication. When positively reinforced, the group member who specializes in irrelevant and digressive contributions is apt not only to continue this practice, but his or her messages are apt to become more highly irrelevant and digressive.

Negative feedback is particularly important in groups experiencing communication problems or where communication efforts are serving to lower the quality of communication. Whereas positive feedback often serves to increase the amount and intensity of undesirable communication behaviors, negative feedback should have the effect of extinguishing such behaviors or at least of *alerting group members to the need to take corrective action.*

Many communication systems have built-in feedback loops that automatically make adjustments when a given standard or norm is exceeded. For example, the thermostat in the home heating system feeds back information to the central unit, which activates the unit automatically when the

36   temperature in the home exceeds or falls below a certain point. Human beings have a similar, automatic feedback mechanism that controls body temperature. When body heat exceeds a given point, we automatically begin to perspire to reduce body heat. The reader should note that he or she need make no conscious effort to read this internal body feedback and induce perspiration.

Unlike the systems described above, *the small-group communication system is not automatically self-correcting.* Feedback received by group members does not automatically trigger a mechanism that corrects the errors they have been making as communicators. Indeed the most outrageously ineffective and inefficient communication behaviors often occur repeatedly in the small group because there is no built-in safeguard to assure that corrective actions will be taken. This fact means that group members have a very special responsibility. They must make *conscious, intelligent* use of the corrective potential that negative feedback gives them. When negative feedback reveals that there is a qualitative insufficiency in their efforts to communicate, they must take immediate corrective action.

Measurement of Communication Performance

This chapter has been designed to illustrate that the quantity and quality of interaction within the small-group communication system may vary dramatically. Certainly, individual members vary substantially with regard to the efficiency and effectiveness with which they exchange meanings. To improve their performance, group members must have some precise way of measuring the adequacy of their own communication as well as the adequacy of those with whom they are attempting to communicate.

The Quantitative Approach   The structure of small-group communication is very important. Perhaps the most basic question we can ask is who said what to whom with what effect. The frequency with which a member attempts to communicate with other group members, and with the group as a whole, can have great diagnostic significance. *When we know the frequency of communicative acts and the overall pattern of such acts, we can make some rather precise inferences about the communicative efficiency of the group. Moreover, the frequency and pattern of communicative acts in the group may significantly affect the quality of communication.*

As a communicator, the member of the small group may function either as a sender or receiver of messages. As a sender, he or she may attempt to reach one other member, some combination of members, or the entire group with any of his or her messages. Bostrom has developed a number of useful measures that give us a clear picture of the sending and receiving attempts that are made in groups. The six quantitative indexes of communicative participation used by Bostrom are as follows:

1. The "sends" ratio = the ratio of the individual's 1-to-1 sends compared to the total 1-to-1 sends in the group.
2. The "receives" ratio = ratio of 1-to-1 receives of the individual compared to the 1-to-1 receives of the whole group.
3. "Group-sends" ratio = ratio of the individual's 1-group sends compared to the total 1-to-group sends.
4. "Receive-send" ratio = the ratio of individual receives to messages sent by that same individual.
5. "Selectivity ratio" = the degree to which an individual concentrates his or her sends on a few members or spreads them out evenly over the group.
6. "Centrality index" = the sum of the group sends ratio and the individual receives ratio.[28]

The initial application of these ratios to thirty discussion groups produced some interesting results. In the first place, *communicative interaction in small groups is far from random; it tends to take on predictable patterns.* More important, good discussants were higher in one-to-one, one-to-group sends and centrality, although they were lower in the receive-send ratio. Good discussants had fewer receives than sends. Discussants who sent more than they received were the most satisfied with the groups. Finally, the more messages a member sent, the less selective he or she became.[29]

In one sense, these findings run counter to the advice one finds in traditional discussion texts. Those who were rated by other group members as good discussants and who were themselves most satisfied with the group talked more than they listened. Furthermore, the high sender tended not to spread his or her messages evenly among all the group members. However, what the group members perceived as "good communication" may not be good communication when evaluated more carefully and objectively.

---

[28] R. N. Bostrom, "Patterns of Communicative Interaction in Small Groups," *Speech Monographs* 37 (1970), 260–61. The quantity of interaction in the small group can be affected by general seating arrangement and one's position in that arrangement. Discussants' positions vis-à-vis one another and the consequent communication channels available to them are referred to as communication networks (the circle, chain, Y, and the wheel are among the different types of networks studied). In his summary of the research literature on communication networks, Marvin E. Shaw, *Group Dynamics: The Psychology of Small Group Behavior* (New York: McGraw-Hill, 1971), pp. 137–148, notes the possible effects of discussants' seating positions and type of network on interaction in the small group. Seating position as well as "availability of channel" may affect the amount, flow, speed, and efficiency of communicative interaction.

[29] Ibid., pp. 262–263.

38

Some additional conclusions seem warranted, based on our research and experience with groups: (1) the "sends" and "group-sends" ratios are useful quantitative measures of an individual's communication—very low scores on these two measures suggest that the member must work actively to step up his or her sending activity if he or she is concerned about a positive image and to assure more efficient utilization of human resources in the group; (2) a low score on the selectivity ratio may suggest that the sender is consciously avoiding those members with deviant opinions or that he or she seeks out those who positively reinforce him or her; and (3) an inordinately low receives ratio may suggest that the sender's messages characteristically reflect such a qualitative insufficiency that other members consistently avoid responding or disregard his or her remarks.

Clearly, these ratios can provide much useful quantitative information about the nature of communication in the small group. They can be easily computed. Therefore, the reader is urged to compute such ratios for his or her own group and discuss the results with the group in an attempt to take corrective action where the group feels such actions are justified.

If a group wishes to avoid the somewhat time-consuming task of tabulating this type of information by hand, they are directed to PROANA5 (PROANA is short for process analysis, and 5 stands for the size of the group to be analyzed). Using six measures of the frequency and direction of communication interaction in the small group that are similar to the ratios described earlier, PROANA5 differs in that the data are computer-processed. The computer print-out that results provides the group with a detailed analysis of their own discussion.[30]

"Sends" and "receives" ratios provide useful information about the frequency and direction of contributions in the small group. They do not provide information about the type of contribution, however. The ratios alone do not tell us how many acts of agreement we have had, for example, or what type of communication is most apt to follow agreement. Significantly, we now know that certain communication acts are much more apt to follow a given type of act than another. Indeed "if the preceding act was an agreement, it is highly probable that the next act will also be an agreement, particularly if we know that the same person provides both behaviors."[31] This reflexive or mirrorlike quality of small-group communication has important practical implications. If we realize that confusion is apt to beget confusion or that high-level abstractions are apt to trigger other high-level

---

[30] E. M. Bodaken, W. B. Lashbrook, and M. Champagne, PROANA5: A Computerized Technique for the Analysis of Small Group Interaction," *Western Speech* 35 (1971): 112–113. PROANA5 is designed to measure the degree of (1) *balance of participation,* (2) *communication line usage,* (3) the degree to which *clique groups interfere* with total interaction, and the degree of (4) *communication propensity* and (5) *leadership.*

[31] E. L. Stech, "Sequential Structure in Human Social Communication," *Human Communication Research* 1 (1975): 174.

abstractions, the need for effective corrective action becomes apparent.

Clearly, the sequence of communication acts in the small group is predictable and occurs in patterns. Recent research confirms that communication in the small group differs "markedly from random patterns; the 1-to-1 and 1-to-group messages make up most of the total. In other words, Bales' analytic scheme should be sufficient to describe most of the communication in a small group, and further study of group behavior probably ought to focus on these two types." [32]

Bales has developed what has probably become the most used system for recording the frequency and type of communication in the small group. Bales's category system is geared to the finding that all contributions in the group can be classified as task behavior (categories 4–9) or interpersonal behavior (categories 1–3 and 10–12). Table 2.2 shows the percentage of contributions that are recorded in each category for the *average group*— these figures were compiled after IPA (interaction process analysis) had been applied to large numbers of groups.

Communication that is characteristic of the average group cannot be equated with what is desirable, however. For this reason, Leathers has recorded the percentages for each category that he expects to find in the *ideal group.*

You will note that the ideal group differs from the average group primarily in terms of interpersonal behavior. This is no accident. We have found that categories 1–3 and 10–12 are particularly useful diagnostic indicators. Groups that deviate markedly from the ideal group in those categories are apt to experience very serious communication problems.

For example, a group that is low on solidarity behavior is one where individuals will sacrifice little for the group while concentrating on their own objectives. In such groups, members will rarely volunteer to do additional work for the group. When combined with a high level of antagonism, group interaction is apt to be stiff, formal, and inefficient. Because group members tend to be preoccupied with their own ends, they tend to do a lot of "sending" and little "receiving" while making a perfunctory effort to gain the active participation of other members of the group.

Categories 2 and 11 are also valuable diagnostic indicators. By definition, a group that is high in category 11 and low in category 2 is probably experiencing unacceptable levels of tension. There may be limited interaction and/or withdrawal because members are already so uncomfortable that they are reluctant to make a contribution that will further raise the level of tension. In one classroom group, a young member actually reported that he felt as if he might have a heart attack because the level of tension was so high; the group was locked in a leadership struggle. Role conflict abounded, and the group had developed no mechanism for releasing tensions. Clearly, such a group has little prospect for either the efficient or

---

[32] Bostrom, "Patterns of Communicative Interaction in Small Groups," pp. 259–260.

40   effective exchange of meanings that is characteristic of good group communication.

Finally, the amounts of agreement and disagreement can often have a significant impact on communicative interaction. A group with very little agreement tends to become lethargic; and the members, insecure and dissatisfied. We all need reinforcement of our behaviors and ideas to sustain and increase the vigor and frequency with which we participate. Conversely, too much agreement can also be undesirable. We have found that group members must use the reward of agreement selectively. No matter how inane or irrelevant his or her contribution, the discussant who is positively reinforced tends to increase the *length* of his or her contributions. Excessive positive reinforcement in the form of agreement typically produces digression. We recall one example vividly. One of the members of the group had said little for forty minutes and was obviously unprepared. Finally, he mumbled a comment of little relevance and substance. To his surprise, another group member told him his idea was valuable. The discussant blinked, did a double take, and then said, "Oh ya, I would like to expand on my idea." He then proceeded to ramble for about fifteen minutes.

Finally, the line between too much and too little disagreement is a very thin one in the small group. Those who advocate the virtual elimination of disagreement may not have carefully considered the consequences. Groups with little disagreement are apt to produce inferior products because ideas have not undergone the filtering process associated with *critical* interaction. Conversely, an excessive amount of purposeless disagreement is apt to produce the conflict climate discussed in Chapter 7.

In sum, Bales's interaction process analysis is a valuable tool and easy to use. Simply assign a number to each person in your group. The letter *O* is used to designate comments directed to the group as a whole. If member 1 turns to member 2 and says, "Frankly, I think you are an ass," the contribution would be recorded 1–2 in category 12. Once you have made a complete record of the contributions in your group, you simply compute a percentage for each category. Whenever the interaction profile for your group deviates markedly from the profile for the ideal group in Table 2.2, you should stop and determine what corrective actions must be taken.

The Qualitative Approach   The quantitative approach to small-group communication is valuable for the reasons already stated. Only by inference, however, does it tell us anything about the quality of communication within the group. It tells us little, if anything, about the accuracy with which meanings are being exchanged within the small group.

Group members must have some method of determining whether their efforts to communicate are sufficient or insufficient qualitatively. As we indicated earlier in this chapter, feedback probably provides the most useful information as to the adequacy of a discussant's efforts to communicate. It is important to know whether one's messages seem to produce

TABLE 2.2*
BALES'S CATEGORIES FOR INTERACTION PROCESS ANALYSIS

Category	Tallies	Average Group	Ideal Group	Your Group	Percentage
1. Shows Solidarity: raises other's status; gives help, reward		3.4	10		
2. Shows Tension Release: jokes, laughs, shows satisfaction		6.0	6		
3. Agrees: shows passive acceptance, understands, concurs, complies		16.5	20		
4. Gives Suggestion: direction, implying autonomy for other		8.0	8		
5. Gives Opinion: evaluation; analysis; expresses feeling, wish		30.1	21		
6. Gives Orientation: information, repeats, clarifies, confirms		17.9	15		
7. Asks for Orientation: information, repetition, confirmation		3.5	4		
8. Asks for Opinion: evaluation, analysis, expression of feeling		2.4	3		
9. Asks for Suggestion: direction, possible ways of action		1.1	1		
10. Disagrees: shows passive rejection, formality, withholds help		7.8	11		
11. Shows Tension: asks for help, withdraws 'out of field'		2.7	1		
12. Shows Antagonism: deflates other's status, defends or asserts self		0.7	0		
	Total:				

* Bales's categories as shown here first appeared in Robert F. Bales, *Interaction Process Analysis*, Cambridge, Mass.: Addison-Wesley, 1950, Chart 1, p. 9. Used with permission. Average scores reported in the second column are based on interaction process analysis recordings of a large number of groups observed by Bales. Ideal group scores reported in the third column are estimates by Leathers.

42   confusion or tension or inflexibility or all three, for example. Such feedback signals the sender that something is wrong and that corrective action must be taken.

To make full use of the corrective potential of feedback, the discussant must know what to listen and look for in the feedback responses he or she receives. Research by Leathers over the last decade at UCLA and the University of Georgia has been designed to provide that information.

Ultimately, of course, the discussant must be able to read the feedback he or she receives and take immediate corrective action when necessary. To develop that capacity, however, we suggest that the discussant make audio and videotapes of the discussion in which he or she takes part. Then he or she should systematically study the feedback received to see whether it consistently reveals certain undesirable qualities.

The discussant may study either the verbal or nonverbal feedback he or she receives or both. To study the verbal feedback to your messages, begin by carefully examining the nine scales that comprise Leathers's feedback rating instrument (see Figure 2.1). These scales are designed to measure the nine dimensions that characteristically make up the verbal feedback response.[33] Every feedback response you receive should be rated on each of the nine scales. For example, let us assume that you rated ten of the verbal feedback responses to your messages on scale 1; your ratings were 1, 1, 3, 2, 4, 1, 1, 2, 2, and 1. To determine your average rating on this scale, you would add the numbers together and divide by 10. Your mean rating of 1.8 on this scale reveals that verbal feedback to your messages is very

FIGURE 2.1
LEATHERS'S FEEDBACK RATING INSTRUMENT

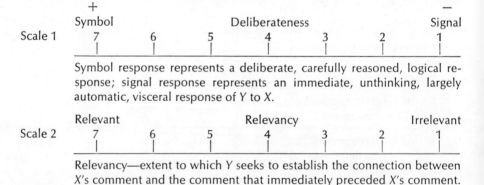

	+						−
	Symbol			Deliberateness			Signal
Scale 1	7	6	5	4	3	2	1

Symbol response represents a deliberate, carefully reasoned, logical response; signal response represents an immediate, unthinking, largely automatic, visceral response of Y to X.

	Relevant			Relevancy			Irrelevant
Scale 2	7	6	5	4	3	2	1

Relevancy—extent to which Y seeks to establish the connection between X's comment and the comment that immediately preceded X's comment.

[33] D. G. Leathers, "The Feedback Rating Instrument: A New Means of Evaluating Discussion," *Central States Speech Journal* 22 (1971): 32–42, describes the development of the LFRI and illustrates how it is used. See D. G. Leathers, *Nonverbal Communication Systems*, pp. 214–220 and pp. 253–255, for a detailed treatment of the factor-analytic development of the LNFRI and illustration of how it can be used.

FIGURE 2.1 (Cont.)

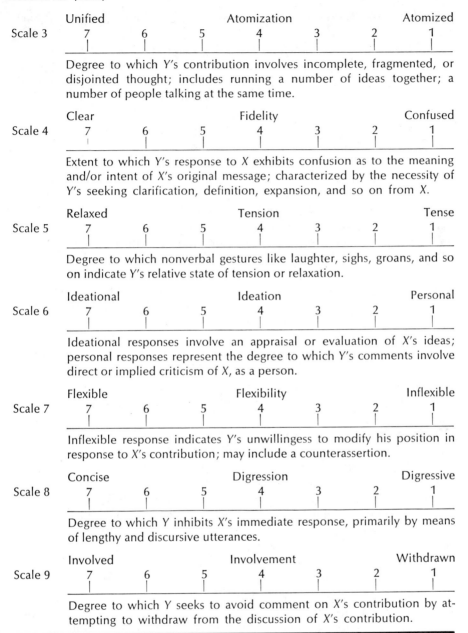

Scale 3

Unified			Atomization			Atomized
7	6	5	4	3	2	1

Degree to which Y's contribution involves incomplete, fragmented, or disjointed thought; includes running a number of ideas together; a number of people talking at the same time.

Scale 4

Clear			Fidelity			Confused
7	6	5	4	3	2	1

Extent to which Y's response to X exhibits confusion as to the meaning and/or intent of X's original message; characterized by the necessity of Y's seeking clarification, definition, expansion, and so on from X.

Scale 5

Relaxed			Tension			Tense
7	6	5	4	3	2	1

Degree to which nonverbal gestures like laughter, sighs, groans, and so on indicate Y's relative state of tension or relaxation.

Scale 6

Ideational			Ideation			Personal
7	6	5	4	3	2	1

Ideational responses involve an appraisal or evaluation of X's ideas; personal responses represent the degree to which Y's comments involve direct or implied criticism of X, as a person.

Scale 7

Flexible			Flexibility			Inflexible
7	6	5	4	3	2	1

Inflexible response indicates Y's unwillingess to modify his position in response to X's contribution; may include a counterassertion.

Scale 8

Concise			Digression			Digressive
7	6	5	4	3	2	1

Degree to which Y inhibits X's immediate response, primarily by means of lengthy and discursive utterances.

Scale 9

Involved			Involvement			Withdrawn
7	6	5	4	3	2	1

Degree to which Y seeks to avoid comment on X's contribution by attempting to withdraw from the discussion of X's contribution.

signal; that is, other discussants are responding to your messages in an immediate and visceral way. This finding may lead you to conclude that there is something wrong with your messages. To get the complete verbal feedback profile for these ten messages, you would apply all nine scales

44   to each of the feedback responses and compute a mean rating for each scale.

For any scale, ratings between 4.5 and 3.5 would be considered average. Mean ratings below 3 suggest that you are receiving markedly negative feedback and that corrective action should be taken. For example, a mean rating of 1.5 on scale 4 reveals that you are receiving very confused feedback and that your messages probably have very low codability. In addition, a rating of 1.8 on Scale 5 and 2.2 on Scale 8 indicate that the verbal feedback you are receiving is very tense and digressive.

You might, of course, attribute some of the confusion, tension, and digressiveness in the verbal feedback responses directed to you to the ineptitude or stupidity of the respondents. More likely, however, the presence of these negative feedback qualities suggests some deficiency in your efforts to communicate. The key question you must seek to answer is "Why do other group members consistently provide me with this type of negative feedback?" Once you have determined the answer, you must take the necessary actions to raise the quality of your own communication.

Although the information provided in the verbal feedback response is very useful, we believe the nonverbal portion of the feedback response is even more useful. Recent research indicates that the "receiver" provides the "sender" more information in the form of nonverbal than verbal feedback.[34] This is probably true because receivers often consciously control the nature of their verbal feedback in such a way as not to offend a sender of high status or a sender whom they like.

For rating the quality of nonverbal feedback one receives, the procedure is the same as with verbal feedback; you do need a full, videotaped record of the discussions in which you took part. You apply Leathers's nonverbal feedback rating instrument in Figure 2.2 to the nonverbal portion of all feedback responses that you receive. Here you concentrate on facial expressions, gestures, posture, and the way the receiver uses the space available to him or her. For purpose of illustration, take the following example. Again using ten feedback responses to your message, you find that the mean ratings on scales 1, 2, and 8 of the LNFRI are 1.1, 1.5, and 2.3 (you know, therefore, that the nonverbal feedback you are receiving exhibits much uncertainty, withdrawal, and hostility). Your task is to determine what qualitative insufficiency in your messages produced these negative qualities in the feedback responses.

By using both the LFRI and the LNFRI, you will have a complete, precise record of the feedback you are receiving. With this valuable information, you are then in a position to take corrective action.

Part 3 of this book focuses in detail on those factors that serve to impair the effective and efficient functioning of the verbal and nonverbal com-

---

[34] D. G. Leathers, "The Process Effects of Positively and Negatively Incongruent Messages" (Winter 1975), an experiment in the University of Georgia series.

FIGURE 2.2
LEATHERS'S NONVERBAL FEEDBACK RATING INSTRUMENT

Confident 7	: 6	: 5	: 4	: 3	: 2	: 1	Uncertain
Involved 7	: 6	: 5	: 4	: 3	: 2	: 1	Withdrawn
Attentive 7	: 6	: 5	: 4	: 3	: 2	: 1	Inattentive
Pleased 7	: 6	: 5	: 4	: 3	: 2	: 1	Displeased
Deliberative 7	: 6	: 5	: 4	: 3	: 2	: 1	Spontaneous
Responsive 7	: 6	: 5	: 4	: 3	: 2	: 1	Unresponsive
Clear 7	: 6	: 5	: 4	: 3	: 2	: 1	Confused
Friendly 7	: 6	: 5	: 4	: 3	: 2	: 1	Hostile
Analytical 7	: 6	: 5	: 4	: 3	: 2	: 1	Impulsive
Interested 7	: 6	: 5	: 4	: 3	: 2	: 1	Disinterested

munication systems. In that section, particular emphasis is given to techniques that can be used to deal with small-group communication problems. Relatedly, Part 4 examines those interpersonal and task outcomes that result from communicative interaction in the small group.

SUPPLEMENTARY READING

Baird, J. E., and Gouran, D. S. "An Analysis of Distributional and Sequential Structure in Problem Solving and Informal Group Discussions." *Speech Monographs* 39 (1972): 16–22.

Dittmann, A. T. *Interpersonal Messages of Emotion.* New York: Springer, 1972. Chapter 5.

Hare, A. P. "Theories of Group Development and Categories for Interaction Analysis." *Small Group Behavior* 4 (1973): 259–304.

Leathers, D. G. "Process Disruption and Measurement in Small Group Communication." *Quarterly Journal of Speech* 54 (1969): 287–300.

Saine, T. J.; Schulman, L. S.; and Emerson, L. C. "The Effects of Group Size on the Structure of Interaction in Problem Solving Groups." *Southern Speech Communication Journal* 39 (1974): 333–345.

Strodtbeck, F. L. "Communication in Small Groups." In *Handbook of Communication.* Edited by I. S. Pool and W. Schramm. Chicago: Rand-McNally, 1973. Chapter 20.

Thayer, L. *Communication and Communication Systems.* Homewood, Ill.: Richard D. Irwin, 1968. Chapters 9, 10, 11, and 12.

Ruben, B. D. "General System Theory: An Approach to Human Communication." In *Approaches to Human Communication.* Edited by R. W. Budd and B. D. Ruben. New York: Spartan Books, 1972. Chapter 7.

QUESTIONS AND EXERCISES

1. Which of the eight intragroup forces identified in this chapter have affected your own behavior in the small group? Was the impact on your behavior desirable or undesirable?
2. Communication in the small group is a continuously interacting, never-ending process. Study the continuous strip illustrated here and suggest

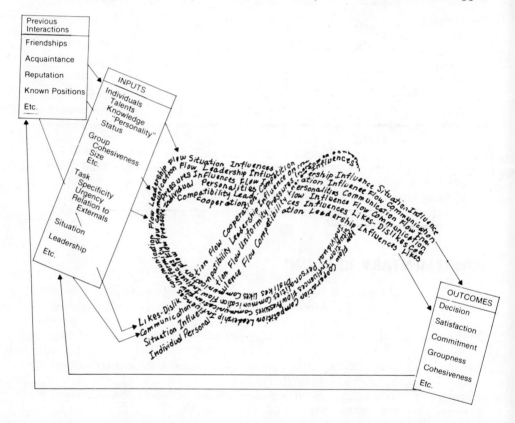

how the factors are interrelated. Explain how these factors relate to those described in this chapter. Then propose a schematic model of your own design that suggests how the small group functions as a system.
3. We indicated that language in the small group is used nonproposition-ally, arbitrarily, discontinuously, nonfluently, redundantly, and restrictively. Are these features of verbal interaction in the small group always undesirable? If your answer is no, illustrate how the nonpropositional, discontinuous, or redundant use of language might be advantageous.

4. Why is it particularly important that your messages have high codability?
5. We indicate that the small group communication is not automatically self-correcting. Illustrate how you might use this knowledge to make discussion more effective.
6. Listen to the audiotapes you have made of your group meetings and prepare a paper analyzing the verbal interaction in your group. In that paper identify the major examples of the functional and dysfunctional use of language. Indicate what steps group members might take to improve the use of language in the group.
7. Using the same tapes, prepare a one-hour analysis of the verbal communication in your group, and present it to the class. If you believe indexes such as the "sends," "receives," and "selectivity ratio" are particularly important, concentrate on the quantitative dimensions of interaction in your group. If you believe group members made ineffective use of the feedback they received, concentrate on the qualitative dimensions of interaction.
8. In what ways might conformity pressures exert a favorable influence on interaction in the small group?

3 The Uses of Small Groups

Groups are everywhere. They are personal, social, educational, spiritual, vocational, professional, and so on. Group interaction is initially experienced in the family, but this is only the first of a continuing series of small groups that influence the kinds of persons we become and teach us acceptable ways of relating to others, fulfilling our needs, satisfying our ambitions, and so on.

Interaction among persons in small groups for decision making or information exchange is an ancient process even though schools have offered courses about it and people have studied it systematically only in recent decades. It is possible that people met together to talk over at least some of their problems before they started recording their own history. The Bible reports a series of conferences that Moses and his brother, Aaron, held with the Egyptian pharaoh; the question for discussion was, "Should the Children of Israel be released from bondage?" The uses of discussion in ancient times, however, probably resembled only partially those we see around us today. The number and diversity of discussions have been increased through the centuries by changes such as increasing population and its developing mobility, the growing complexity of societies and interdependence of peoples, improving methods of communication, and many others.

There are two major causes for the expanding use of discussion. First, through the centuries, power and control in a nation, society, group, or organization have shifted from a single ruler or small clique of insiders to the larger group that makes up the nation, society, or organization. Obviously, such a shift meant that methods had to be developed for discovering what policies large numbers of group members favored. When many are involved in decision making, talk and discussion are essential. Secondly, people have tended to substitute decision by talking it over for the barbaric methods of violence and war. Even the use of intrigue seems to have lessened over the long years, perhaps through the influence of ethical and religious thought and possibly even through the greater likelihood of exposure and wide condemnation by way of mass communication.

It is clear, of course, that these two are not completed causes; the evolution is still going on. There are many contemporary instances of rule by a single autocrat, both in nations and in smaller organizations such as industrial firms, churches, schools, or labor unions. Neither have we eliminated force, violence, war, and intrigue. Nevertheless, it would be difficult to deny that the world has moved and is still moving in the direction of distributing power among the many rather than the few and of utilizing talk, negotiation, and compromise in place of violence and war.

Contemporary Uses of Small-Group Communication

It would be almost impossible to enumerate all the situations in which small-group communication is employed or to estimate the number of committee and board meetings, study groups, interactions for therapy, and similar gatherings that occur on any given day. Instead of trying to enumerate the kinds of groups, we may find it more illuminating to sketch some of the more important situations and uses in order to suggest the complexity and extent of small-group communication today.

DISCUSSION IN POLITICAL AFFAIRS

Discussion of several kinds is employed by legislative bodies at all levels. On almost any campus, the student governing body uses committees to study problems, to reach decisions, and to make recommendations for action. In some cases, the student council or senate may be small enough to sit as a discussion group in its sessions where legislative policy is adopted. Where a governing body is large, of course, it must adopt more formalized rules of procedure and decide by majority vote. The nature of the discussion taking place is thereby modified. Such modified discussion occurs in the formal sessions of state legislatures, the Congress, and the General Assembly of the United Nations. We are not concerned in this book with the large parliamentary assembly. Vital to the operation of any legislative body, however, are many smaller group meetings, which clearly use the type of small-group communication that concerns us here.

At the community and county level, city councils, park district boards, school boards, county boards of supervisors, public health boards, and similar groups make extensive use of discussion both in their formal meetings and in their subgroups and committees. State legislatures and the Congress accomplish their purposes through standing and special committees, which conduct studies, hold hearings, deliberate, and recommend. Some states also have political party caucuses that meet to discuss pending legislation. Official state boards and commissions, as well as a large number of agencies at the national level, such as the Interstate Commerce Commission, Federal Communications Commission, Federal Power Commission, Civil Aeronautics Board, and the Securities and Exchange Commission, are other governmental groups that use discussion method. The United Nations has its Security Council, Trusteeship Council, Social and Economic Council, and many other agencies that strive for agreement through collective talk.

In addition to the functions of these official bodies, there are other functions of government that require group deliberation. Among the most interesting of these at the international level are diplomatic and political negotiations.

SMALL GROUPS IN BUSINESS AND INDUSTRY

Business and industrial organizations also make much use of small-group communication. Most firms have found that spreading participation in decision making results in better decisions and greater commitment to carrying them out. For one thing, industrial and corporate organizations have become so complex that decision making by one "strong" person is no longer possible or effective. More and more, large organizations have turned to committees and task groups for decisions.

DISCUSSION IN OTHER ORGANIZATIONS

These same tendencies toward widespread use of discussion have become characteristic in most other kinds of organizations.

Most religious leaders participate regularly in study groups and problem-solving discussions within their churches and often take part in interchurch meetings within ministerial associations, ecumenical conferences, and the like. Labor union officers engage in group sharing of information and in deliberation within their unions and also in labor-management negotiations involving working conditions, workers' grievances, and employment contracts. Farmers are involved in numerous meetings where they discuss new agricultural methods and agree on policy in relation to legislation that affects them. Teachers are familiar with committee work and with informational and decision-making meetings at both departmental and school or college level, as well as with discussion groups at their regional, state, and national professional conventions. Medical societies use group methods to exchange ideas about new developments and to reach decisions on matters of public health and their professional interests.

Discussion procedures are commonplace on a campus among both student and faculty groups. Student government organizations and housing associations use committees and executive boards to make policy and regulate activities, as do the religious foundations, the YM-YWCA, student interest clubs, and dozens of other groupings. Faculties have their committees on courses and curricula, discipline, educational policy, athletics, and so on, along with councils of department chairmen and deans, faculty senates, and similar policy-making bodies.

Lawyers, too, use discussion. The frequency of out-of-court settlements appears to be increasing; the oral discussions that result in a settlement are sometimes held in the judge's chamber. One indication of the trend is the use of arbitration to settle disputes not involving points of law. The method is to have the disputing parties agree on arbitrators whose decision, after they talk over the problem, is binding.

USING GROUPS FOR SELF-INSIGHT AND THERAPY

Increasingly today small groups are used to help "normal" persons understand themselves and others better and also to offer therapeutic insights through group interaction to persons with serious adjustment problems. Carl Rogers has called the intensive group experience "the most rapidly spreading *social* invention of the century."[1] These group sessions are given a wide variety of names:

sensitivity-training sessions
encounter groups
confrontation groups
T-groups (for training)
training laboratories
human relations training groups
human potential-awareness groups
awareness experiences
sensory awareness groups
personal growth laboratories
synanon (usually for drug addicts)
marriage enrichment groups
marriage encounter groups
therapy groups
sociodrama
psychodrama
Gestalt groups

[1] Carl Rogers, *On Encounter Groups* (New York: Harper and Row, 1970), p. 1.

creativity workshops
organizational development groups
body awareness groups
team-building groups

Rogers illustrates the purposes of such groups in recounting two influential sources of their development just after World War II. One was the inspiration of Kurt Lewin; he and his students began their T-groups at Bethel, Maine, to provide training in human relations skills. They later organized the National Training Laboratories to extend the intensive group experience to schools, industries, and other institutions. Another major influence originated at about the same time at the University of Chicago, when Rogers and his associates created a program for preparing counselors to deal with the problems of returning war veterans. This staff felt that cognitive training alone was not enough to prepare counselors, but "experimented with an intensive group experience in which the trainees met for several hours each day in order to better understand themselves, to become aware of attitudes which might be self-defeating in the counseling relationship, and to relate to each other in ways that would be helpful and could carry over into their counseling work." [2]

This attempt succeeded, Rogers feels, by integrating "experiential and cognitive learning in a process which had therapeutic value for the individual."

> The Chicago groups were oriented primarily toward personal growth and the development and improvement of interpersonal communication and relationships, rather than having these as secondary aims. They also had more of an experiential and therapeutic orientation than the groups originating at Bethel. Over the years this orientation toward personal and therapeutic growth has become merged with the focus of training in human relations skills, and the two combined form the core of the trend which is spreading so rapidly throughout the country today.
>
> Thus the conceptual underpinnings of this whole movement were initially Lewinian thinking and Gestalt psychology on the one hand, and client-centered therapy on the other.[3]

Such groups in an almost endless variety of forms are used extensively now to give the individual greater self-insight and self-knowledge about his or her adjustments and relationships, whether a counselor, social worker, teacher, executive, and so on, or a person requiring professional help with adjustment problems. They also serve to provide better understanding of group functioning, and of interpersonal behavior in groups, including communication skills.

It is important to emphasize the *differences in function and operation*

[2] Ibid., pp. 2–4.
[3] Ibid.

between groups providing such intensive group experience and those task groups in natural settings—such as decision-making boards and committees—that are the primary interest in this book. Sensitivity or encounter sessions operated as decision-making groups would be unsuccessful in achieving their desired ends, just as sensitivity session procedures would be inappropriate for decision-making discussion.

It is equally important to study the similarities. Some of the self-insights and understandings of group functioning that are such vital outcomes of many intensive group experiences may give clues to more effective operation of task groups in natural settings.

Types of Group Discussion

Communication is vital to all these uses of groups, but in this book we are concerned primarily with task groups using interactive discussion. For purposes of analysis and study it will be useful to suggest some of the types of group discussion and to specify what kinds are of greatest interest to us here.

To establish a reasonable classification is no simple matter because purposes, groups, task assignments, and situations are so variable. It seems plausible, nevertheless, to describe differences introduced by variations in purpose, the presence of nonparticipants, and the patterns of communicative interaction.

Purpose

Discussion is most often employed to achieve one of two basic purposes, information sharing or decision making, or some combination of these two.

Participants in informational discussion exchange data, insights, and ideas for the purpose of learning. The outcome, they hope, is increased understanding. In decision-making, problem-solving, or policy-determining discussion, a group is attempting to decide what to do or to believe. The outcome is a decision or a policy. Obviously, these purposes are often combined in the same discussion; a group usually must exchange information preparatory to deciding; a staff of workers at the regular weekly meeting may engage on one occasion in simple, informational discussion and on another may share information and also reach decisions on items of business. Information sharing is characteristic of study groups, workshops, staff meetings, briefing sessions, and round tables, whereas decision-making groups are more often called committees, conferences, boards, and councils.

Presence of Nonparticipants

The most common type of discussion occurs when a small group meets face-to-face with only the group members present. All those in the room are participants, and all communicate, making the discussion private, or closedgroup.

In contrast, some discussions are public and are held for the benefit of a listening audience. Participants must take other communicators into account as they do in private discussions, but, more importantly in the public situation, they must take the audience into account. Complex differences are introduced by the presence of nonparticipants.

Public discussion may use many different formats, and each may be employed either for information sharing or decision making.

PANEL In the panel type of public discussion, a small group of experts or well-informed persons discuss a problem for the benefit of an audience. The distinctive feature of the panel is the communication pattern. Participants engage in direct, conversational interchange of ideas. The communicative interchange is similar to that which is characteristic of the closed-group committee, conference, or round table. Probably, this format is the one most frequently used in public discussion.

DIALOGUE The dialogue is similar to the panel, except that there are only two communicating participants. The interchange is directly conversational. Often one of them is an expert on the problem for discussion, and the other supplies more questions than information.

SYMPOSIUM Here, too, a small group of experts or well-informed persons discuss a problem for the benefit of an audience; the distinguishing characteristic is again the communicative pattern. Each participant delivers a relatively short speech without being interrupted, giving his or her view or explaining one aspect of the problem. Speakers follow each other in turn until all participants have been heard.

FORUM The term *forum* is used in three ways. The first is applied to participation by the listening audience after they have heard a public discussion or some other type of presentation. If the audience hears a panel discussion and is then invited to question and make contributions, this portion of the meeting is designated a *forum*. Thus the whole discussion should properly be called a *panel-forum*. Similarly, there can be a *dialogue-forum* or a *symposium-forum*.

Using the concept of forum to mean general audience participation after some type of presentation makes it possible to classify a *lecture-forum* as a type of public discussion. After the speaker delivers his or her lecture, an audience forum period follows. In the same way, these other types can be classified as public discussions: *debate-forum*, in which audience participation follows a set of formal debate speeches advocating affirmative and negative positions on a proposition; *film-forum,* where audience discussion concerns a motion picture that the group has just seen; and forums in which the vehicle for audience discussion is a radio or television broadcast heard by the whole group prior to the forum period. Obviously, any of these formats could be used either for enlightenment or problem solving.

A second sense in which the term *forum* is used applies to a type of discussion in which members of the audience may participate from the beginning of the meeting. This form has at times been called an *open forum.* The entire meeting is devoted to discussion by the whole audience as participants. No formal presentation precedes audience participation.

The third usage of the term *forum* designates a whole series of regular public discussions on related problems. Sometimes a group of people who want to meet regularly on common problems will call their organization and the activity a *community* forum.

HYBRIDS

A few discussions combine features of closedgroup and public discussion.

COMMITTEE HEARING One of the most important tasks of a committee is to investigate problems. Only on the basis of accurate information and thorough understanding can it make intelligent recommendations to the parent body. An effective device for acquiring understanding quickly is the committee hearing. Instead of sending out researchers to seek facts, important committees can invite well-informed persons to appear and offer information and opinions. Congressional committees even have the power to subpoena witnesses.

A committee's deliberation among its members is closedgroup, as we have seen. When a witness appears during a hearing, however, a new element has been added—the discussion is no longer private; the procedure takes on some of the characteristics of public discussion. At important congressional committee hearings, reporters are usually present; often these hearings are open to the general public. Indeed some have been televised on national networks. If, during an interval between hearing witnesses, the committee engages in procedural deliberation that under other circumstances would be closedgroup but that now has press and nation overhearing, the committee discussion will certainly be altered. Members cannot communicate without taking the listeners into account in some sense.

CASE CONFERENCE Another closedgroup-public hybrid has been used as a learning device. Two or more participants engage in a conference in front of a listening audience. The participants are expected to proceed as if the conference were taking place in a real closedgroup situation. Often they are assigned roles; that is, they play the part of someone who would be involved in such a situation. The listening audience overhears for the purpose of learning from the procedures acted out by the participants.

The term *case conference* has been applied to other forms of discussion. It is sometimes used to designate a closedgroup discussion by all members of a group about an actual case or situation. For example, a group interested in juvenile delinquency might discuss a particular case of a juvenile offender. His offense and treatment by the authorities would be described in detail; general discussion would follow. This type is similar to a closed-group round table.

Communicative Interaction

Discussions vary in the kind of communicative interaction permitted and expected in the situation.

The most frequent kind is the direct conversational interchange characteristic of committees, conferences, and public panels. Here participants speak up, usually without recognition, when they feel moved to make a comment, interrupt each other, and in other ways talk much as they would in conversation. Each individual alternates as speaker and listener, usually with some rapidity; comments from one person lasting as long as two minutes are uncharacteristic.

In some discussions, such as a symposium, participants deliver uninterrupted speeches as part of the meeting. Some public panel discussions will have a symposium feature where members explain their view in a formal speech before participants interact conversationally as a panel.

As we noted, the audience is sometimes invited to participate after a symposium or panel. This forum period involves imprompu speeches from the floor, consisting of questions or comments.

In this book we will concentrate primarily on discussion theory and procedures in the closed small group concerned with decision making. Thus our major interest will be in communicative interaction that is directly and informally conversational.

Gains from Group Interaction

Small groups have employed discussion in wide-ranging activities and diverse situations because it has some obvious strengths. The gains accruing from collective action where, for example, a group benefits from a division of labor among members have been called the *assembly effect*.

In surveying such gains, of course, we must be careful not to overstate the case.

Some enthusiasts for group procedures have made exaggerated claims for the beneficial outcomes of togetherness. On the other hand, some critics of group action, recognizing the exaggeration of the overenthusiastic, have failed to see the very real virtues that can result from group interaction in many situations. The student of discussion must make a realistic appraisal of the strengths as well as the limitations of group effort in decision making as contrasted with the work of the individual.

We must keep in mind while considering the strengths and limitations of discussion that groups and the individuals who make them up differ from each other in an amazing variety of ways. Generalizations of any kind must be treated with extreme caution. One group may be composed of five highly gifted individuals and a brilliant leader, whom the other five are willing and eager to follow. If we give this group a specific, limited question on which they are already well informed and which they are motivated to discuss, we will not be surprised when the group is highly productive. These same individuals would also be impressively productive if they worked on the problem separately. If we give these same five talented persons a dull, uninformed leader, who creates a hostile climate during the discussion, and also a complex problem on which information is not readily available, they might well be more productive working separately. No doubt, in many situations a brilliant, highly motivated individual would produce better decisions than some groups of mediocre, unmotivated, or hostile participants.

Our problem, then, is to understand the conditions under which groups are productive and efficient. Under what conditions is there a gain from group interaction? What kinds of tasks need group discussion? What kinds of leadership, participation, member attitudes, situations, and so on enhance productivity? What are the limitations and exceptions? Under what conditions are group productivity and harmony lessened? Although we have some experimental evidence and much careful observation to suggest answers to questions such as these, every statement we make must be approached tentatively and cautiously.

GROUPS MAY PRODUCE BETTER DECISIONS

In most situations, groups apparently produce higher-quality decisions than could an equal number of equally able individuals working separately. Some of the experimental evidence on group versus individual productivity is derived from performance on tasks such as guessing the number of beans in a bottle or working simple arithmetic problems in the presence of other people, tasks rather far removed from decision making on important political, social, economic, or business problems. However, there is now enough evidence involving complex discussion topics to suggest that there often is gain from the interaction of group members.

The gain is explained by many diverse factors. Some tasks and situations lend themselves to group discussion whereas other problems can be better solved by the individual executive. Then, too, in many situations there is no alternative to group action, and hence comparison with individual productivity becomes meaningless. A single star cannot play a basketball game by himself; moving the ball down the court requires a team functioning as a coordinated unit. In the same sense, many manufacturing operations today are too complex for a single executive to know and perform all the tasks required. Thus a group interaction of production engineer, design specialist, sales manager, financial consultant, tax expert, and personnel director is mandatory. In these situations, the question is not whether executive action would be more efficient than group discussion but how to make the executive committee of the plant work smoothly in spite of the difficulties encountered in interaction.

Groups Have More Resources Than Individuals Have Because each person's background, experience, and exposure to knowledge are uniquely different from those of every other person, a group has access to more information; and their combined thinking results in some new insights for everyone. A pooling of experience and information means that someone is more likely to think of the breakthrough idea at the moment it is needed.

Collins and Guetzkow have synthesized the experimental research in social psychology that is relevant to group processes for decision making. They find support for the proposition that "for tasks which involve creating ideas or remembering information, there is a greater probability that one of several persons will produce the information than that a single individual will produce it by himself." [4]

Groups Are More Productive When the Task Allows a Division of Labor Most often, groups discussing complex problems can bring to bear the unique talents of each member and also can take advantage of having several members by dividing up assignments both before and during discussion. In preparing for a particular discussion, members can divide responsibility for becoming informed.

The experimental evidence indicates that groups are usually no better than individuals on relatively routine tasks or on simple assignments such as solving arithmetic problems. Groups tend to be superior, however, on tasks profiting from a wide range of possible solutions where much is to be gained by criticism and selectivity and by originality and insight. A group can evaluate a wide range of solutions, but this will be a gain only if the task requires a large number of alternatives for arriving at a good outcome.

[4] Barry E. Collins and Harold Guetzkow, *A Social Psychology of Group Processes for Decision-Making* (New York: John Wiley & Sons, 1964), p. 20.

A group assigned a task involving quantitative judgments can be more accurate than individuals working separately, perhaps because the pooling of judgments reduces random error.

Through interaction members can improve on the thinking of other members, censoring out poor ideas, discovering fallacious reasoning, and in other ways taking advantage of their combined intelligence, experience, and information.

Members Are Often Stimulated by the Presence of Others   In the discussion situation, members of a group may be motivated by social stimulation to strive harder to contribute and to help the group succeed. It is possible that members will be stimulated to think of ideas that otherwise would not have occurred to them and perhaps to recall long suppressed information and insights. Brainstorming uses group pressure to promote "creative ideation"; members "hitchhike" and improve on the remarks of others.

LIMITATIONS AND EXCEPTIONS   Under some conditions, individuals are superior to groups. Group productivity varies enormously, depending on the nature of the task and situation, quality of leadership, abilities of individual members, availability and quality of information, and other factors. Thus it is unrealistic to expect that groups will always be superior to individuals in efficiency and quality of decisions. Because individuals working alone also differ in capacity, motivation, and so on, it is equally clear that individuals are superior to groups only under certain conditions.

Individuals working separately seem able to produce a larger quantity of alternative suggestions for action than will a group, although the group has more potential ideas than can be expressed in a limited period of group interaction. Separate individuals do not have the benefit of criticism and group judgment leading to selecting the best alternative, and those working alone do not have any way of combining or pooling alternatives.

On some routine tasks or on tasks where only one person can work at a time—such as writing a report or investigating facts or doing research—an individual effort is, no doubt, better than group action. An executive may be better equipped to make day-to-day decisions in managing an organization than could an executive committee even if it were in continuous session. If the group needs a report written or a matter investigated, it usually should refer the task to an individual or two or to a subgroup such as a committee. The group can then conserve its time by being required only to consider whether to accept or to modify the finished product.

A group can best establish policies and evaluate the efficiency of appointed administrators, but an executive can make better decisions about purchasing typewriters and hiring secretaries. The board of directors might profitably discuss these matters only if the annual cost of typewriters became an unreasonable drain on the company's resources or if a rapid turnover of secretarial employees were seriously interfering with worker morale. A group that finds itself spending time each month deliberating on such problems as the quantities and brands of typewriters is probably not using its discussion time intelligently.

GROUP MEMBERS MAY FEEL STRONGER COMMITMENT

There is normally a stronger allegiance to a decision when those affected have participated in its formulation. A single administrator can make a policy decision, but rarely can he carry it out alone. Those who must translate it into action feel more satisfied with the decision, more involved in it, and more willing to work for its execution if they have helped to hammer it out.

Anyone can confirm this tendency by noticing that he or she is more sensitive to praise or criticism of one of his or her own statements than he or she is to reactions related to statements of others. In the opposite way, it is easier to feel indifferent or resistant to edicts forced upon one by another. This is the essential difference that makes democracy superior to dictatorship; whereas dictators can decide and act more quickly and efficiently, they are eventually undone because others are not so committed to their ideas as they are.

LIMITATIONS AND EXCEPTIONS   It must not be assumed that stronger commitment always results from interaction. Hostility may be heightened instead of being reduced. It may be a group discussion experience that causes an individual finally to withdraw from membership rather than to have his loyalty increased. Whether commitment to group decision is won depends on a complexity of factors.

Other Limitations

DISCUSSION IS UNSUITED TO SOME TASKS

Not all problems lend themselves to group solution. Some metaphysical questions could never be settled by interaction, just as some questions cannot be answered empirically. Questions asking, "Is God dead?" and "How many angels can dance on the head of a pin?" are not matters where persons can expect to come up with an answer by talking around a table. If the group benefits from such interaction, it will be for reasons other than learning the group's answer to the question.

A group should not waste their time considering trivial matters, such as those of taste or personal preference. A board of busy persons once spent an hour debating the wording of a sentence in a report. Some preferred one wording, whereas others liked different language choices. The composition of the sentence was not directly related to the purpose of the report; so their deliberation was not particularly constructive. If a minor point could be decided one way as well as another, the group should let an executive decide or decide quickly by majority vote.

DISCUSSION TAKES TIME

Discussion almost always requires substantial amounts of time. Autocratic decisions are speedy by comparison. If problems are complex and controversial, there are rarely shortcuts to thorough understanding and deliberation. Discussion cannot often be used fairly when members are in a hurry for a decision. For the leader to say, after two or three persons have spoken, "We don't have time to talk about this fully, but would you all agree that we should do so and so?" is to stampede the members. They are in no position to disagree without being disagreeable. Only if the proposal is so outrageous that all the members spontaneously howl out their disgust is the stampede likely to be stopped. Whether the proposal expresses the will of the group when they are silent after such a plea from the leader, no one can know. To find out requires additional communication from them.

DISCUSSION CAN BE WASTEFUL

Not only is group discussion time-consuming, but it also often wastes some of the time it requires. Unless a group has unusually able leadership, members spend some of their time in false starts and unproductive byways. Discussers may talk at length, for instance, before they wake up to the fact that they have no power to do anything about the problem or that they do not need an answer. The result for the person who places a high value on efficiency may be frustration or even disgust for the method.

DISCUSSION CAN SUBSTITUTE TALK FOR ACTION

Division of responsibility among group members sometimes encourages the substitution of talk for constructive action and decision making. Most group members find it easy and pleasant to talk, and there is a danger that visiting together will become an end in itself. It may appear that what is occurring is worthwhile because it seemingly is sanctioned by the group when, in actuality, what is happening is not constructive at all. Many unnecessary meetings and not a few unnecessary organizations are perpetuated primarily because talking together is a pleasurable habit. There is nothing wrong with enjoyable communication in congenial groups, of course; most social events involve such activity. What is deplorable is pointless, meandering talk disguised as constructive discussion.

Groups in some situations may tend to be indecisive. Because no one person is directly responsible for action, all often do nothing. No one member of a committee, for example, can be singled out as the source of delay, and, consequently, the group may spend much longer than they should in making up their minds. A chairperson may quite properly claim that his or her hands are tied until the members choose to act. The net result may appear as inefficiency to an outsider waiting for a decision; such an outsider may say he or she is being given the run around. A humorist long ago observed incisively, "If Moses had been a committee, the Children of Israel would still be in Egypt!"

Here, then, are some of the strengths and weaknesses of discussion. It is clear that discussion is often a powerful tool for good. The times call for much collective action, and to use discussion ably is a positive virtue. Group action and group efficiency are important considerations in our culture and in many others. The strengths of group discussion can be applauded and put to constructive use even though we recognize realistically its limitations.

SUPPLEMENTARY READING

Burgoon, Michael; Heston, J.; and McCroskey, J. *Small Group Communication: A Functional Approach.* New York: Holt, Rinehart and Winston, 1974. Chapters 3–8.

Davis, James H. *Group Performance.* Reading, Mass.: Addison-Wesley, 1969.

O'Banion, Terry, and O'Connell, April, "Is an Encounter Group Something Like a Discussion Group." In *The Shared Journey: An Introduction to Encounter.* Englewood Cliffs, N.J.: Prentice-Hall, 1970. Chapter 9.

Rogers, Carl. *On Encounter Groups.* New York: Harper and Row, 1970.

Steiner, Ivan D. *Group Process and Productivity.* New York: Academic Press, 1972. Chapters 2 and 3.

QUESTIONS AND EXERCISES

1. Discussion for information sharing is used in many different kinds of situations. The objective of this exercise is to decide when an informational discussion can be called by a specific name.

   a. Divide the class into groups of four or five. Each group is to consider examples of

      Study groups
      Workshops
      Staff Meetings
      Briefing Sessions
      Round Tables

   b. A person from each group is to report the agreement about the purposes of each of these types.

2. Go through two consecutive issues of a metropolitan newspaper, and record the meetings that may involve discussion. Attempt to estimate how discussion is being used.
3. Write a paper on the use of discussion in a campus organization, a state legislature, the Congress, or the United Nations.
4. Keep a journal of your communicative activities for a week. Decide how often you have participated in small-group communication.

Part 2
PREPARING FOR GROUP INTERACTION

4   Planning

embers of a group often feel that their time was largely wasted in group deliberation or, at least, that the time available was not used effectively. This fault may stem from poor planning and sometimes from the total absence of planning. Careful planning can mean the difference between effective and haphazard decision making.

In using the materials in this chapter, we face two hazards. This book is not a how-to-do-it manual, but in planning there is a temptation to lay out the steps and say, "Do it this way and succeed." We must resist the cookbook approach, however, because achieving good discussion is not as simple as cake baking. We must try instead to suggest the factors to be understood and taken into account in the planning stage.

The second hazard is the temptation to address this chapter to a designated leader. The person in charge of a specific discussion seems to be the one who should be responsible for planning. What he does in advance is important, of course, but his efforts alone are not enough. Other members must help. They must understand what advance preparation contributes and why it is vital. Furthermore, one advantage of group action is that members can divide the labor of preparation.

ANALYZING REQUIREMENTS

The initial step is to determine what is required for a productive discussion within the situation. Demands are as varied as the types of discussion and kinds of circumstances.

Participants must be chosen and leadership responsibilities assigned to a designated leader or divided among members. After the type of discussion and situation is specified, a question must be selected and worded appropriately. Members must secure information and resource materials. The leader responsible for guiding the discussion may want to draw up an outline. Then the group must plan the physical arrangements. In the classroom setting, students will usually want to provide some kind of evaluation machinery for making an appraisal of the discussion.

If a group is to face multiple problems, as will usually be the case, an agenda is needed. This will list the problems to come up and the order of considering them. For an item of great importance, participants and leadership must be taken into account; the question, recognized and stated; resource material, secured; guiding outline, drawn up; physical arrangements, planned; and any prediscussion meetings, arranged.

The care and extent of advanced planning required will be determined by a number of factors, such as the nature of the group and the persons involved, the nature of the task, and the situation. If an executive committee responsible for a manufacturing plant meets every two or three days and handles largely routine decisions, little planning may be required for a particular meeting. Members are familiar with each other, and each participant is an expert in the area he represents, whether in sales, engineering, production, or finance.

In contrast, a special conference of executive vice-presidents from the company's plants located throughout the country may require meticulous planning for success. If an executive is designated as leader for the conference, he must also decide to what extent he should involve other participants in the preparation stages.

Exercise in Evaluation

We can illustrate what is required by supposing that we wish to explore three topics:

1. Increasing personal awareness (members share information and opinions)
2. Reaching a decision in a committee (members analyze the problem and agree on a course of action)
3. Resolving conflicting recommendations of two groups (members hear both proposals and try to reconcile them)

PERSONAL AWARENESS SHARING

1. Divide the class into small groups, and simultaneously in buzz sessions share personal insights, opinions, and feelings on a topic mean-

ingful to each member personally. Groups will meet for thirty minutes on three different days, beginning with no assigned leadership.
The objective is for *each* member to state explicitly what *every* other
member of the group believes about the topic.

2. After the three sessions are completed, members are asked to complete a number of evaluative scales giving ratings (5—to a very large
extent; 4—to a large extent; 3—to an average extent; 2—to a small
extent; 1—to a very small extent) in response to such questions as to
what extent the following took place:
   a. Did the group develop a climate promoting free, permissive talk?
   b. Did members communicate in ways encouraging the others to talk
      again later?
   c. Did members develop increasing compatibility and understanding
      of each other?
   d. Did members share their true feelings and beliefs?
      Members will score their ratings and compare and discuss how
      each evaluated the three sharing sessions.

COMMITTEE DECISION MAKING

1. Select from the class a group of five to seven. Have them select a
leader and a question of policy they feel strongly about. Ask them to
discuss in front of the class for forty-five minutes, analyzing the problem and agreeing (if possible) on a course of action.
2. Following the discussion, observers from the class should evaluate
the session by responding to two kinds of questions:
   a. How satisfactory was the decision reached?
      (1) To what extent did the decision represent the substance of the
          entire discussion?
      (2) To what extent are the members agreed on the decision
          reached?
   b. How effectively did the group use its time?
      (1) How adequately did the group analyze the problems involved?
      (2) How much time was spent on irrelevancies?
      (3) How thoroughly were alternatives discussed?
      (4) Did the members operate cohesively and cooperatively?

INTER-GROUP CONFERENCE

1. The class should elect three persons to role-play Teamsters' Union
representatives and three to represent trucking companies. The dispute is over the union drivers' demand for a 30 cent-an-hour raise.
The union and management delegates are to meet separately, outside
of class, to decide on the position they will take and their strategy.

In front of the class, the two delegations will conduct a conference where they attempt to reach a settlement.

2. The conference will then be evaluated by a four-member observer team appointed by the instructor. The observers will each have five minutes to evaluate the aspect each has concentrated on: (a) quality of the outcome, (b) quality of contributions by each member, (c) indications of intergroup cohesiveness and cooperation, and (d) indications of member satisfaction with the outcome.

Now for the *planning* questions: After the three exercises are completed, the class should ask what kinds of problems were encountered in

- Choosing participants
- Specifying leadership
- Selecting and wording questions
- Using information
- Planning physical arrangements
- Evaluating

IDENTIFYING PARTICIPANTS AND LEADERSHIP

Participants for classroom discussions are most easily selected by discovering clusters of students interested in a particular problem such as the United Nations, the grading system, regulation of marijuana, capital punishment, and so on. Certainly, members should not be assigned to a group unless they are interested in the subject for discussion.

In the assigning of students to decision-making groups, it is important that there be some measure of disagreement in the attitudes of members toward the problem. If the question is whether marijuana should be decriminalized and if all the participants agree beforehand, the discussion will not be very exciting or even necessary. Similarly, a conference involves controversy.

The membership of many groups is predetermined, and planners are not responsible for choosing and inviting persons to participate. For some discussions, however, selecting the participants is necessary. They will be chosen for knowledge of and interest in the problem and for special competence in communication and discussion.

Suppose the mayors of two adjoining cities must plan a conference to iron out some jurisdictional disputes in the areas of their common border. They must decide who, in addition to themselves, should attend. Which officials would be included would depend on the nature of the disputes and their individual competencies. If the disputes involved enforcing traffic regulations on streets dividing the cities, they would obviously consider their chiefs of police and perhaps their city engineers and directors of traffic. Among the available officers who could be invited, however, they might choose participants according to competence. Perhaps the police chiefs could not be gracefully excluded, but any others might be added only if they could be expected to make a particularly helpful contribution.

Usually, continuing groups have a designated leader, but often a group meeting for one or two sessions will elect a leader from among the participants after they assemble. In this event, however, the person chosen will be handicapped in having almost no time for advanced planning.

Questions for Discussion

An early step in preparing for a particular discussion is agreeing on the question. To be productive, groups must discuss questions, not statements, single words, or phrases.

Suppose that a board of directors has just learned during a meeting that, on the night before, burglars, probably youngsters, broke into the plant and poured motor oil over machinery and office equipment. The board has a problem, and much lively talk will result. A fascinating half hour may be consumed in considering any one of these questions: What is wrong with our youngsters these days? Have the American people lost all respect for property rights? What satisfaction do people get from doing malicious damage? Don't the schools train young people to know right from wrong? Why can't parents keep their children out of mischief? Why can't the police lock up all the burglars? These questions are interesting, but only indirectly related to the board's problem. The discussion will be of minimum value unless the group concentrates on a question or questions directly relevant to the group. Members can weigh the relevancy of questions by applying tests such as these:

Does this group need an answer to this question? Questions to be fruitful must be related to the group's interests and functions. The board of directors may be curious about the role of parents, schools, and police in preventing juvenile crime, but these matters are of indirect concern. Of more immediate concern to the board are questions such as these: What changes, if any, should be made in present arrangements for protecting the plant at night? Should additional men be assigned to the night watch crew?

Is this group competent to answer this question? Groups can waste happy hours considering questions that they cannot be expected to answer. The matter of police efficiency in locking up burglars is a problem for penologists and sociologists. The question, "What satisfaction do people get from doing malicious damage?" must be answered, if it can be answered, by psychologists and psychiatrists. The board of directors cannot profitably spend time discussing such questions.

Does this group have power to act upon the decisions agreed upon, or is it in a position to recommend to a group that does have power to act? The board of directors should not spend time discussing whether the police department should try harder to apprehend burglars and how policemen should be deployed to achieve increased vigilance. Rather, the board should consider whether it should recommend to the police department that it provide increased protection. This board cannot profitably decide what parents, schools, or other agencies should do. Similarly, the Security Council of the United Nations should not discuss, "What should be the Russian foreign policy toward China?" This group cannot set Russian policy, and the Kremlin would not be influenced by this group's recommendations.

Is this question one that requires collective thinking and interaction of the group, or could it be answered more adequately by research or by a single executive? The board's discussion will be inefficient if it asks, "Was the watchman asleep last night?" or "How did the burglars get inside the plant?" These questions must be answered by investigation, and usually such queries can most efficiently be pursued by a single individual. Probably, the board would direct an executive to investigate and recommend an answer to a question such as, "Should the chief of the night crew be replaced?"

Can the group answer this question in the time available? The requirements here are obvious. If the question is crucial, additional sessions must be scheduled, or a subgroup must be made responsible, or the question must be divided into more limited components, or some other method must be found for deciding.

SOURCES OF QUESTIONS

In most groups, problems arise from the functioning of the group; are internal to the operation, task, or responsibility of the group; or grow out of social, economic, or political circumstances or specific events outside the group that are related to the group's interests and functions. Here the challenge is to recognize what is the real question for discussion.

Questions come from many sources.

INTERESTS OF THE GROUP If a particular section of discussion students share some common concerns, fruitful questions can emerge from these concerns. A number of class members, for example, may be majoring in teacher education and hence interested in discussing the grading system, the differences between high school and college teaching, federal support of education, or other related matters.

The shared interest in studying discussion can also suggest topics: What are the possible leadership styles in discussion? To what extent should a designated leader exercise control over the group? What are the advantages of designating a leader in contrast to dividing leadership responsibilities?

INTEREST OF INDIVIDUALS Students may wish to suggest questions related to their individual interests and to their major fields of study. A student in liberal arts may want to discuss the standards for judging a man a success in our culture. A scientist or engineer may suggest as a topic, "Are scientists responsible for the uses made of their technological creations?" The premedical major may favor such questions as mercy killing and abortion.

CAMPUS AFFAIRS Perennial problems of the campus are always potential sources of discussion questions: To what extent should students have a voice in administering the college or university? To what extent do final examinations accomplish their stated purposes?

CURRENT EDUCATIONAL, POLITICAL, ECONOMIC, OR SOCIAL PROBLEMS Contemporary conditions in politics, business, education, religion, and so on may be sources of interesting discussion questions. Any particular discussion could be restricted to the problem at the local, state, national, or international level.

SPECIFIC EVENTS Another source of questions—and perhaps the most dramatic source of all—is the specific event or incident that touches the interests of the group. On campus a topic may be suggested when some decision of the college administration stirs controversy. Some international incident or local or regional catastrophe may suggest questions for classroom discussions.

KINDS OF QUESTIONS

Questions proposed for discussion can be of many kinds, and it is helpful if participants are aware of them. One especially useful differentiation among types is to distinguish among questions of fact, value, and policy.

QUESTIONS OF FACT Questions of fact deal with truth and falsity. Is this so, or is it not so? Does this characteristic exist, or does it not? Is this happening? For example, the question, "Are we in a business recession?" is a question of fact.

Such questions vary from those that are easy to answer to those so difficult as to be unanswerable with present knowledge. The difference lies in the extent to which the problem is subject to empirical verification. Obviously, we would not discuss questions of fact that could be answered by research, such as, "How many men in the United States are now unemployed?" However, a group might well discuss a question that can be partially answered by empirical methods but involves a judgment about the quality of the evidence. Examples are, "Is there a connection between cigarette smoking and lung cancer?" and "What evidence is there for a belief in flying saucers?"

The query, "Is there a God?" can be classified as a question of fact because either there is or there is not, but no amount of discussion could answer the question at the present time.

We should note that the answer to the question, "Are we in a business recession?" depends partially on what is meant by the word *recession*. Thus questions of fact that result in lively discussions are not so simple as they may seem at first glance.

QUESTIONS OF VALUE   A question of value asks for judgments that involve the attitudes and feelings of participants: How good is *X*? How shall *X* be evaluated? An example of a value question is, "Is capital punishment justified?" Here, again, part of the discussion must center on the meaning of *justified*. Also, the question of value goes a step beyond the question of fact, but it must embrace information before the value questions can be answered. We must agree on the *functions and purposes* for which capital punishment has been used before we can deal with justification.

QUESTIONS OF POLICY   Questions of policy ask, "What action should be taken?" "How shall we proceed in the future?" Often the word *should* appears in the question of policy: "Should youthful criminals be given stiffer punishment?" "Should the United States increase foreign aid?"

Reaching a decision on a question of policy almost always involves questions of fact and of value. Two examples may make these relationships clearer.

Suppose we have some persons on the campus who want to eliminate compulsory physical education. The policy question is, "Should the college (university) abolish the physical education requirement?" Antecedent to reaching a decision are questions of fact, such as, "Are students physically fit?" and questions of value, such as, "Is a physical fitness program a desirable part of a sound educational program at college level?" We may decide that students are not physically fit and that a fitness program is desirable; even so, the answer to the policy question is not automatically that the present program should be retained. The group is free to decide that the present program should be abolished and that a different method for guaranteeing fitness be put in its place. Thus all three kinds of questions are reasonable discussion tasks.

Another illustration could be encountered if a school were considering adopting an honor system for the administration of final examinations in place of providing proctors. A question of fact to be considered early may be, "Would an honor system for administering examinations work successfully on this campus?" A question of value would be, "Is an honor system a desirable thing?" Only after facing such questions as these could a group answer the decision-making question, "Should we recommend an honor system for this campus?"

NARROWING AND LIMITING

Questions selected must not be so broad that they encompass almost endless possibilities. Such questions as these are too broad: "What steps can be taken to promote the interest of young people in world affairs?" "What additional services can the university provide for students?"

The question should be narrowed and limited to the time available for discussion. A good question is, "What steps, if any, should be taken to ease East-West tensions?" It would be possible, however, to spend months or even years discussing this question. Planners of a forty-minute discussion should limit themselves to a tiny portion of this larger problem. A narrower limitation would be, "Should the United States try to improve relations with Cuba?" Even this question is complex for a short discussion. Perhaps a more realistic limitation for a short discussion would be, "Should the United States encourage businesses to trade with Cuba?" Further narrowing could be achieved by limiting the question to trade in nonmilitary merchandise or to automobiles.

Also, the question should be limited to a single problem; it should not be double-barreled, as in, "Should the United States nationalize the railroads and the coal mines?" It is difficult enough to discuss one complex problem at a time.

WORDING THE QUESTION

A final requirement in planning for a discussion topic is the wording of the question. The wording should be

OPEN TO ALTERNATIVE ANSWERS   Preferably, the question should be phrased so that it cannot be answered yes or no. It is not always possible to avoid the yes-or-no phrasing, but the many-sided question is usually more satisfactory for discussion. Some questions are unacceptable because, if taken literally, they could be answered in one word and the discussion would be over: "Should students study more?" The answer is yes. A better phrasing would be, "To what extent are students interested in academic achievement?" A yes-or-no question that is somewhat better is, "Is there a difference in the quality of undergraduate education offered by small colleges and large universities?"

Sponsors who phrase a yes-or-no question usually are interested in a much more complex answer than an affirmative or negative response. If a question were phrased, "Are examinations desirable?" the participants would probably discuss some such question as, "Under what conditions do examinations contribute to the educational development of students?" The question should be worded this way in the first place.

Some questions, of course, can be phrased most directly as yes-or-no questions. For example, there is no desirable alternative to the kind of policy question that asks about a change in a particular law such as, "Should capital punishment be abolished?" In some situations this is also the best way to narrow a problem to manageable proportions. If a group does not have time to discuss the question, "What policy should be applied in cases of student dishonesty?" it may be wise to discuss the more limited yes-or-no question, "Should students be expelled for copying during final examinations?"

CLEAR A statement that persists among the military is that any order that can be misunderstood will be misunderstood. This statement can certainly be applied to discussion questions. Vagueness must be avoided. What is meant by the question, "Should the United States adopt the policy of striking the enemy first?" or by this question, "Is the trend toward scientific education progress?" The wording here must be clarified, or the discussion will be out of focus from the beginning. If the first question is asking about preventive war, it should be worded to ask, "Should the United States initiate immediately a preventive war against nation X?"

UNBIASED The question should be impartially worded. It should not suggest the bias of those who worded it, as in, "Should the antilabor right-to-work laws be repealed?" Value judgments should be left to the participants. Also, the wording should not suggest the hoped-for outcome, as in, "Wouldn't you agree that University X is the best university in its conference?"

CONCISE Because participants need to grasp the question and keep it in mind throughout the discussion, it should be worded efficiently and succinctly. Doubtless the following example is exaggerated, but certainly anyone involved would be discouraged with this wording: "Would a lowering of personal income taxes or of corporation taxes and a shift in the rediscount rate controlled by the Federal Reserve Board be effective deterrents for control of recessionary tendencies in our economy, or are these proposals just impractical measures that sound good superficially?" This question was actually proposed as a subject for discussion.

Exercise

A group wishes to organize a discussion on the general topic of juvenile crime. Members then suggest these questions:

- Why is the crime rate increasing?
- How can we prevent juvenile crime?
- What are ways of punishing or rehabilitating youthful offenders?
- How can the rate of juvenile crime be reduced?
- What are the failures of parents in juvenile crime?
- How can the church help?
- Should juvenile offenders be given stiffer sentences?
- Is youthful crime a breakdown in cultural organization?
- Should parents be punished for the crimes of their children?
- Should chronic offenders be placed in special schools?

Decide on the three best questions for a discussion by a panel before a listening audience.

Planning Physical Arrangements

Another responsibility is to arrange the physical surroundings in which the discussion will occur. Thought should be given to time of day, meeting room, and such obvious aspects of physical comfort as adequate light, heat, and ventilation. Some hours of the day are more conducive to active thinking than others, although some kinds of informality can best be achieved around a luncheon table. Participants should be comfortable, but not extremely so; a group cannot do its most efficient thinking if, for example, members are given an open invitation to relax as they might if seated in soft, overstuffed lounge chairs. A comfortable straight-backed chair with padded seat is preferable. Members are usually more productive when seated at a table where they can take notes and have reference materials easily accessible.

Ideally, every participant should be located so that he or she can look directly at each other person without turning his or her chair. This arrangement is not easy to achieve and may explain the popularity of the round table notion, although round tables are not commonly available. When a group is seated at a rectangular table, persons located on the sides cannot face everyone at once:

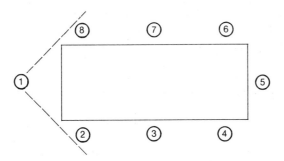

member 3 cannot look at 2 and 4 at the same time. Nevertheless, he or she can turn from 2 to address 4 or 5 without turning his chair.

With this arrangement, the designated leader should seat himself or herself at position number 1 or 5, because he or she can then face everyone directly, although still unable to look every person in the eye at the same time. The leader can turn from number 8 to 2 with only about a 90-degree movement of his or her head; the shift to face any others is even less. Surprisingly, from the leader's position, the angle of shift is greater at a round table when he or she turns from the person on his or her right to the one on his or her left. The angle would approximate what it is in the diagram if the leader were seated at position 3. The disadvantage with a rectangular table is that only members 1 and 5 have a good view of every-one simultaneously. At a round table, every member has as direct a view of everyone else as it is possible to provide when there are more than three persons in the group.

More important than such rather obvious matters as furniture arrange-ment and temperature control is the question of which members to place where, in relation to each other and the leader. One consideration is power structure within the group. Because the designated leader plays an influential role, it is usually undesirable to place the most powerful per-sons next to the leader. Such a concentration of highs will make it even harder for low-status persons to speak up or to disagree, especially if the highs seem to take similar positions. Another consideration is the talkative-ness of members. A person known to be a high participator can be placed in the least desirable physical location, and he or she will probably take an active part just the same, whereas the timid, shy or reluctant communi-cator can be placed in a prominent position, such as one near the leader, where talking is easier.

Studies of physical arrangements in discussion indicate a relationship between seating position and communicative interaction. When members are seated in a circle, they tend to talk more readily to those opposite than to those next to them, at least in some kinds of situations. When a rectan-gular table is used, those who become high participators and who may emerge as leaders tend to choose the ends of the table or a central posi-tion. Those who talk least are inclined to take seats at the corners.[1] Of course, individuals manage "personal space" as they assess intimacy and stress in the particular situation.[2]

SUPPLEMENTARY READING

Barnlund, Dean C., and Haiman, Franklyn S. *The Dynamics of Discussion*. Boston: Houghton Mifflin, 1960. Chapter 4.

Bormann, Ernest G. *Discussion and Group Methods*. Second Edition. New York: Harper and Row, 1975. Chapter 13.

Collins, Barry E., and Guetzkow, Harold. *A Social Psychology of Group Processes for Decision-Making*. New York: John Wiley & Sons, 1964, pp. 88–106.

[1] A. Paul Hare and Robert F. Bales, "Seating Position and Small Group Interaction," in A. P. Hare, E. Borgatta, and R. Bales, *Small Groups: Studies in Social Interaction*, rev. ed., New York: Alfred A. Knopf, 1965, pp. 427–433.

[2] Lawrence B. Rosenfeld, *Human Interaction in the Small Group Setting*, Columbus, Ohio: Charles E. Merrill, 1973, p. 198.

Gouran, Dennis S. *Discussion: The Process of Group Decision-Making.* New York: Harper and Row, 1974. Chapter 9.

Johnson, David W., and Johnson, Frank P. *Joining Together: Group Theory and Group Skills.* Englewood Cliffs, N.J.: Prentice-Hall, 1975. Chapters 3 and 10.

QUESTIONS AND EXERCISES

1. Suppose you are in charge of planning a discussion where two participants are extremely influential and powerful, whereas the others are new to the group and may feel inadequate. Explain how you would take these facts into account in arranging for the discussion.

2. The following questions have been proposed for discussion by a panel of college students. The program is to be televised regionally and is to last fifty-nine minutes. Some of these questions are satisfactory, and some are not. Evaluate them by applying the requirements for adequate discussion questions.

   a. The federal government should provide help, through legislation, to meet future demands for more and better educational facilities.
   b. Should students in this college with an *A* in a course prior to the final examination be exempted from the final examination?
   c. Does Russia fit into the picture of world affairs?
   d. Should the university committee on student affairs be so dominated by the faculty?
   e. What should be done to secure peace?
   f. What action, if any, should be taken to alleviate the parking problem on this campus?
   g. Should there be high taxes on economy?
   h. How can the United States best promote friendly relations with the newer nations of Africa?

3. Your department is planning a career day for those completing degrees, emphasizing job choices, opportunities, interviewing techniques, résumé preparation, and so on. Three guest speakers are coming for the day: a vice-president for personnel of a large manufacturing plant, a successful teacher from a local community college, and a managing director of a major television station.

   Divide the class into two task groups. The purpose of the exercise is to propose a plan for the discussions *with students* to be held during the day to achieve maximum information exchange for the benefit of those seeking jobs.

   A. Group 1 is to plan the discussions involving small groups for not more than seven persons. Analyze what the situation calls for, specify the physical arrangements, suggest the questions to be used to begin the discussion, and *write* the publicity flyer to be distributed to attract students.

B. Group 2 is to plan the discussions involving large numbers of students (such as classes or a large meeting for from fifty to one hundred). Analyze requirements, specify physical setting, suggest the questions to be addressed, and *write* the publicity flyer to be used to attract students.

Have each group report its proposal to the class and critique each of the recommendations for achieving the purposes intended.

5 Securing and Using Information

Groups need sound information as a basis for logical conclusions. Good decisions do not flow from a pooling of ignorance. Because nothing constructive can result simply from collective group thought if the thinking consists of unsupported opinions, an uninformed group will reach a poor decision.

A study conducted at the University of Michigan[1] suggests that the use of facts may be even more important in some situations than in others. In careful observation of seventy-two decision-making conferences in business and government, measures were made of two kinds of conflict: substantive conflict, consisting of the number of supportive comments made contrasted with the number of disagreements expressed; and affective conflict, defined as the extent to which trained observers noted member frustrations or interpersonal clashes. Estimates also were made of the amount of consensus resulting from the discussion.

For groups in substantive conflict, those having more factual knowledge and making more extensive use of the facts were more likely to resolve conflict and reach consensus. Significantly, also, the chairmen of groups that experienced high substantive conflict but went on to reach consensus worked much harder at the task of making use of information than did chairpersons where groups did not reach agreement. Chairpersons whose

[1] Reported in Barry E. Collins and H. Guetzkow, *A Social Psychology of Group Processes for Decision-Making* (New York: John Wiley & Sons, 1964), pp. 106–119.

groups achieved consensus made three times as many attempts to elicit factual information from participants.

Use of facts did not give the same results for groups in affective or interpersonal conflict. In these groups, consensus was related to partial withdrawal from the total task by concentrating on simpler agenda items, to lack of personal interest in the outcome, and other factors.

What should be noted is that when members disagree about a policy, groups sometimes can resolve differences by looking at the facts. Certainly, in cases where information is clearly needed, members cannot progress beyond differences until they obtain the information.

Sources of Information

The college student is already familiar with the basic sources of information, and we should not in this kind of book take time for a complete treatment of research methods. What we will do here is to review the basic sources of information in order to help members of a group check on every possibility.

PERSONAL KNOWLEDGE

Most decisions made by small groups concern problems with which the member participating has had some acquaintance and knowledge. When the participant can use some of his or her own experiences of the past, he or she will talk with enthusiasm and involvement. It is also likely that each member's background has been unique, and thus for a member to overlook any past experience that would be helpful is to deprive the group of a bit of information that can come only from this one source.

OBSERVATION

In preparation for discussion of some topics, members may be able to make a special observation of relevant conditions. In this event, too, there is gain from the member's feeling that he or she has become personally involved in the problem. Members will usually report on their observations with enthusiasm, and for them the problem has become more vivid. Of course, personal observation is limited to certain kinds of problems.

If the group feels it will benefit from making personal observations, members must keep in mind three requirements for acceptable investigation. The first is seeing accurately. The observer must place himself or herself in a position to observe and spend sufficient time on the scene to see exactly what is there. Another essential is reporting accurately. This requisite involves exact use of words. The observer must be able to report so precisely that listeners who did not see will understand what was witnessed. A third requirement is reporting fairly. The observer must attempt to describe what he or she saw without regard to whether he or she liked what was seen. If the observer favors federal aid to education and has observed the operation of a federal program in the local schools, he or she must be careful not to make his or her report sound more favorable than the conditions warrant. After the observer has reported on the situation accurately and fairly, of course, he or she is free to draw any conclusions from the facts just as other members can introduce their own opinions in response.

INTERVIEW

A very valuable source of information for many discussion groups is the interview with persons who are in a position to know pertinent facts. Students preparing for a discussion on penalties for violations of automobile regulations probably would gather most of their information by talking with the director of traffic and parking, members of the discipline committee, and students who had violated the regulations.

A number of cautions must be kept in mind in connection with interviewing. Not every person in an official position knows enough about a particular problem to be worth the time and thought required for a good interview. Also a person in a position to know may not have been on that particular job long enough to answer the questions. In learning about parking violations, for example, the investigator may go to the chief of police and find that the latter only carries out instructions for issuing tickets and knows nothing about reasons for policy. The director of traffic and parking may be responsible for policy but may be so new in the job that he or she has not yet learned why the regulations are as they are. Thus the investigator should make some discreet inquiries about who knows the most about what before he or she uses up investigation time.

Another caution is that the interview should be planned carefully in order to be courteous and also productive. The interviewer should ask for an appointment at a convenient time, specify the nature of his or her visit, and respect time limits established in advance. He or she should plan the questions carefully and should not waste time by probing outside the authority's competence. Questions should deal directly with the area of expert knowledge. It is especially important to avoid asking for information that can be obtained by reading what the authority has written or that is readily available in printed sources.

A special kind of pencil and paper interview is the public opinion poll or survey. If a group is discussing academic study habits or conditions, it may be useful to ask members of a housing group to fill out a survey giving the hours they study, the places they study, and similar information. It must be remembered that formulating opinion questions and sampling questionnaires is a high-level skill and the student may need expert guidance in the use of this technique. Sometimes the investigator determines the outcome of a poll by careless wording of questions.

READING

The most important single source of information, of course, is the library. The discusser must be proficient in locating materials of many different kinds.

REFERENCE WORKS Useful as sources of general information are encyclopedias such as the *Britannica* or the *Americana* and their annual yearbook supplements. To begin learning about the treatment of juvenile offenders, for example, the discusser may read first a general article in a good encyclopedia on juvenile courts or children's courts. At the end of a major article there usually is a short list of excellent references on the subject.

Even more valuable for many purposes are special reference works such as the *Encyclopedia of the Social Sciences*; encyclopedias on religions, education, and other special subjects; and dictionaries, specialized yearbooks, and atlases.

Biographical information is at times important to the discusser. *Who's Who* and *Who's Who in America* are familiar. There are also numerous biographical dictionaries for well-known persons in a particular state or region and in specialized fields such as those listed in *American Men of Science, Leaders in Education, Directory of American Scholars,* and *Who's Who in Engineering*. When a discussion group is evaluating a proposal by some authority, it is helpful to know who he or she is and what his or her qualifications are. For some kinds of subjects, especially, the opinions of experts form the best guides for judgment by a group. If a group were discussing questions such as, "What evidence is there for a belief in telepathy?" or "Can life as we know it exist on Mars?" expert opinion would be the controlling information; in such cases, the group should learn about the background of each alleged expert.

MAGAZINES Because most discussions deal with current problems, magazine articles are often the best sources of up-to-the-minute information. To locate helpful articles quickly, the researcher must use indexes to periodicals.

PAMPHLETS Pamphlet materials are somewhat harder to locate than are books and magazine articles. However, there are two dependable indexes listing many of these publications. *Public Affairs Information Service* lists publications of all kinds, including pamphlets, that deal with current problems in public affairs. H. W. Wilson Company's *Vertical File* also indexes pamphlets. The difficulty comes in finding these ephemeral materials in a particular library or in having time to order copies. The indexes give names and addresses of organizations that have published each pamphlet, along with the price if a charge is made. Cost is usually nominal, and many are supplied free upon request to the sponsoring organization.

Special interest groups publish materials on many topics. Names and addresses of such organizations can be obtained from directories such as the *Guide to Public Affairs Organizations,* the *World Almanac,* and the U.S. Department of Commerce publication *Trade and Professional Associations of the United States.* If a group were discussing hospitalization insurance, for instance, an inquiry to the American Medical Association would probably bring a supply of relevant pamphlet materials.

The discusser must be a careful reader of such materials. They are almost always published to promote the interests of the organization paying the printing bill and must be evaluated in that light. However, they often contain much accurate and useful information. The reader must separate the helpful facts from the special interest pleadings.

GOVERNMENT PUBLICATIONS   Official publications prepared by government officials can sometimes be valuable sources of information. The researcher should be especially familiar with the *Congressional Record,* which contains official proceedings and speeches in both houses of Congress and an amazing accumulation of articles in the appendix. Committees of the two houses hold extensive hearings on a large variety of subjects; published transcripts of committee hearings are storehouses of information, expert testimony, and opinions.

Other government publications can be located through a monthly catalog of *United States Government Publications.*

STATISTICAL INFORMATION   Facts in the form of statistical tables can be vital in some discussions. Fortunately, this kind of information is readily available in many different places. The U.S. Department of Commerce issues an *Abstract of the Census* and the *Statistical Abstract of the United States,* which contain a variety of facts on population, education, business, and so on. This department also publishes information on domestic and foreign trade in its monthly *Survey of Current Business.* The Department of Labor has a similar publication, *Monthly Labor Review,* giving facts on employment and similar matters. Statistical data of various kinds appear in such popular periodicals as *World Almanac* and *Information Please Almanac. Statesman's Year Book* supplies much statistical information on the nations of the world.

Gathering Information

A small group is often faced with the task of becoming well informed on a complex problem in a short time. Unfortunately, the shortage of time seems to be almost a universal characteristic in discussion. A committee may be required to report in two weeks; a city council meets every Monday evening and considers several complicated matters each time—and, in between, members are busy making a living. Preparation time for discussion is nearly always shorter than the members would wish.

Compensating somewhat for this handicap is the gain from a group's opportunity to divide the labor of collecting information. To mention this approach is not to suggest that any member can thereby abdicate his or her responsibility for becoming informed. However, a division of labor can eliminate unnecessary duplication of effort and make preparation more efficient. It should be emphasized that all members must be informed, and there are certain sources that all should consult, so that there will be a basis for common understanding of the problem.

Collins and Guetzkow, basing their reasoning partially on the work of Donald T. Campbell, have explained what makes intellectual division of labor possible. Each member of a group has available to him information from three sources: (1) his own direct observation and research, (2) observations of the investigations of others, and (3) verbal contributions of other group members: "In terms of the final information (or acquired behavioral disposition as Campbell would call it), *knowledge and habits gained through any of the three sources can contribute to the group product.* . . . Although one group member must first 'learn' or observe on his own, the rest of the group can assimilate the same knowledge with less effort than was involved in the original learning. In short, the verbal statements of a single group member are an important and efficient source of knowledge for other group members." Collins and Guetzkow go on to state a proposition recognized in essence by Aristotle and supported by recent experimental evidence: "The group is most likely to accept a member's contribution (a) when it is well supported by evidence, (b) when it is logically sound or internally consistent, and (c) when it is consistent with past experience." [2]

Although a group preparing for discussion should use division of labor, there are also some risks if a member fails to perform his or her task or if some members are confused by their fragmented reading. They must decide carefully how to divide the work because some persons will be better at particular assignments.

Evaluating Information

With regard to relying on others, the important questions concern observer credibility. We want to know what other observers have learned, but which reports can we believe? Have they recorded the information we need, or must we guess from indirect references they happen to make?

[2] Ibid., pp. 37–39.

READING CRITICALLY

Deliberate lying and distortion do not occur too often in printed media although there are enough instances of fabrication to make the discerning reader wary. Biases and hidden interests of those controlling information releases can mislead the reader. Some amusing examples of this occur in television as well as publishing. Ford Motor Company once insisted on the deletion of a picture of the Chrysler Building, and a railroad sponsor took out a bit of dialogue from a program using the line, "I'd rather fly." A program on Andrew Carnegie had an uncomplimentary remark about John D. Rockefeller; the reference was deleted because a Rockefeller was on the board of the sponsoring corporation. Many newspapers have long been accused of trimming their editorial sails so as not to offend their advertisers.

Only occasionally, however, is there flagrant fabrication. One such incident occurred in Times Square when a white woman told police that a black stranger forced his attentions on her and stabbed her husband. Later the wife admitted the stabbing was done by a white man, a former friend. She confessed that she and her husband, while the husband lay bleeding on the sidewalk, made a whispered agreement to lie about the assailant's identity. The government's deliberate misrepresentation of the facts about the Vietnam War, Watergate, and the activities of the CIA and FBI have resulted in the media being more critical in accepting the government's version of the facts.

Perhaps even more troublesome to the investigator than intentional deception is the more common unintentional distortion. One cause is brevity. There is rarely enough space in the newspaper or magazine to report the whole truth. Something must be left out or condensed. The source must make a selection and naturally leaves out what suits him or her least. Thus another cause for inaccuracy is human bias and limitation. Inexperienced observers may not see the right things even though they were right on the scene. Given an experienced observer and adequate opportunity to observe, the reporter cannot tell someone else everything he or she saw and heard and felt. Also, time seems always to be short; the story is covered hastily, written up quickly, and printed hurriedly. The amazing thing is that a news magazine, for example, is as accurate and helpful as it is when it must appear every week and compete for the very latest in news coverage.

Still another obstacle to accuracy is that reports must be put into words, which are fragile vessels for saying precisely what the observer wants to say and nothing more. Even if reporters have ample time for observation and ample media space for their reports and are completely honest and control their biases, the language they use may still admit unconscious slanting according to the way they look at the world.

EVALUATING SOURCES

How do investigators check on the reliability of their sources? For one thing, they do not depend on a single source but read as widely as possible. For another, in addition to being analytical and tentative in their approach, they are cautious about interpreting the language of the report. Then, too, they ask some direct questions about information and about the observers responsible for the information:

1. Is the information accurate? Can it be confirmed by two or more sources?
2. Is the information recent? Conditions may have changed, and the most recent information available is the kind needed in discussion. For this reason, the discusser will usually find books and general reference materials less helpful than current periodicals.
3. Is the information complete? Does the information collected describe only part of the picture? The only cure for incomplete information, of course, is to do additional research.

Questions testing the credibility of observers, authorities, and experts who have given testimony of interest to discussion groups must be somewhat broader. An authority may be an institution as well as an individual expert. A newspaper, a magazine, a church body, a labor union, or a research organization may express a collective opinion, and this position may be cited as the basis for decision. Reports and opinions can be evaluated by asking about competence and trustworthiness.

First, *is the authority competent?* In order to have confidence in authoritative testimony, the expert must be competent in general; that is, have special training, knowledge, and experience and have a reputation for honesty and accuracy; in addition, he or she must have special competence in the particular subject matter on which he or she is testifying. One of the requirements for special competence is that the authority have been in a position to observe the matters on which he or she can testify as an expert.

The statement of an authority should not be confused with the testimony of a witness to a particular event. In court, any person who has general competence (for example, normal intelligence and eyesight) can testify to events he or she observed firsthand. Inferences can be based on statements made by such ordinary witnesses, but authoritative testimony is much broader and more important. A witness, for example, may establish the existence of an event, such as the presence of a suspect at the scene of a murder, but only an expert can be relied on for an opinion as to whether a particular gun fired the fatal shot.

These same tests may be applied to evaluate sources of information. A magazine or newspaper, for instance, must establish a reputation for general honesty and reliability, as well as for special competence in particular areas where its testimony carries authoritative weight. Otherwise, readers can have no confidence in inferences based on facts or opinions from such sources.

Secondly, *is the authority unbiased?* An authoritative statement is not just an ordinary opinion. In an election campaign, partisans on either side say, "In my opinion, candidate X is the man best qualified for this office," but these statements are not expert testimony. An authority weakens the weight of his or her opinion as an expert if he or she has a reason for bias; moreover, the expert is expected to be objective in his or her evaluations even if he or she does have a personal prejudice.

The most convincing expert testimony is obtained when an authority offers an objective opinion in spite of the fact that he or she may have personal reasons for disliking what his or her judgment tells him or her is the case. A person in this position giving ordinary testimony is sometimes called a *reluctant witness,* and a similar designation might be given an authority who expresses an opinion contrary to his or her private interests.

Using Information

Much careful research can be wasted unless the information is contributed when the group needs it. Members must be well enough informed to supply it; and if they fail to recognize what is needed at a particular time but attempt to contribute it five minutes later, the efficiency of the group will be impaired. If the group needs certain information that no member can supply it is often wise or necessary to adjourn the meeting and assemble again when the proper facts are obtained. A discussion simply cannot proceed properly without the right facts. Irving Lee has commented on the number of situations in which "the speaking took fire almost in inverse ratio to the thinness of the argumentative fuel." [3] The designated leader of a group should insist—patiently but firmly—that the relevant facts be brought out when they are needed.

In contributing facts, members should remember that discussion is a cooperative, sharing enterprise. They should listen carefully to information presented by others and try to build upon it by adding relevant facts that further illuminate the situation. They should be eager to capitalize on the specialized knowledge and unique background experiences of other members. At the same time, the members must not allow their respect for the group to dull their critical analysis of the facts and experiences presented by the other members. In these ways, they demonstrate their understanding that facts do make a difference in the quality of the group product and

[3] Irving Lee, *How to Talk with People* (New York: Harper and Row, 1952), p. xi.

at the same time make their maximum contribution to the group's knowledge of the total problem.

INFORMATION PROCESSING

It is not easy to explain how individuals process information as they work with others in a group to reason their way to sensible conclusions. They must in a particular context examine facts and the inferences that logically follow, and they must deal with *probable* outcomes rather than certain truths.

As Mortensen notes, each person "is an integrated system of complex and interdependent functions designed to interpret events in ways that are consistent with its past experience and existing physical and psychological state."[4] The same person may respond to similar cues differently in various situations because he or she may react at one of several levels of meaning or view the information against a backdrop of alternative interpretations. After assigning meaning and choosing the preferred interpretation, he or she must still integrate the information into already-held concepts and make it appropriately consistent with the situation, task, and so on while taking into account the others in the group.

Some persons are more or less closed-minded when others offer information conflicting with their past experiences and beliefs, whereas some group members are more open to new interpretations. Burgoon suggests that persons with "low tolerance for ambiguity" have difficulty seeing unfamiliar situations flexibly.[5] They then may grow impatient when a group wishes to consider all alternatives fully. March and Simon posit an extension of this difficulty, called *uncertainty absorption,* when inferences are communicated to the group instead of the detailed information on which the inferences are based:

> Through the process of uncertainty absorption, the recipient of a communication is severely limited in his ability to judge its correctness. Although there may be various tests of apparent validity, internal consistency, and consistency with other communications, the recipient must, by and large, repose his confidence in the editing process that has taken place, and, if he accepts the communication at all, accept it pretty much as it stands. To the extent that he can interpret it, his interpretation must be based primarily on his confidence in the source and his knowledge of the biases to which the source is subject, rather than on a direct examination of the evidence.[6]

[4] David C. Mortensen, *Communication: The Study of Human Interaction* (New York: McGraw-Hill, 1972), p. 70.

[5] Michael Burgoon, "Amount of Conflicting Information in a Group Discussion and Tolerance for Ambiguity as Predictors of Task Attractiveness," *Speech Monographs* 38 (June 1971): 121–124.

[6] James G. March and Herbert A. Simon, "Communication," in *Dimensions in Communication,* Second Edition, edited by James H. Campbell and Hal W. Hepler (Belmont, Calif.: Wadsworth Publishing Co., 1970), p. 76.

Uncertainty is increased when the information that must be absorbed is complex and when the group must deal with unfamiliar concepts couched in unfamiliar language.

Careful use of information is essential to group deliberation, but information is usually presented in bits and pieces; it must be organized in some meaningful way. Facts must be interrelated so that valid inferences may be drawn from them. The process of recognizing interrelationships among data and reaching inferences involves reasoning. The reasoning process is really quite simple; we reason every waking hour and on the whole do so quite competently. Admittedly, we encounter difficulties as we undertake to think our way through complex and unfamiliar problems, but there is little mystery or complexity in the process itself. Most reasoning errors arise from ignorance of reasoning patterns and from mental carelessness. We must examine patterns of inference and learn to recognize fallacies in reasoning, errors resulting at least in part from carelessness.

THE TOULMIN MODEL OF ARGUMENT

An extremely useful model for describing a logical process of reasoning is Stephen Toulmin's *The Uses of Argument*.[7] His model for recording the interrelationships of evidence and conclusions is based on simple concepts and easily grasped rules.

What we will do here is explain Toulmin's layout in simple form, argue that it is usefully applicable to discussion, and urge the student to look at Toulmin's book for further understanding.

We begin with an assertion: George is a student in this college. When we make this statement to someone we *claim* it to be true. If our statement is challenged, we must attempt to produce the support we had for making it in the first place. If it is said, "How do you know for a fact that George is a student here?" we may respond, "He is attending one of my classes." This statement then is the *datum* or fact that is the basis for our assertion. We can propose the first relationship between *data* and *claim*:

Datum ⟶ So Claim

George is a member
of one of my classes ⟶ So, he is a student
in this college.

Now the other person has a right to ask about the step from data to claim. Is there an appropriate and legitimate (logical!) connection? What is needed at this point, Toulmin says, "are general, hypothetical statements, which can act as bridges, and authorise [sic] the sort of step to which our

[7] Stephen Toulmin, *The Uses of Argument* (Cambridge, England: Cambridge University Press, 1958). Also available in paperback.

particular argument commits us." He calls these connecting bridges *warrants*. Persons who appear in a classroom and sit among other students listening to the instructor are presumed to be students. George has been coming to this classroom since the first day of the term and sitting among others known to be students; the widely accepted notion that those attending a class are students is authorization or warrant for our assertion that George is a student. We can represent these three elements schematically:

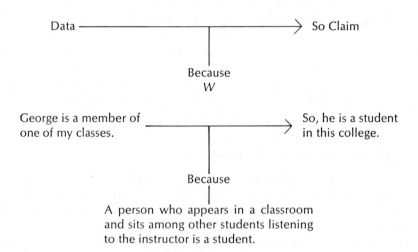

Data ⟶ So Claim

Because
W

George is a member of one of my classes. ⟶ So, he is a student in this college.

Because

A person who appears in a classroom and sits among other students listening to the instructor is a student.

The warrant may seem incidental and obvious in some cases. Its task is to record explicitly the justifiability of the step involved from data to claim. It also is a more general statement than the pieces of data; it may be authorization for a large number of specific data–claim relationships.

Now we can start to recognize the differences introduced by dealing with subjects from different fields. There are many kinds of warrants. In some fields it is fairly easy to establish the validity of warrants and see the data–claim relationships they authorize. There are simple ways of establishing that a person is enrolled as a student in a particular college. As we move into the political realm, however, and talk about invasion of another nation's territory leading to war, we cannot be certain that relationships are so invariable. Thus we must protect ourselves against making unreasonable claims and offering warrants that cannot establish an unvarying relationship. Some warrants in some areas justify a data–claim step only if we are willing to allow for exceptions or to express some qualifications in making the statement. Toulmin thus adds a fourth element, a *qualifier*, to the data, claim, and warrant already introduced. Now we can qualify the step from data to claim and say that because George is a member of one of my classes, he is *probably* a student in this college or *almost certainly* a student here or *presumably* a student here.

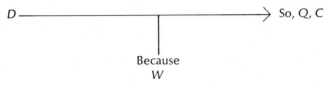

Also, the qualification step introduces the possibility of stating the *reservation* or *rebuttal,* as Toulmin calls it, that can be cited as recognition that the data–claim relationship may not hold. The reservations indicate circumstances in which the warrant would not be valid and would be set aside. It is possible that George is only masquerading as a student. If he is, the general warrant that those who attend and listen are students will not hold in this case. The Toulmin layout enables us to foresee this possibility and allow for it. We are thus less likely to make a mistake in reasoning. We can also state our assertion less rigidly and positively; we are not forced into an all-or-nothing claim:

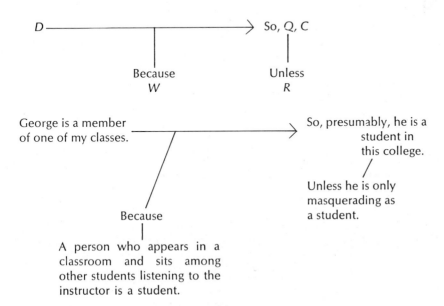

The final element in the layout is *backing* for the warrant. We must ask why a warrant has authority or why this particular warrant is sound. Backing varies with the field, also. The kind of support needed to show that a person who attends a class is a student may be quite different from backing for the warrant that invasion of any nation's territory will lead to war. To complete the Toulmin scheme, we can represent our argument in this way:

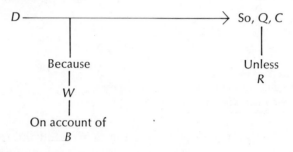

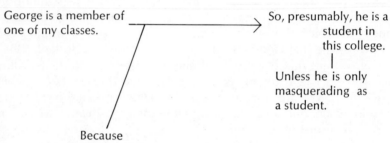

It is in providing the backing for warrants that traditional inductive forms come into use. Support may be in the form of specific instances, examples, analogy, or any of the other kinds.

We should note that there can be more than one fact in the data and that we could have several data all related to the same claim. We can allege, for example, that Mary, Sue, and Jim are students in the college by pointing to the same relationships already established. Likewise, there can be multiple reservations and additional backing. George may not be a student even though we have presumed he is one because he is actually another instructor sitting in the class to observe teaching technique or a student from another college who is a visitor or an alumnus of the college who has received permission to audit this one course. If someone questions whether our backing for the warrant is sufficient, we may need to quote an authority such as the dean of the college to the effect that anyone attending classes is presumed to be a student.

We should be able now to lay out a more complex argument in this manner. Suppose we have asserted that the Russians are more likely than we are to place men on other planets first. Our reason for making this claim is that they have developed rockets with greater thrust (data).

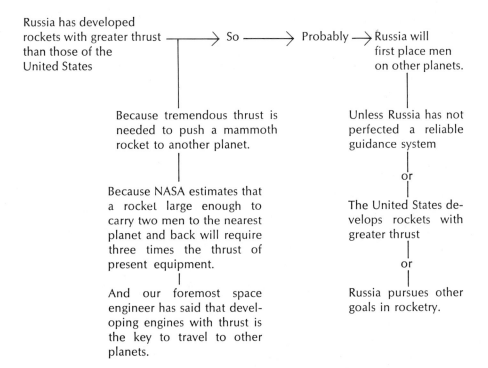

Russia has developed rockets with greater thrust than those of the United States ——→ So ——→ Probably —→ Russia will first place men on other planets.

Because tremendous thrust is needed to push a mammoth rocket to another planet.

Because NASA estimates that a rocket large enough to carry two men to the nearest planet and back will require three times the thrust of present equipment.

And our foremost space engineer has said that developing engines with thrust is the key to travel to other planets.

Unless Russia has not perfected a reliable guidance system

or

The United States develops rockets with greater thrust

or

Russia pursues other goals in rocketry.

This cause-to-effect relationship is reasonable, for it is recognized that tremendous thrust will be required to push to other planets the necessarily mammoth rocket (warrant). This warrant can be questioned and hence may require backing. Even though the claim may seem a reasonable inference from these data, in view of the warrant with its backing, Toulmin recognizes that it is wiser to talk about probability than certainty. Hence between data and claim he supplies a qualification, such as *presumably, probably, perhaps, in 98 percent of the cases,* or whatever seems supportable by the circumstances. Also, there is always the possibility that the outcome will be interfered with by intervening causes; hence there is a place for reservations; unless some other force prevents it, the claim seems reasonable.

When a group reasons by the process Toulmin described, it is proceeding in a manner that is comparable to the scientific method. Scientists attempt to maintain an objective view by striving to keep themselves and their feelings outside the problem. They try to make measurements precise as well as objective and to make definitions operational. They collect information exhaustively and suspend judgment until the facts are in. Even then they accept conclusions tentatively, being the first to insist on revising their own findings in the light of newer data. Scientists do not merely guess about the way nature may be ordered, although they do not reject the use of hunches, intuition, and creative conjecture. What they do do is state a hypothesis carefully and then test it experimentally or by controlled observation. They then restate it with more confidence, or they forget it and try something else. They do not keep pushing it because it was their idea or because they like the sound of its expression. They move forward by building on what has been learned before, one step at a time.

A small group cannot stop and run experiments, of course. But members can emulate the respect of scientists for facts, their care in checking on the reasoning process, their willingness to revise and to hold views tentatively, and their willingness to be reflective.

Ehninger and Brockriede, in their book *Decision by Debate*,[8] have extended the Toulmin model to the reasoning process used by the debater. They illustrate its use in causal relation, generalization, and analogy. They also show how this same layout of argument can be used where the datum is a statement from a credible authority and where the argument is in the "emotional mode" of proof. These authors call this last form the use of *motivational* proofs. Finally, they discuss fallacious reasoning in terms of the Toulmin system, explaining unwarranted claims, deficient warrants, ignored reservations, and overstated claims along with the more familiar kinds of fallacies. Because careful reasoning is as critical to the discusser as to the debater, the student seeking additional help in applying the Toulmin system is urged to consult the Ehninger and Brockriede book.

This Toulmin model is worthy of careful study. It enables the reasoner to be properly cautious by qualifying his or her claims. He or she avoids rash inferences pretending inevitability by noting the reservations (that is, in Toulmin's terms, rebuttal) that may alter his or her claims. If his or her data statement is questioned, he or she can make this statement a claim and back up to construct a new model supporting it. Finally, the Toulmin

[8] Douglas Ehninger and Wayne Brockriede, *Decision by Debate* (New York: Dodd, Mead, 1963), Chapters 8–12.

model enables the reasoner to support warrants. In the example given, he or she may back the warrant by citing specific instances of rockets that required certain amounts of thrust, through analogy, with authoritative statements, or by any combination of these and other inferential patterns.

The Toulmin scheme should also lend itself easily to discussion groups. Although it may seem blunt to say, "I'm not sure that your reasoning is sound," it may be easier to say, "What were you considering the warrant that connects your data and claim in this case?" A group approach should be possible in citing additional data for a particular claim or backing for a warrant. Any system that promotes sound reasoning will certainly be a welcome contribution to the conscientious discussion group.

It should be noted that there are a number of kinds of reasoning in which we can proceed from the data to the claim in the Toulmin model. These methods are based on different assumptions that need to be made explicit in order to minimize the likelihood that we will reach false conclusions.

INDUCTIVE REASONING

With this method of generalization, we may cite a number of specific instances that have a common characteristic. We, therefore, tend to believe that the claim, or conclusion, may well be true.

This kind of inference can be tested by asking questions such as these: (1) Have enough instances been examined to justify a generalization? (2) Are the instances examined typical or representative of all the members of the class of objects covered by the generalization? This test asks whether the sample is biased.

The problem of sampling is familiar in connection with public-opinion polling. The pollster wishes to select a random sample of the population. If he or she wants to know how much money Americans expect to invest in government bonds during the next year, he or she must avoid asking only bankers. The proportion of bankers interviewed must be similar to the proportion of bankers in the total population; included in the sample must be a proper proportion of all other socioeconomic groupings in the nation.

A third question to ask is, "Are there negative instances?" The reason here is obvious. The generalization based on a sample is questionable if negative examples turn up.

Inductive reasoning thus involves a complex chain of interlocking inferences. Viewed from one perspective, this chain partly consists of drawing, from pieces of evidence that form a related pattern, a conclusion, generalization, general statement, or general premise. But once a generalization or general premise is established, it is possible to move again in a specific direction by applying the general statement to a particular instance. A deductive inference, then, moves from the general to the specific.

DEDUCTIVE REASONING

Deductive inference is customarily presented as a syllogism:

> All teachers are scholars.
> Jones is a teacher.
> Therefore, Jones is a scholar.

There are here three statements: a major premise, or generalization, which has been established, perhaps inductively, by other reasoning methods; a minor premise, which asserts that a particular instance can be classified within the category of events covered by the generalization in the major premise; and a conclusion, which follows from the first two statements.

The form here is crucial. Note that there are also three terms: the major term is *scholars,* the condition of existence that we are establishing in the particular case of Jones; the minor term is *Jones,* the particular instance about whom we are making a deduction; the middle term, *all teachers,* is most vital to the validity of the syllogism—in the major premise it includes any and every teacher within the category of teachers, and in the minor premise it places Jones within this category. If every single example of teacher has the condition of being a scholar and if Jones is indeed one of these instances of teacher, then it follows that he exhibits the characteristic common to everyone in the category, scholarship.

This deductive pattern is labeled a *categorical* syllogism because the major premise asserts categorically, that is, without exception, that all members of a class have a certain characteristic.

The logic of deductive reasoning can become rather complex in all the possible ways the major premise, minor premise, and conclusion can be true or false. From the perspective of the Toulmin model, however, we can see that what is most important is that all of the parts of the deductive process be carefully scrutinized in order to prevent false conclusions. What may appear to be logically true at the outset may be clearly false upon closer examination.

CAUSAL RELATIONSHIPS

Causal relationships are perhaps the most pervasive of all the reasoning patterns; that is, the "if this, then that" relation is present in many inferential processes. The underlying notion of such relationships is that the universe is a logically ordered whole with an interlocking unity and that nothing happens without an explainable cause. An event is the result of an earlier event, and it, in turn, leads to other consequences. Reasoning by causal relation involves breaking into this endless chain at some point in time.

If reasoners observe an event and look backward in time to the forces responsible, they are reasoning from effect *to* cause. When they go out-doors and find the ground wet, they infer that it has recently rained. They infer, when a friend receives a failing grade in a course, that he or she has limited ability, poor study habits, and/or low motivation. If the small for-eign car captures a substantial proportion of the market this year, this event is an effect, and they wish to discover the causes that explain the phenomenon. They may examine possible causative factors and infer that the most plausible are desire of buyers for economy, for a feeling of pres-tige resulting from owning a European product, and for satisfaction result-ing from appearing to be a nonconformist. Notice the wording *most plausible*. The inferential connection between effect and alleged causes is more tenuous than that involved in the method of specific instances.

Cause-to-effect reasoning occurs when we recognize events in the present and reason that these causes will bring about future effects. Care-less driving may lead to an accident; detected crime is followed by pun-ishment; a lowered rediscount rate results in increased borrowing. We reason that production of a small American car will have the effect of re-ducing sales of imported models.

Here the probability of error is even higher than in effect-to-cause rea-soning. The inference is tenuous for the same reasons that effect-to-cause inferences are, and, in addition, we are usually predicting the future; a mulitude of intervening causes may prevent the expected result. Foreign manufacturers may lower prices or introduce a dramatic innovation that increases the appeal of their automobiles; or import duties may be de-creased, preventing American manufacturers from meeting the price competition.

A third causal relationship is effect-to-effect reasoning. Here we infer that one effect will be accompanied by another effect of the same cause. If lessened American demand for small foreign cars results in decreased imports, another effect will be lower profits for these foreign manufac-turers, and still another will be the collection of lessened import duties by the United States.

The questions usually asked to test causal relationships are the following:

First, *does the alleged causal relationship actually exist?* If a supersti-tious person tells his friends he or she is having bad luck because he or she broke a mirror, they naturally question whether his or her misfortunes are related to the breakage. No such relationship has been established in past experience; other causal explanations for his or her bad luck can almost always be discovered.

To attribute an effect to an unrelated circumstance is to commit the fallacy of false cause. A common form of this error is labeled *post hoc, ergo propter hoc* (literally: after this, therefore because of this). The postwar increase in juvenile delinquency was sometimes alleged to be an effect of World War II, but the mere fact that it followed the war does not establish that the war was responsible.

Secondly, *is the alleged cause a sufficient explanation for the attributed effect?* One of the gravest risks in employing causal reasoning is that of oversimplification. Rarely does a single cause explain a complex phenomenon. What was the cause of the Great Depression? Even when observers are wise enough to look for multiple causation, it is sometimes difficult to be sure that particular causes were alone influential enough to bring about the alleged effect.

Thirdly, *are there intervening causes that may prevent the alleged effect?* In the example given earlier, the actions of foreign-car manufacturers may intervene to alter what would otherwise be a reasonable cause-to-effect relationship.

ANALOGY

Reasoning from analogy, or resemblance, is a particularly useful inferential pattern for discussion. In the analysis of problems, it is often desirable to know what has happened in other places under similar conditions. In evaluating a proposed solution, discussers properly ask, "Where has this proposal been tried and how successful was it?" The analogical pattern is one in which we predict certain outcomes in the situation under discussion because these features emerged in a situation having similar characteristics or involving similar relationships.

In any discussion of compulsory national health insurance for the United States, it would be desirable to examine carefully the operation of such a system in Great Britain. Those favoring the proposal here would infer that the beneficial effects in Britain should operate similarly in the United States because of the resemblance between the two countries, peoples, and medical systems.

There is only one crucial test of this reasoning pattern: Are the situations being compared similar enough so that what resulted in one could reasonably be expected to occur in the other? The resemblance must not only exist generally; the two situations must be alike in those specific areas with which the assertion deals. In the case of national health insurance, for the analogy to be sound, the medical problems, financial aspects of medical care, and attitudes of doctors and patients toward state-directed medical care in the two nations must be sufficiently similar. Those who oppose such a system in America would be likely to say that conditions in the two nations have too little resemblance for the analogy to carry much weight.

AUTHORITY

Another common inferential pattern is one in which we reason that a condition exists or a policy is wise because respected authorities—those who presumably understand them best—say so. Economists are asked to estimate the probability of a business decline; psychologists can explain personal behavior; educational experts can evaluate proposals for improving schools.

It must be observed at once that for many purposes argument from authority offers weak and unreliable inferences. Often as many respected authorities can be cited on one side of a controversy as on the other. As Shakespeare observed, "The devil can cite Scripture for his purpose." On the other hand, there are areas of investigation and controversy in which authority is the most fruitful and sometimes the only source of inference. Suppose discussers ask whether the United States should finance a project to send manned spacecraft beyond the moon. Citizens, that is, nonexperts who must pay the bills, can appropriately consider the question. In analyzing the problem, they must ask whether man can survive on or near other planets. Who can answer this question? They must turn to experts and listen to their opinions; and at this point in time inferences can be only opinions. The fact is that most discussers cannot interpret data transmitted by rockets and must rely on authoritative knowledge. In evaluating testimony of authorities, we ask about their competence, opportunity to observe, credibility, and so on.

SIGN AND CIRCUMSTANTIAL DETAIL

As has been said, inferences are based on pieces of data, or evidence. When interrelationships or organizational patterns begin to emerge, it is possible to draw inferences and to have increasing confidence in them. Two other kinds of patterns in which inferences are not usually drawn unless there are a number of interrelated pieces are sign and circumstantial detail.

A discussion of reasoning from sign is often omitted from current textbooks, perhaps because it can be considered in part as causal relationship and partially, at least, as argument from circumstantial detail. Both will be treated here because it is desirable to be familiar with these terms. Perhaps also such treatment will make the other forms clearer. Certainly, the overlapping among patterns should not be a cause for concern; all the reasoning forms are interrelated.

Whereas the patterns discussed so far offer instances or comparisons or causes or authoritative statements on which inferences are directly based, a sign supplies only indirect evidence that a condition exists. A sign is a symptom or outward manifestation of a condition that cannot, at least at the moment, be directly determined. A doctor diagnoses disease by basing an inference on signs: fever, blood count, spots on the skin, nausea, and so forth.

Increasing unemployment and declining inventories may be signs of a business decline. Of course, these symptoms may also be considered effects of conditions that contribute to that decline. A racing fire engine is a sign of a fire, and indirectly its mission is the effect of the fire—the bell would not have rung and the chase begun without a fire report—but the clanging engine rushing by is not an effect of the fire in the same direct sense that property damage and financial loss are effects.

Whatever the overlapping with causal relation, reasoning from sign is useful in discussion because so often in complex problems causes and effects are not yet clearly identifiable. What are the causes of juvenile crime, and what are the best methods of combating it? Is such crime increasing? Concrete answers are scarce, but it is possible to study signs that suggest causes of improvement or failure where various solutions have been tried and it is possible to discover signs of increasing or decreasing criminal acts.

The argument from circumstantial detail also is based on indirect, or circumstantial, evidence. From assorted bits and pieces emerges an interrelated picture that seems to make all the pieces fit together. Most familiar here is the use of circumstantial evidence in connection with criminal trials: There is no witness although the accused was seen emerging from the building at the approximate time of the murder; he had a motive; he owns a gun of the caliber used; he cannot account for his movements that day; and a coat button clutched in the victim's hand was similar to those on his coat. Similar reasoning is sometimes appropriate in discussion. It may be difficult to assemble direct evidence, but there are indirect circumstances that may add up to a composite picture. Signs are obviously fallible—there may be smoke but no fire, at least no unwanted fire—and the indirect nature of sign and circumstantial detail requires us to proceed with special caution in using these inferential patterns. Tests are also difficult to apply. There are two questions that provide some protection from error:

1. Are there a sufficient number of signs (and/or circumstantial details), all pointing toward the same conclusion, to make the inference seem reasonable? From an increase in unemployment alone a reasoner would hesitate to forecast a business decline, but the combination of a large number of indirect indications lends credence to an inference.
2. Is there corroboration for the inference suggested by signs (and/or circumstantial detail) from other kinds of reasoning? A confirming generalization based on specific instances or an authoritative statement, for example, would do much to increase confidence in the conclusion.

FALLACIES OF REASONING

In addition to fallacies arising from violations of the reasoning patterns discussed, errors of inference can result from inattention to language and from the substitution of emotional for rational thinking. If language is used ambiguously or vaguely, inferences will be distorted, and misunderstanding will result. Using a word in two senses may create the fallacy of equivocation: "Crackers are better than nothing; nothing is better than ice cream; so crackers are better than ice cream." Discussers must stop often to define terms and make meanings precise.

There are also some common fallacies that rise when emotionalism is confused with rationality. Some persons are tempted to resort to emotional thinking when they are afraid that their rational arguments are too weak to prevail. Of course, emotionalism is not always intentional; every person is guilty of nonrational thinking at times.

One emotional argument is to attack the source rather than the idea. This fallacy is called *argumentum ad hominem,* or "poisoning the well." The attack is on the man rather than his argument. Another is to argue for acceptance of a policy because others have endorsed it. An idea must be judged on its merits; because it is approved "by millions" or because "everybody favors it" or because generations of ancestors believed in it cannot alone justify it. Small groups should be sensitive to the weaknesses in such thinking. They should try to be certain that all their statements are true; that is, accurately represent actual events in the real world. They will be skeptical of a deduction that asserts that any outcome is absolutely certain, any association invariable, or any conclusion inevitable.

Discussion typically consists of direct, conversational interchange and brief communications from each participant interspersed with the short contributions of others. Rarely in lively discussion does any member have the opportunity to present an extended, closely developed chain of reasoning. Rather, the pieces of evidence and inferences are contributed in bits by various members. Hence each participant must recognize what is happening when the materials are fitted together for a conclusion. Otherwise, a member who is not following the reasoning will introduce an unrelated piece of evidence or opinion that leads in another direction; the result will take the group off on a tangent.

Another difficulty encountered in applying reasoning in a small-group situation stems from the fact that the reasoning patterns studied in isolation for analytical purposes do not often appear in pure form. Two or more forms, when interrelated, are more confusing to recognize, yet strengthen the soundness of conclusions. In fact, it may be unwise to attempt a sorting out of types—when all the evidence and inferences of various kinds fit together into a reasonable pattern, our thinking is probably approaching validity. If a group first agrees that a causal relationship seems to exist between increasing unemployment and a business decline, the relationship will seem more plausible if someone describes a similar situation in the past—the method of analogy—in which a business decline apparently resulted from decreasing employment. Even greater weight will be added if collectively they can cite six examples of past recessions, supporting a tentative generalization—using the method of specific instances —that rising unemployment preceded a business decline. Finally, they may add authoritative testimony—a number of experts expressing the opinion that these two phenomena are causally connected.

It should be repeated that in lively discussion these corroborative patterns will not be presented in this orderly, one-step-at-a-time fashion. Different members with varied experiences and knowledge will contribute the pieces as they are recalled. At some point the group must review the contributions and summarize them in an integrated form.

Discussers should not hesitate to ask the group to halt temporarily and test their collective reasoning. Also, it is wise to ask, for example, whether an analogy is an isolated resemblance or whether enough similar cases are known to expand the comparison to a generalization based on numerous specific instances or whether authoritative opinion coincides with the inferences suggested by signs and circumstantial detail.

Still another difficulty encountered by members using reasoning in group situations is the pressure generated by group conformity. Often the person who is seeing most clearly the relationships among the facts presented over a period of many minutes will be the only one who at first analyzes the implications in the way he or she does. The discomfort that comes to a person when he or she is a minority of one may operate to discourage him or her from pressing his or her view. Yet his or her interpretation could well be the one the group will accept later or would have accepted had he or she shared his or her views with the group.

Social influence can help group productivity if it stimulates members to better thinking. The presence of several members means wider experience and more knowledge brought to bear. Several opinions may mean the better alternative will be chosen by the group judgment. When members conform or suppress their ideas merely to win group approval or to avoid being out of step, however, the group product is being damaged by social influence. Members must be willing to speak up even at the risk of some criticism. If the group has already created a permissive climate, of course, there is freedom to express a different or unpopular view.

Some persons apparently are so unsure of their own views that they are perfectly willing to go along with a group on almost any basis. They just assume that the group's reasoning will be sounder than their own. Such an assumption can be damaging to the group effort, obviously. It may mean in some groups that one or two bold persons are doing almost all the real thinking for the group. It certainly reduces the contributions the conformists could make if they would become full participants. Members who recognize unsound reasoning or fallacious thinking but who hesitate to point it out for fear of group disapproval are canceling out one of the values of using group effort. Here, too, the group should create a climate of frankness and a direct "let's all look openly but not defensively" attitude toward exploring all aspects of the problem.

Using reasoning during the discussion, then, becomes an assignment in seeing the logical parts of the problem as a whole in spite of its disjointed presentation, of resisting conformity pressures, and, most important, of using reason clearly without becoming entangled in rigid complexities or syllogistic absolutism. It is extremely important, as we have said, to test reasoning for validity.

SUPPLEMENTARY READING

Burgoon, Michael, "Amount of Conflicting Information in a Group Discussion and Tolerance for Ambiguity as Predictors of Task Attractiveness." *Speech Monographs* 38 (June 1971): 121–124.

Collins, Barry E., and Guetzkow, H. *A Social Psychology of Group Processes for Decision-Making.* New York: John Wiley and Sons, 1964. Pp. 106–119.

Ehninger, Douglas, and Brockriede, Wayne. *Decision by Debate.* New York: Dodd, Mead, 1963. Part III.

Goldberg, Alvin A., and Larson, Carl E. *Group Communication: Discussion Processes and Applications.* Englewood Cliffs, N.J.: Prentice-Hall, 1975. Chapter 4.

Gouran, Dennis S. *Discussion: The Process of Group Decision-Making.* New York: Harper and Row, 1974. Chapters 5 and 6.

Lee, Irving. *How to Talk with People.* New York: Harper and Row, 1952.

Mortensen, C. David. *Communication: The Study of Human Interaction.* New York: McGraw-Hill, 1972. Chapters 3 and 4.

Toulmin, Stephen E. *The Uses of Argument.* Cambridge, England: Cambridge University Press, 1958. Chapter 3.

QUESTIONS AND EXERCISES

1. Choose a discussion question of current importance. Assume that you are responsible for providing participants with a complete bibliography on the subject. Prepare an exhaustive list of the sources—library and nonlibrary—to which you would send them.
2. Plan a discussion on a question of public concern. Begin the preparation of a cooperative bibliography; that is, assign to specific members of the group responsibility for securing relevant bibliographical items from each general category of reference sources. One member can be responsible for recent books; another, for general reference works; a third, for current magazine articles; and so on.
   a. When each person has secured his or her bibliographical entries, pool the lists and type copies of the combined bibliography for all members.
   b. Have each person give an oral report on his or her category, telling the others what to expect in each reference, discussing which articles everyone must read to be well informed, and so forth.

3. How much research must members of a group do before they are qualified to discuss a problem? If members of a group admit that they are not as well informed on the subject as they would like to be, should they disqualify themselves from discussing the problem? Should problem-solving discussion be engaged in only by experts on a problem?

4. Lyman Bryson has said: "Properly speaking, discussion is controversy. It is talk in which opinions are contrasted and judged. It is controversy over judgments that belong properly in the realm of opinion. Discussion is not a means, except incidentally, for discovering facts ... Very few important questions can be settled by fact alone. When all the available facts are in, the important issues of life arise." Is he saying that persons need not seek facts before discussing? That discussion by nonexperts is futile? That facts are not-important in discussion?

5. What kinds of reasoning and/or additional facts will be needed to solve the following problem, reported in a student newspaper: "About eight hundred University of Illinois students became ill simultaneously early Sunday in two men's residence units, Forbes and Hopkins halls, calling for some diagnostic detective work by health agencies. The ailment was only a mild diarrhea. There was little nausea or vomiting, which differentiates it from usual cases of food poisoning. . . . An unusual aspect of the case is the fact that men living in Garner Hall, which is fed from the same kitchen, were not stricken. The students eat in separate dining rooms, serviced from a central kitchen. A factor pointing toward the food service, however, is that men who failed to eat dinner there Saturday night 'uniformly were exempted' from the illness, the health director said. Items of food served are undergoing analysis. . . ."

Part 3
COMMUNICATIVE INTERACTION IN THE SMALL GROUP

6 Phases in Group Interaction

Groups interacting for decision making and even groups meeting for human relations training or therapy move through different phases or stages of development. To understand these developmental phases, we must consider them from two different perspectives. The first is descriptive; what phases or stages do groups move through when interacting for decision making and for other purposes? Secondly, what must group members understand about the nature of these phases if they are to help groups use their time and resources effectively?

What phases a group moves through in particular circumstances depends on a number of factors. One is the group setting and the purpose for bringing members together, whether a task such as decision making is primary and social-emotional needs are secondary or whether the group assembles to deal with personal and interpersonal needs where, in Tuckman's words, "the group exists to help the individuals deal with themselves and others." [1]

Another is the nature of the group's leadership and the degree of structure. A designated leader such as the chairman of the board may be more conscious of "efficient" and "orderly" phases leading toward a decision stage than would be true in an unstructured group where leadership and direction must emerge as matters secondary to interpersonal interactions.

---

[1] Bruce W. Tuckman, "Developmental Sequence in Small Groups," *Psychological Bulletin* 63 (1965): 384–399.

110   A third factor is the time available to the group. Much of the research on developmental sequences is based on studies of what Bormann has called "zero-history" groups,[2] strangers assembled to complete a specific task in a single, short session. Phases of interaction in such a situation will be quite different from those in continuing groups such as a board of trustees, for example, meeting monthly to exercise responsibility for a particular institution.

We can examine first what the research literature tells us about developmental phases, gaining some insight into the influences of these kinds of factors. Then we can consider the nature of such developmental phases in relation to group interaction for decision making.

Developmental Phases

Because decision-making task groups are composed of human beings who also have needs as persons, much of the early interaction in such groups is taken up with orientation of persons to the others present and to the nature of the task, with getting to know something of the others, with estimating the situation and how each member is relating to it, and similar person needs. Even when the group later "gets down to work," much of the communication consists of dealing with social-emotional needs and feelings. The interrelationships between task-related and person-related interaction and the phases groups pass through have been described from a number of approaches.

BION

W. R. Bion developed a theory of group activity through the study of neurotic patients in therapy groups, observing that certain emotional states are associated with any work the group is assigned. Although the group will engage in recognizable, task-related, goal-oriented activity, this kind of activity does not account for all the interaction. Bion identified three kinds of emotional states, or "cultures" that combine with work: dependency, pairing, and fight-flight.

Stock and Thelen,[3] reporting a research program based on Bion's theories, say "a group can be described at any given time as operating in a work-dependency culture (seeking support and direction from outside the group), a work-pairing culture (finding strength within the group), a work-fight-flight culture (avoiding by fighting or running away), or as being in

[2] Ernest G. Bormann, "The Paradox and Promise of Small Group Research," *Speech Monographs* 37 (August 1970): 211–217.

[3] Dorothy Stock and Herbert A. Thelen, *Emotional Dynamics and Group Culture* (Washington: National Training Laboratories, 1958).

some transitional phase. In each case the work aspects of the group's activities are suffused and influenced by the emotional state or concern." They described the development of groups "in terms of successive phases of varying duration in which one work-emotionality culture gives way to another." Groups in their development moved toward more effective integration of work and emotionality.

BENNIS AND SHEPARD

Working with "self-study" groups of students and building also in part on the work of Bion, Bennis and Shepard [4] found two phases in group development: dependence, in which members dealt with prescribed rules and authority, followed by interdependence, in which they were concerned with affection, intimacy, and personal relationships.

Each of these two phases had three substages, making six phases in all. The earliest was "dependence-flight," where members reduced uneasiness by acceptance of the proposed structure and leadership or by discussing external matters, and so on. Next came "counterdependence-fight," in which they expressed hostility to the leadership and struggled with establishing their own group structure, followed by a third subphase of dependence, called "resolution-catharsis," where the group begins to define itself and realize ways to become effective.

Whereas much of the dependence phases was occupied with arrangements of leadership and power, the *interdependence* phase consisted of "enchantment-flight," "disenchantment-fight," and "consensual validation." As the groups resolved their problems of unity and structure, they maintained harmony in the early stage of interdependence by avoiding conflicts. This "flight" behavior was followed by "disenchantment-fight" when conflict was brought into the open. The final stage, "consensual validation," involved resolution of interpersonal conflict and completion of task assignment. These six stages, of course, were not distinct but blended together in a continuous process, although not one that moved steadily forward. Sometimes groups backed up, meandered, or moved forward in uncertain jumps.

Although their work primarily involved human relations groups, the outcomes seem to provide insights into other kinds of interaction as well.

ZALEZNIK AND MOMENT

Zaleznik and Moment view the phases of group development as movement upward through "levels of work." [5] Beginning with "low-level work,"

---

[4] Warren G. Bennis and H. A. Shephard, "A Theory of Group Development," *Human Relations* 9 (1956): 415–437.

[5] Abraham Zaleznik and David Moment, *The Dynamics of Interpersonal Behaving* (New York: Wiley and Sons, 1964), Chapter 5.

112 members get acquainted, react to each other, relate personal anecdotes revealing their opinions as persons, and in other ways size each other up. The second level of work, according to Zaleznik and Moment, involves a kind of "warm-up" for considering issues; members exchange superficial comments that sound like examination but actually do little to describe the group's real problems.

When members begin looking at relevant data in some depth, the group has moved up to the third level of work. The group can explore an issue for some time, clarifying and defining without actually beginning serious exploration. These first three levels could be characterized as "getting ready."

In reaching "top level work," the group operates as a group rather than as an aggregation of individuals. Members are open to others' ideas, feedback is immediate, and communication is "more valid." The initial emotionality of uncertainty and unease gives way to this fourth level of "involvement in the task itself," where "new insights and ideas emerge spontaneously and are tested immediately and openly."

SCHUTZ

A number of theorists have conceptualized phases of group development as *linear*, explaining that a group first does thus and so, moving then to another phase, followed by a third, and so on. Schutz[6] hypothesizes three linear phases, but he also begins to suggest the notion of circularity and of spiraling; that is, that a group repeats itself and moves "forward" by falling back or circling around.

His research suggests that each person has three basic interpersonal needs: for inclusion, control, and affection. Based on observation of social workers, psychologists and psychiatrists meeting as "group process training groups" for thirty to forty-five weekly sessions, Schutz found the groups achieving integration by moving through three phases in this order:

1. *Inclusion Phase.* Members began by verbal sparring about identity: "Will I be unique in this group or one of many indistinguishable from the others?" "How much do I wish to commit my real self?" These are what Schutz calls "boundary problems"—of entering into the boundaries of that group and establishing belongingness. In this phase are found "goblet issues." This image comes from the cocktail glass, or goblet, sizing up the others and deciding whom to talk to and how openly. An exchange on the harmless topic of "the weather" may not be about the weather at all; each may be deciding about the other as person, using idle weather-talk to evaluate and "locate" the other person.

[6] William C. Schutz, *The Interpersonal Underworld* (Palo Alto, Calif.: Science and Behavior Books, 1966), Chapter 9.

2. *Control Phase.* After resolving inclusion problems, members moved to questions of sharing responsibility, distribution of power, and control. Groups sometimes had competition for leadership, struggled with rules of procedure, and in other ways attempted to adjust to a comfortable level of control and direction for the group.
3. *Affection Phase.* The third stage meant emotional integration as persons accepted the group as group and found the right amount of "affectional interchange" and intimate involvement. At this stage "each member is striving to obtain for himself in the group his most comfortable amount of affectional interchange and most comfortable position regarding initiating and receiving affection."

Schutz observes, as do other authors, that these are not distinct phases. In early meetings, inclusion problems are uppermost, later control questions are most prominent, and, finally, questions of affection are dominant. All three kinds of problems may receive some notice in all stages, and some persons especially may find one of the problems so powerful as to "transcend the current group issue." Schutz emphasizes also that this cycle of three phases may recur and that a group must exist over a long period of time for the phases to become fully developed.

This author offers a "principle of group resolution" as well as one of integration. When the groups observed were within three meetings of termination, the sequence of phases described above were *reversed.* Members first dealt with affection as they anticipated an end to their organization; they recalled, for example, earlier disagreements and explained again what they had really meant, so that there would be no hard feelings. This seemed to help them accept their coming separation. Then the group focused on the leader, discussing whether they should have complied with or rebelled against his wishes. Finally came problems of inclusion: whether the group should somehow continue and how much each was really committed to membership.

These approaches to phases in group development give insights into ways groups balance social-emotional needs as persons and the task assignment of the group. Throughout a decision-making discussion members may need to deal from time to time with their relationships to each other and to the group as group, but such concerns are probably more critical early in a group's formation and perhaps again when the group is to terminate or a particular person must end his or her membership. If such matters become dominant momentarily during other phases, it may be because some event or external pressure forces the group to examine problems of inclusion and affection. Problems of control, or leadership, will also usually be worked out reasonably early in a group's life, although competition for the leadership may break out at any time, or members may be unhappy with the structures and rules of procedure being followed, thereby causing the group to give renewed attention to such control problems.

We can now turn to conceptions of the phases in group development as they relate more directly to decision-making groups.

BALES AND STRODTBECK

Observing small groups engaged in problem-solving tasks, Bales and Strodtbeck[7] analyzed communicative interaction to discover the phases groups went through in moving toward a decision. They divided each problem-solving session into three equal periods so that an equal number of interactions occurred in each period. They then analyzed each initiation and reaction using Bales's system of interaction process analysis.

They found each of the three phases characterized by qualitatively *different* types of interaction. In the first phase, the greatest emphasis was on problems of orientation, with fewer contributions involving evaluation and control. Interactions occurring with highest frequency in this early period were asking for orientation, information, repetition, confirmation and giving orientation, information, repetition, confirmation.

After the initial phase, interactions involving orientation tended to decrease, and the highest frequency of communicative acts concerned problems of evaluation. This means that in the second period there were a larger number of communications asking for opinion, evaluation, analysis, expression of feeling and giving opinion, evaluation, and analysis, and expressing feeling or wish.

In the third or final phase, problems of control reached their highest peak, whereas evaluation declined. Acts involving orientation continued to decline in frequency throughout the second and third phases. Problems of control at this stage involved asking for suggestion, direction, possible ways of action and giving suggestion, direction, implying autonomy for others.

Another important finding was that, throughout the discussions, both positive reactions and negative reactions tended to increase. Bales and Strodtbeck hypothesize that orientation may need to come before evaluation: "speaking to the other in evaluative terms implies previous orientation." Furthermore, "the attempt to control the situation by joint action implies both previous orientation and evaluation." If a group under the conditions they have set up tends to move from orientation, to evaluation, to control, they feel, then, as the group moves toward agreement on a decision, there will be increasing strains on the group's solidarity and social-emotional relationships. The number of negative reactions seems to build to a peak near the end, where disagreement over proposals must be expressed and where tension and antagonism are most apparent. But positive reactions also build up as members resolve their differences and confirm their agreement, with positive tension reduction building to a sudden

---

[7] Robert F. Bales and Fred L. Strodtbeck, "Phases in Group Problem-Solving," *Journal of Abnormal and Social Psychology* 46 (1951): 485–495.

peak at the very end as members accept the outcome and show the tension release and solidarity through joking, laughing, and expressions of reassurance. As the researchers write, "We note joking and laughter so frequently at the ends of meetings that they might almost be taken as a signal that the group has completed what it considers to be a task effort, and is ready for disbandment or a new problem."

Bales and Strodtbeck are careful to point out that this phase movement may not occur under all conditions. No doubt, the nature of each phase would be altered by a large number of circumstances. They speculate that a serious struggle within the group for status or leadership would affect the type of communications. Phases would be changed also with different kinds of tasks and different amounts of information possessed by members and so on.

FISHER

Aubrey Fisher, too, found that different kinds of interactions were dominant in the phases groups move through during decision making. As a researcher interested in the functions of communication in affecting decision emergence, he studied each unit of communicative interaction by categorizing them along three dimensions:[8]

Dimension One:
  A. Asserted
  B. Seeking
Dimension Two:
  1–Interpretation
  2–Substantiation
  3–Clarification
  4–Modification
  5–Summary
  6–Agreement
Dimension Three: (Applied only to categories 1 and 2 above.)
  f–Favorable toward the proposal
  u–Unfavorable toward the proposal
  a–Ambiguous toward proposal

He also recorded origin of a proposal and reintroduction of a proposal.

Fisher reports four phases characterized by distinctive interaction patterns.

1. *Orientation Phase:* Clarification and agreement statements were highest in this phase. Members were unsure of their position and tended not to be assertive or opinionated. Agreement was more ambiguous

---

[8] B. Aubrey Fisher, "Decision Emergence: Phases in Group Decision-Making," *Speech Monographs* 37 (March 1970): 53–66.

than reinforcing, perhaps to encourage social facilitation and getting acquainted rather than to reinforce ideas, for opinions were expressed tentatively.

2. *Conflict Phase:* In the second phase, members became more definite and willing to dispute. Communications unfavorable to proposals and those disputing the substantiation offered by others were more frequent here than in any of the four phases. Fisher observes that "members in the second phases are aware of the direction the groups' task behavior is heading, of the relevant decision proposals which are emerging . . . [and] typically express either a favorable or an unfavorable attitude toward those decision proposals rather than an attitude of ambiguity." Views are also held more tenaciously; members attempt to persuade those who disagree.

3. *Emergence Phase:* Members in the third phase gradually reduced conflict and argument, offering fewer unfavorable reactions to proposals. There were more interpretations followed by interpretation, as well as more favorable comments followed by other favorable comments. Members tended not to defend positions so tenaciously. Ambiguity, however, again increased. Fisher explains: in the orientation phase, "ambiguity served as the initial expression of tentatively favorable attitudes," whereas in the third phase, it functioned "as a form of modified dissent. That is, the group members proceed to change their attitudes from disfavor to favor of the decision proposals through the mediation of ambiguity." Thus, decision and agreement begin to *emerge* in phase three.

4. *Reinforcement Phase:* Members began to become aware that they were moving toward a decision in the final phase. Argument lessened, whereas interpretation and favorable reactions to interpretations increased. There were fewer unfavorable substantiation units and fewer ambiguous substantiation units in phase four, whereas comments for decision proposals were constantly reinforced. Dissent virtually disappeared as members moved toward unity of opinion.

SCHEIDEL AND CROWELL

Although Fisher in his research report and others have recognized that groups do not actually move forward in the linear, one-phase-at-a-time fashion suggested by the models so far presented, it was a study by Scheidel and Crowell [9] that has best described the way members back up, repeat, and circle around while moving forward in a kind of "spiral" fashion.

After studying idea development during problem-solving discussions, they hypothesized that while a group is moving toward a solution, it is

---

[9] Thomas M. Scheidel and Laura Crowell, "Idea Development in Small Discussion Groups," *Quarterly Journal of Speech* 50 (1964): 140–145.

following a circular course in which members spend one-fourth of their comments confirming statements already made and another fourth clarifying and substantiating. "This oral play on an idea and the verbalizing of concurrence," they say, "are probably the ways by which a group gets its anchoring." One member "reaches forth" with an idea, which is then tested through elaboration, "clarification, substantiation, and verbalized acceptance."

These authors offer a spiraling model to replace the simpler conception of linear development in group reasoning. This notion of a spiraling development suggests that a group moves onward in the sense that it makes progress toward a decision and outward in the sense that it elaborates, agrees and disagrees, and, one hopes, confirms and solidifies at the end. This conception is a reasonable one, and we must be certain not to think of forward movement as a simple, mechanical, stage-by-stage list of isolated activities. Rather it is a complex, developmental set of interactions unfolding spirally as the group moves forward.

TUCKMAN

In an article reviewing a large number of studies of phases in group development, Tuckman[10] has attempted to synthesize agreement on phases and at the same time to discuss theoretical considerations explaining group development. Although the model emerging from his study is a linear one, his conclusions are worth reporting because of his synthesis.

Considering studies of groups in a therapy setting and the human relations training-group setting, as well as "natural groups" assigned a task such as decision making, Tuckman proposes a developmental model consisting of four stages.

1. The first stage he calls *forming*. This is what several others have labeled the orientation phase, characterized by testing the climate and the others present, by established dependency relationships with leaders, and so on.
2. The second phase is *storming*. This is the stage Fisher has called the conflict phase. There is polarization around ideas and persons and some resistance to group influence.
3. The third stage Tuckman calls *norming*. Resistance lessens in this stage whereas group feeling and cohesiveness increase. Members faced with a task assignment can more directly express meaningful personal opinions and evolve standards for weighing decisions. This stage is similar to Fisher's *Emergence Phase*, and it resembles somewhat Zaleznik's and Moment's "top-level work."
4. The final stage is labeled *performing*. Here group energy is concentrated on the task. Members are integrated enough as a group to

---

[10] Tuckman, "Developmental Sequence in Small Groups," pp. 384–399.

work effectively and collectively as a unit. This phase is similar to Fisher's final *reinforcement* stage and also to "top-level work" and to Bennis's and Shepard's "consensual validation" during the interdependence phase.

Using Knowledge of Phases

Once group members understand the phases typical of decision making discussion, what use can they make of this knowledge when they are members of such task groups?

There is no lack of prescriptive advice because, as Jacques Barzun says, "discussion must not go off in all directions like a leaky hose."

It is common to hear discussion participants talk animatedly without any sense of direction. The talk often wanders aimlessly, pursuing this tangent and that byway, sometimes traveling in great circles and doubling back over the same ground without recognizing the familiar terrain. It is not uncommon to hear a committee chairman greet his colleagues with the disquieting question: "Well, what are we supposed to talk about today?"

To attempt guidance of a discussion without any sense of the phases of interaction would be as inefficient as taking a journey without a map. The motorist would be forced to approach each highway intersection, locate a passerby, and call out, "Which road should we take to reach the next village?" Perhaps a similar question for the erratic discussion leader is, "Well, what shall we talk about next?" Discussion without planning is often chaotic, wasteful of time and energy, and frustrating for everyone.

If aimless meandering were not so common among discussion groups, it would seem too obvious to suggest that productivity requires planning. Apparently, it is not obvious, and thus we should emphasize its value in contributing to orderly forward movement. Whoever during discussion is responsible for the guidance function of leadership should think in advance for his understanding, if for no other use, about the stages likely to be encountered during decision making.

In a study of seventy-two conferences in business and governmental groups, one of the characteristics observed was the orderliness of the discussion. Collins and Guetzkow report that "those meetings in which discussion is orderly in its treatment of topics, and without backward references to previously discussed issues, tended to end in more consensus, despite large amounts of substantive or affective conflict. When participants discussed but one issue at a time, instead of simultaneously dabbling in two or three, it was more possible for the group to reach consensus." [11]

---

[11] Barry E. Collins and Harold Guetzkow, *A Social Psychology of Group Processes for Decision-Making* (New York: John Wiley and Sons, 1964), p. 111.

If the guidance function consists of helping the group to discuss one issue at a time and to be orderly in its treatment to topics, we must decide what issues or topics must be considered during a discussion and what order is likely to be most productive.

VARIATIONS OF PATTERNS

Carl Larson reports a study[12] comparing the effectiveness of various patterns of analysis in small-group problem solving. It may suggest clues about use of phases because it compared four different "analysis forms":

A. *No Pattern:* The group was given no "systematic analysis form" to follow, "theoretically duplicating," according to Larson, "conditions which exist when groups deliberate with no systematic analysis form governing their deliberations."

B. *Single Question Form:* Based on a description of the reasoning characteristics of successful and unsuccessful problem solvers, the pattern of the single question form consisted of adherence to an outline as follows:

1. What is the single question, the answer to which is all the group needs to know to accomplish its purpose?
2. What sub-questions must be answered before we can answer the single question we have formulated?
3. Do we have sufficient information to answer confidently the sub-questions?
4. What are the most reasonable answers to the sub-questions?
5. Assuming that our answers to the sub-questions are correct, what is the best solution to the problem?

C. *Ideal Solution Form:* The ideal solution form of analysis was adapted from the pattern proposed by Kepner and Tregoe.[13] Groups were instructed to follow this outline:

1. Are we all agreed on the nature of the problem?
2. What would be the ideal solution from the point-of-view of all parties involved in the problem?
3. What conditions within the problem could be changed so that the ideal solution might be achieved?
4. Of the solutions available to us, which one best approximates the ideal solution?

D. *Reflective Thinking Form:* Following a traditional reflective thinking pattern, the reflective thinking form of analysis consisted of using these questions:

1. What are the limits and specific nature of the problem?
2. What are the causes and consequences of the problem?

[12] Carl E. Larson, "Forms of Analysis and Small Group Problem-Solving," *Speech Monographs* 36 (November 1969): 452–455.

[13] Charles H. Kepner and Benjamin B. Tregoe, *The Rational Manager: A Systematic Approach to Problem Solving and Decision Making* (New York: McGraw-Hill, 1965).

3. What things must an acceptable solution to the problem accomplish?
4. What solutions are available to us?
5. What is the best solution?

Larson found the traditional reflective thinking pattern less effective than the more recently developed forms of analysis. Problem-solving "accuracy" was facilitated more by the "ideal solution" and "single question" analyses than by the reflective thinking form.

Stech[14] asked in a study whether discussion is a random process or whether there is some orderliness in sequencing of comments. He found that on a ranking task small groups exhibited a "fair degree of predictability"; that is, that it was possible to predict somewhat satisfactorily the extent to which statements "induced predictable succeeding statements." This suggests there is some orderliness in discussion but that it is not "a very logical, reasoned kind of response system," based on the fact that it was only partially predictable. An incidental finding of the Stech study was the suggestion there may be less tension and interpersonal difficulties when there is efficiency of structure. As he notes, "too much constraint can lead to problems between people just as too much randomness can cause difficulties in completing the task."

Brilhart and Jochem, in asking whether one pattern is more effective than another, found also that the traditional reflective thinking pattern was less effective than two other forms, brainstorming and a pattern based on the phases discovered by Bales, orientation, evaluation, and control. Of the three patterns, brainstorming produced more and better solutions.[15]

PHASES IN A PARTICULAR DISCUSSION

Members and designated leaders should anticipate the stages a group is likely to move through in a particular situation. It may be possible to think ahead of time about the alternatives open to the group, and for some important discussions those responsible for leadership may find it useful to develop a tentative "blueprint" of the possible phases.

Such a developmental outline is a series of questions that may help the group to progress from the initial problem to an acceptable outcome. It should be only a guide, followed flexibly rather than rigidly, but it may serve to help members restrain erratic shifting from questions of analysis to solution to evaluation and back to analysis. For an exchange of information, the "blueprint" in mind may be as simple as these questions:

1. What do we mean by the question for discussion?
2. What are the facts?

---

14 Ernest L. Stech, "An Analysis of Interaction Structure in the Discussion of a Ranking Task," *Speech Monographs* 37 (November 1970): 249–256.

15 J. K. Brilhart and L. M. Jochem, "Effects of Different Patterns on Outcomes of Problem-Solving Discussion," *Journal of Applied Psychology* 48 (1964): 175–179.

A decision-making discussion may be somewhat more complex:

1. What is the nature of the problem?
2. What are possible alternative solutions?
3. What standards must a solution meet to be acceptable?
4. What proposal best satisfies the problem and the standards? By focusing on one of these questions at a time, the group can perhaps be more effective in moving forward.

Members must keep in mind how these developmental questions fit into the larger phases we have noted of orientation, evaluation, control, and so on. When asking about the definitions of the question or the nature of the problem early in a discussion, members will be concerned with relationship problems of orientation, getting acquainted, sizing each other up, and so on. Later, considerations of evaluation and other concerns will become more important.

It must also be realized that a developmental outline is not an agenda, which is a listing of the order of items to be taken up at a complex organizational meeting dealing with many matters. Planning the agenda is, of course, important, for an entire meeting should be conducted in an orderly fashion. An agenda for a board of directors meeting might look like this:

 I. Reading of minutes of last board meeting
 II. Reports of committees
   A. Engineering
   B. Sales
 III. Unfinished business
   A. Salary increases for office personnel
   B. Final plans for annual stockholders' meeting
 IV. New business
   A. Revised policy on scheduling summer vacations
   B. Proposal for increasing the capital stock
   C. Other new business

Many of these items may be relatively simple and quickly covered. But the proposal under IV. B., increasing the capital stock, may be complex; to consider it and reach an acceptable decision may require thorough and lengthy discussion. For this item, the chairman of the board may wish to work out a developmental "blueprint" that outlines the questions that the group may wish to answer as it moves toward a decision.

ADAPTING TO THE SITUATION

The degree of structure a group will find desirable in a particular situation is a function of the nature of the task, the kind of leadership, the time available, and similar factors. Members can expect an early stage of orientation and interpersonal "sizing up" even when faced with an urgent decision-making task, but this stage will be more obvious and will last longer if the group and the problem are new. In contrast, a board of trustees meeting regularly to control the affairs of a university may require little time at each monthly meeting for orientation. Indeed, because the members are usually busy and distinguished citizens giving their time without recompense, they will probably accept a high degree of structure in the phases they move through while making decisions. If their designated chairman is inefficient in using a developmental pattern, they will likely be uncomfortable, whereas in some other situations members may be equally uneasy with carefully controlled decision-making phases.

What is important is that members of groups be aware of what is appropriate and effective in particular situations, expecting to move through phases such as orientation, conflict, emergence of proposals, and reinforcement with varying emphases and durations.

In addition to orientation toward the other persons, members can expect to spend some time in most decision-making discussions with orientation toward the problem. Often discussions begin, after some interpersonal interchanges, with questions of definition and limitation. Members must also seek and give information and opinions, and this process may spill over into the stage Fisher calls the "conflict phase." Groups must supply the background information on which they can base a satisfactory decision.

Later, most decision-making groups will include evaluation at some stage. Members will be proposing possible solutions; each alternative course of action must be evaluated.

For many problems, the evaluation procedure will prove very confusing because some members will look at the proposal from one set of standards and other members in quite a different way. When this happens, there must be another subphase dealing with criteria, spelling out which set of standards is to be applied in evaluating each proposal. For example, if a student-faculty conference is held on substituting a pass-fail grading system for the present A-B-C-D-F system, the students and faculty would undoubtedly approach alternatives with different standards for judgment. The students may want a grading system that reduces student tension, motivates students to take an interest in the subject, and removes the grade-point average as the measure of an individual's worth to society. On the other hand, the faculty may feel that a grading system must reward outstanding students, give highest status to those with the most intellectual talent, and serve to identify those who can benefit from graduate school. If they take these two philosophical positions, they probably will not agree on a decision. The students may press for a major move toward pass-fail grading; and the faculty, for no change or a token measure such as allowing a pass-fail option for one course a semester. If they were to agree on the criterion that in designing any grading system the faculty's judgment must be given first priority, they might agree on a policy close to the faculty's position. If, in contrast, they establish as the first criterion that a grading system must serve to motivate students to learn, they may reach a different decision.

It is important to reemphasize that developmental phases depend on the situation, the task, the time available, and many other factors. Members should try to understand what is appropriate and effective under particular circumstances.

SUPPLEMENTARY READING

Applbaum, Ronald L.; Bodaken, E.; Sereno, K.; and Anatol, K. *The Process of Group Communication*. Chicago: Science Research Associates, 1974. Chapter 5.

Bormann, Ernest G. *Discussion and Group Methods*. Second Edition. New York: Harper and Row, 1975. Chapter 12.

Fisher, B. Aubrey. *Small Group Decision Making*. New York: McGraw-Hill Book Co., 1974. Chapter 7.

Rosenfeld, Lawrence B. *Human Interaction in the Small Group Setting*. Columbus, Ohio: Charles E. Merrill, 1973. Chapter 3.

Schutz, William C. *The Interpersonal Underworld*. Palo Alto, Calif.: Science and Behavior Books, 1966. Chapter 9.

Tuckman, Bruce W. "Developmental Sequence in Small Groups." *Psychological Bulletin* 63 (1965): 384–399.

QUESTIONS AND EXERCISES

1. Suppose that the president of your college or university has called you, as a campus leader, to his office. He has explained to you his great concern with the symptoms of poor student attitude toward education: student enthusiasm for carnivals, stunt shows, dances, and similar non-academic pursuits; student disinterest in classwork, library study, and special honors for distinguished academic achievement; and student interest in gradepoint averages without particular concern for the acquisition of knowledge and understanding. The president has asked you to plan and lead a closedgroup, problem-solving discussion, using both faculty and student participants; he has specified that he wants from this group specific recommendations for improving the situation. Suggest a developmental outline of the major questions you would expect the group to answer.

2. Apparently, in small-group discussion, a feature of all patterns is that fact seeking, inquiry, or analysis comes before value judgment, generalization, or decision making. In the conducting of a group deliberation using formal parliamentary procedures, however, the general pattern appears to be reversed: a motion specifying an action or proposal must be presented before the matter can be talked about. Can these contra-

dictory positions be reconciled? Are there differences between the two kinds of situations that require these opposite approaches? Which general pattern produces better results? Can the patterns of one deliberation situation be profitably adapted in the other?

3. Divide the class into two discussion groups, 1 and 2. Have each member of the class consider the following problem as if he were about to become the designated leader for a committee discussion (such as a committee of the state legislature).

The question for discussion is, *"Should capital punishment be abolished (or reestablished) in this state?"*

In the *analysis phase* of this discussion, members might consider questions such as these:

A. What do we mean by *capital punishment*?
B. What do we mean by *abolish*?

   (1) Are we considering the elimination of all use of execution, or are we excluding the death penalty for treason?
   (2) Are we limiting our consideration to abolition of the death penalty for criminal violence against the person as distinct from crimes against the state?

In the remainder of the analysis phase, what are the questions you propose for the developmental outline?

(Group 1 will now consider this question for fifteen minutes with the class as audience, attempting to produce an outline of this section.)

In the *solution phase* of the outline, what are the questions you propose?

(Group 2 will next consider this question for fifteen minutes with the class as audience.)

4. Assign a group of five to hold a decision-making discussion on a vital, controversial problem in front of the class, and tape it. Have class members take careful notes about the *structure* or organizational development of the discussion. Then divide the class into two groups, whose assignment is to agree upon the structure of the discussion just observed. Each subgroup will report to the class:

A. The major developmental questions they feel the group dealt with.
B. Their critique of the effectiveness of the sequence of the major phases.

Class members can then agree or disagree with the two reports.

7 The Quality of Small-Group Communication

The nature of small-group communication is shaped by many forces. Some of these are generated by the distinctive and often overriding demands of the group as a social system. Others result from the participants' ineffective use of their own communicative capacities or their failure to deal adequately with communication problems caused by themselves or others. Whatever the cause of the problem or the source of the communication difficulty, there can be little doubt that the quality of small-group communication varies dramatically.

Consider the following situation. C. Dudley Wright, as president of Constitutional Airlines, has just called a meeting of the executive board. The announced subject of the meeting is the proposal that Constitutional Airlines install full passenger facilities in Honolulu, Hawaii. Wright enters the ornate conference room and seats himself at the end of a forty-five-foot-long conference table. While staring at the ceiling, he begins to address the executives of Constitutional Airlines: "As I view the proposed passenger facility in Honolulu I believe that we must confront the problem of convoluted interfacing. As you know, I have long maintained that the Honolulu run should be eliminated, and I am convinced that we must put in complete passenger facilities at Honolulu. Of course, if all of you think as my predecessor, Carruthers Caldwell, thought, we will have quite an experience today. Whatever way we go, however, I think that it is quite clear that we must consider PSA, IRS, FAA, and BMIO. You know, of course, that I have a completely open mind on this question. I am attempting to carry on in the proud tradition that Carruthers started. [This state-ment is accompanied by a subtle but seemingly negative facial expression.] Well, let me get right to the point. To get Constitutional Airlines up to speed, I am absolutely convinced that we must move in Honolulu."

C. Dudley Wright did not function well as a communicator. He made many errors in the brief passage quoted above. Put yourself in Wright's position. Ask yourself what he might have done that he did not do in order to convey his ideas and feelings to the executive board in an effec-tive and efficient manner. More specifically, try to determine how many errors Wright made as a communicator, and attempt to identify the nature of these errors. In the space provided for an analysis of Wright's commu-nication behavior, list Wright's "communication errors," indicate *why* you believe them to be errors, and specify what *corrective actions* Wright should have taken.

ANALYSIS OF C. DUDLEY WRIGHT'S COMMUNICATION BEHAVIOR

_____

_____

_____

_____

_____

_____

_____

_____

_____

_____

_____

_____

Wright made at least eight errors in the executive meeting. In chrono-logical order the errors are (1) using a conference table forty-five feet long (makes balanced interaction among conferees difficult if not impossible); (2) staring at the ceiling as he began talking (eliminated the possibility of using corrective feedback from the conferees); (3) using a high-level ab-straction by identifying the problem as one of "convoluted interfacing" (such an abstraction may have many possible meanings and typically results in much confusion); (4) making an internally inconsistent statement by supporting elimination of the Honolulu run and the installation of passenger facilities in Honolulu in the same sentence (thereby impales the other executives on the horns of a logical dilemma); (5) using implicit reasoning by stating, "if all of you think as my predecessor, Carruthers Caldwell, thought" (because other executives cannot possibly know all the assumptions that Wright is making about Caldwell, they are placed in an untenable position as communicators—they must guess); (6) using four acronymns in succession by referring to PSA, IRS, FAA, and BMIO (it would probably be a miracle if all the other executives knew the *referents* of all four acronyms. Here they refer to Pacific Southwest Airlines, Internal Revenue Service, Federal Aviation Authority and the Big Man in the Inner Office—the chairman of the board); (7) employing an incongruent message (says he is trying to carry on in the proud tradition of Caldwell while flashing a negative facial expression—are we to rely on words or facial expression as the reliable indicator of Wright's true intent?); and (8) reflecting closed-minded thinking by asserting that he has an open mind but concluding that he is "absolutely convinced that we must move in Hawaii" (attempts to communicate with a closed-minded individual are difficult because beliefs are often substituted for facts).

Subjectively, at least, we recognize that Wright's efforts do not represent high-quality communication. They are disruptive for a simple reason. His efforts have had the effect of *impeding rather than facilitating the exchange of consensually shared meanings in the small group.* His communication behaviors functioned to lower the *quality of communication* in this group.

"Very well," you may say, "but can you be more precise? What do you mean by 'quality'?" Let us begin by recognizing that we all engage in a great variety of goal-directed behaviors that are not communication behaviors. The quality of these behaviors is measured by the degree to which they help us achieve our goals in a given area.

Take golf, for example. One's "handicap" is a direct measure of the overall quality of one's golf game. In golf the best players take the fewest strokes to put the ball in the hole; hence any golf-playing behaviors that increase the number of strokes also lower the quality of one's golf game.

The higher your handicap, the lower the quality of your golf game. Thus you know that the individual who carries a "ten" handicap is a reasonably good golfer (a "ten" handicap golfer has demonstrated that typically he or she will need about twelve strokes over the norm, or par, to play an eighteen-hole golf course). The *quality* of his or her golf-playing behavior is high. By contrast, we know that the "thirty" handicap golfer plays poor golf, for he or she will ordinarily take about thirty-seven strokes over par to complete an eighteen-hole course.

Clearly, "ten" handicap golfers engage in many facilitative behaviors that

128   move them reasonably close to achieving the goal of "breaking par." They probably use the proper grip, keep their left arm stiff, and use a complete follow-through. By comparison, the "thirty" handicap golfer typically engages in many behaviors that lower the quality of his or her golf game. Topping the ball, overswinging, and wrapping one's club around a tree are all representative of dysfunctional behaviors.

Although the nature of communication and golf are very different, they share at least one defining feature. Both involve a set of behaviors that can be distinguished from one another on the basis of their *quality*.

In the small group, quality of communication is reflected in the degree to which senders and receivers agree as to the meanings of the messages and responses that are exchanged; that is, meanings must be "shared." Moreover, it is not sufficient that two of the group members agree with one another as to the nature of the meaning one attempted to convey whereas two others disagree as to the nature of that meaning. There must be "consensus" among group members as to the meaning they perceive.[1] Hence high-quality communication in the small group consists of all *effective* and *efficient* exchange of meanings. Anything done by group members that distorts or obscures meaning tends by definition to lower the quality of communication. Similarly, anything that needlessly inflates the amount of time and energy required to exchange meanings contributes to inefficiency.

The C. Dudley Wright example at the beginning of this chapter focused on his communication behaviors. These behaviors were uniformly undesirable in the sense that they lowered the quality of communication in the group. They were disruptive because they served as an impediment to the effective exchange of meanings in Wright's group. Indeed disruptive *factors* or forces in the small group consist of any *communication behavior(s) that cause or contribute to the ineffective or inefficient exchange of meaning.*

Surprisingly, little effort has been exerted to identify factors that disrupt and lower the quality of small-group communication. Even less time has been devoted to the important task of developing a set of techniques that discussants can use to deal effectively with communication problems that they experience in the small group.

If we think back to our golfing analogy for a moment, the contrast is striking. Golf instructors are adept not only at identifying qualitative deficiencies in one's golfing behavior but also in providing practical tech-

---

[1] Quality of communication is not a unidimensional concept. When we write of the effectiveness with which meanings are exchanged in the small group, many readers probably equate "effectiveness" with "clarity" of expression. However, as we point out later in this chapter and in Chapter 8, communication effectiveness may also be defined as the degree to which given communication behaviors are successful in controlling others in the small group or triggering desirable responses. Other defining dimensions of communication effectiveness might also be used.

niques for improving the quality of one's game. For the most part, communication specialists (and authors of books such as this one) have been content with a general description of the behavior they are studying. They attempt neither to make judgments about the quality of the communication nor to apply techniques to deal with qualitative deficiencies.

This chapter is designed to remedy this situation through a twofold focus. First, we identify those factors that lower the quality of communication in the small group and illustrate the effects of the factors on communication quality. Secondly, we provide a new Techniques Test for Resolving Small-Group Communication Problems, which is designed to improve the quality of your own communication in the small group.

Main Sources of Communicative Disruption in the Small Group

A great variety of factors may negatively affect the quality of small-group communication. Here, however, we will concentrate on those factors that we have found to be particularly disruptive in the university classroom and in the research laboratory. The major types of disruptive factors can be classified as message variables, encoder/decoder variables, and group process variables.

We all should be rather familiar with the concept of message. Most of us probably think first of verbal messages. To convey our intended meaning, we know that we have to choose the most suitable words and arrange them in a code that is consistent with the linguistic rules of our community and compatible with the linguistic conditioning of the person(s) who are to receive the message. The person engaged in constructing messages is hardly limited to words as the sole resource, however. Facial expressions, gestures, posture, and vocal cues also convey stable and easily identifiable referents, which may be important parts of messages.

Message Variables Different messages often exhibit distinct and distinctive features. The effective communicator must be alert to such message features when they are apt to result in a marked reduction of the quality of small-group communication. Of the different types of message variables, four have proved to be particularly disruptive: (1) *high-level abstractions,* (2) *implicit inferences,* (3) *facetious interpolations,* and (4) *incongruences.*

Messages that feature high-level abstractions are typically very disruptive. The disruption is particularly severe when the level of abstraction of a given statement is well above that of the general level of the discussion. Our attempt to perceive what others are trying to communicate is a difficult business even under ideal conditions. It can become excruciating when discussants use needlessly abstract terms to express themselves. As the communicator's messages become more abstract, the task of the receivers becomes both more difficult and time-consuming. The message is subject to multiple interpretations, and the amount of "guessing" as to the intended meaning of the message increases.

Abstract messages often represent a severe problem in the small group. Noller recognizes and emphasizes this point in writing that "perhaps one of the primary sources of poor or faulty communications between people and therefore one of the greatest inhibitors of creativity in human relations is a misunderstanding or lack of understanding of the levels of abstraction." [2]

Specifically, a high-level abstraction is a contribution to a discussion wherein the key term is so general as to be susceptible to multiple connotations.[3] To say that Samuel Levine is dean of the College of Liberal Arts at Southwestern University is to be concrete. To say that Levine engages in sophistic pedantry is to be abstract.

The reader can undoubtedly think of numerous instances when he or she became frustrated and confused because a discussant made a needlessly abstract contribution. You are probably not aware, however, of the specific effects of abstract messages on subsequent communication in the small group.

Leathers has examined the impact of abstract messages on small-group communication in a series of laboratory studies. These studies reveal that *abstract messages consistently disrupt subsequent small-group communication, that the degree of disruption increases as messages become more abstract, and that abstract messages consistently are associated with the same, undesirable set of effects.*

Laboratory groups at UCLA were asked to discuss how the university might improve its relationship with the Reagan administration. At selected intervals in the discussions, a "plant" would turn to a discussant who had just spoken and say, "Don't you think this is basically a matter of historical dialecticism?" or "Don't you think that Reagan is really a Jeffersonian Philistine?" Because of the level of abstraction, the discussant who was addressed typically had great difficulty in responding to the abstract message

[2] R. B. Noller, "Some Applications of General Semantics in Teaching Creativity," *Journal of Creative Behavior* 5 (1971): 257. Certainly, we are not implying that the linguistic demands of a situation never require the use of abstract language or that abstract language in and of itself is bad. Indeed Gordon C. Whiting, "Code Restrictedness and Opportunities for Change in Developing Countries," *Journal of Communication* 21 (1971): 43, contends that the use of abstract language to express abstract concepts is characteristic of the elaborated code used by the middle class as opposed to the concrete language of the restricted code that is used by the lower classes. We are suggesting that sudden shifts to much higher levels of abstraction with no intervening attempts at clarification typically have a very disruptive impact on the small-group communication system.

[3] D. G. Leathers, "Process Disruption and Measurement in Small Group Communication," *Quarterly Journal of Speech* 55 (1969): 288.

in an effective and efficient manner. In fact, the response characteristically reflected *confusion, tension,* and *withdrawal.*

A representative sample from the group transcripts should help illustrate the truly disruptive nature of abstract messages:

MESSAGE: Don't you think that Reagan is really a Jeffersonian Philistine?

RESPONSE: He certainly seems to be Jeffersonian and ah, ah, I strongly suspect that he practices Philistinism. [Pause] John, simply to help out the other discussants, perhaps you could define Jeffersonian Philistine. [nervous laughter, glancing at walls and ceiling, pencil tapping, and many contorted facial expressions follow the question about Reagan as a Jeffersonian Philistine]. Oh, I can't even stand to discuss that. Let's drop the discussion right here for tonight, jump in my car, and run over and catch Sammy Davis, Jr., on the Sunset Strip.[4]

Messages that feature implicit inferences are also very disruptive. "What," you ask, "is an implicit inference?" To begin with, we must recognize that the oral discourse among group members is very different from the written discourse of a text or novel. Whereas written discourse is typically composed of complete sentences, complete thoughts, and explicit reasoning, discussion is not. Discussion, in contrast, is a dynamic, interactive type of communication that requires instantaneous modification of one's thinking; one's thoughts are frequently interrupted by other discussants. Because of the frequent interruptions and rapid-fire exchanges, thought continuity is often difficult to maintain in the small group. It is important that the discussants make their ideas and reasoning as explicit as possible. Unfortunately, much of the reasoning and many of the discussants' ideas remain implicit. The most disruptive type of such implicit expressions is the implicit inference.

The implicit inference is defined as a conclusion reached by thought processes that are never revealed to the other discussants. The discussant may have made four or five unstated assumptions before arriving at his conclusion. However, he never shares these assumptions with others in the group. They remain implicit. As a good example of a message featuring at least one implicit inference, let us start with the following conclusion about Senator Ted Kennedy: "Well, given the Kennedy's history, I am not surprised that Teddy is not running for the presidency." Obviously, the discussant arrived at this conclusion only after making a number of assumptions. The exact nature of those assumptions remains a mystery, however. Is the discussant assuming that Ted Kennedy is not running because of his increased responsibility as surrogate father to the children of his assassi-

---

[4] Ibid., pp. 297–298. Subsequent feedback responses to messages that refer to Reagan come from the same article.

nated brothers? Is he or she assuming that Teddy is not running because the Kennedys' sense of political timing is very good and 1984 would be a more opportune year? Is he or she assuming that Teddy will not run because his actions at Chappaquiddick so alienated the public that he would lose? Is he or she making all of the assumptions above and some others? Clearly, such implicit inferences can result in a communication problem in the small group.

Laboratory research reveals that implicit inferences are typically associated with responses that are *signal* (that is, immediate and visceral in nature), *irrelevant,* and *digressive.* The laboratory groups exposed to implicit inferences typically responded in the following manner:

MESSAGE: If everyone thought as Reagan does, nobody would become a college professor.

RESPONSE: No, absolutely not true. Outrageous. That's a ridiculous statement. I couldn't care less about that question; let's talk about the Board of Regents and their responsibility to the people of California. Of course, that is a provocative statement. Yes, indeed, that is a provocative statement that should be examined at considerable length. Before we can make any judgments, I suspect that we must try and infer the way Governor Reagan thinks by looking at the record of his public statements and checking to see if they meet the basic requirements of a valid syllogism.

A third type of message that is often highly disruptive is the humorous interjection or interpolation. Conventional advice to the discussant is that the use of humor will have a beneficial effect on group communication.[5] Humor often conjures up images of the camaraderie of a few beers with the boys after work or a happy hour at the end of the week.

Business executives sometimes attempt to use humor as a tension release. Imagine yourself attending your first board meeting of Citrus International after appointment to the executive committee. Hal Jones, vice-president of operations and a noted practical jokester, turns to you and says, "Lather, we had a hell of a problem here at CI this week. One of our

[5] K. E. Andersen, *Persuasion: Theory and Practice* (Boston: Allyn and Bacon, 1971), p. 185, contends that "the role of humor warrants further investigation. The extensive use of humor as an attention device, as a means of releasing tension, and as a means of facilitating group response seems unquestioned. Humor can be used to turn aside a hostile question or to establish rapport with an unfriendly group. Because humor connotes warmth, friendship, acceptance, communality, it may well affect the communicator's image. Clearly, the function of humor as well as the nature of humor need additional investigation." We would agree that the functions of humor in the small group need further investigation. Although we have little empirical evidence to document the positive functions of humor, we do have laboratory evidence to indicate that some types of humor have a very disruptive impact on the small-group communication system.

big orange crushers came down on Harold Levant and squeezed the juice out of him; he was crushed to death. We wanted to send his foreman, Patton, to break the news to Mrs. Levant, but we hesitated because we knew Patton is rather tactless. However, we finally sent Patton. When Mrs. Levant answered the door, Patton said, 'Are you the widow Levant?' 'No,' she replied, 'I am not the widow Levant; I am Mrs. Harold Levant.' Patton replied, 'You wanna bet.' " In spite of the gravity of the situation, Vice-President Jones could not repress a smile after telling this story.

This aprocryphal story reflects hyperbole as well as bad taste. It is very typical of the decision-making group in at least one respect, however. Many discussants persist in making "wisecracks" in serious, task-oriented discussions. Such contributions are facetious interpolations. The discussant introduces a statement that he intends to be humorous, but his intent as perceived by the other discussants is unclear or ambiguous. Most task-oriented groups exhibit a very low level of tolerance for messages that feature facetious interpolations. Indeed facetious interpolations characteristically seem to impair both the effective and efficient exchange of meanings in the small group.

In laboratory groups, facetious messages typically result in *personal* (critical or insulting feedback directed at the person who has made the facetious contribution) and *inflexible* responses. Here is a typical example from a laboratory discussion:

MESSAGE: Do you realize that Reagan's so far right he was rejected by the Minute Men as a security risk?

RESPONSE: Oh, come on, Dave, you are being so damn subjective I can't be-lieve it. When we started, I really felt a man of your apparent ability would refrain from making such an addlebrained remark. I am convinced that Ronald Reagan is inspired by the purest mo-tives of the dedicated conservative. Nothing has been said to make me think otherwise, and I seriously doubt whether you can con-vince me that Reagan deserves criticism of any kind.

Finally messages that convey two or more meanings that conflict in some way have a very negative impact on the quality of small-group com-munication. "How," you may ask, "can messages convey multiple mean-ings?" Simple misuse of language is one way. A more important source of conflicting meaning becomes apparent after a moment's thought. Think of the number of times an individual has complimented your thinking or at-tire by verbal means, for example, although seeming to contradict this verbal compliment with a negative facial expression.

In this example, meanings are being conveyed by both verbal and non-verbal channels. Such messages are incongruent when the meaning or meanings transmitted through one channel (verbal) are inconsistent with the meaning transmitted through one or more of the other channels (non-

134   verbal).[6] Obviously, the discussant who is forced to decode a message that conveys conflicting meanings is in a real bind.

The following example is based on a laboratory experiment where discussants were forced to deal repeatedly with message incongruences. Although the example is hypothetical, the communicative interaction is almost identical to that which occurred in the laboratory discussions.

Imagine that you are a student at Black Duck State Teachers College and that you are a member of a student group that is discussing steps that might be taken to reinvigorate the college curriculum. You are really into this discussion because it is important to you. As we begin to follow the discussion, you have just stated that you would like to see a new course on behavioral objectives. Randy, the black-haired girl next to you, responds:

RANDY: You know your idea is fascinating. Just fascinating. [As Randy utters these words, she yawns ostentatiously and stares at the ceiling as if she is bored.]

BECKY: [There is a long pause while the other discussants shuffle nervously in their seats. Becky stares at Randy with a look that seems to say, "You bitch." Becky's brow becomes wrinkled as if she does not understand. She turns the palms of her hands upward and spreads arms outward to other members of the group as if asking them for help.] I don't understand. Ah, ah, well, I like it here at Black Duck State; the canoe trips up to Canada are great. In fact, what do you say we plan a trip for next weekend?

The reader can see that the incongruent message was extremely disruptive. Becky's response was typical. Nonverbally, she reflected confusion, hostility, and uncertainty while verbally her response can accurately be characterized as confused, tense, irrelevant, and withdrawn. Indeed the suggestion to plan a weekend canoe trip is certainly the ultimate in withdrawal. Recall that before she was confronted with Randy's incongruent message, Becky was participating eagerly on a subject in which she was highly involved.

Clearly, such message variables as high-level abstractions, implicit inferences, facetious interpolations, and incongruences can and frequently do impair the effective and efficient exchange of meanings in the small group. Such message variables often result in communication problems of long duration that are very difficult for group members to handle. Often the individual members do not know which course of action is the most suitable one for dealing with a specific type of communication problem. To increase your ability to identify such communication problems and your

[6] D. G. Leathers, *Nonverbal Communication Systems* (Boston: Allyn and Bacon, 1976), pp. 238–46.

capacity to deal with them, a Techniques Test for Resolving Small-Group **135**
Communication Problems is provided at the end of this chapter.

Encoder-Decoder Variables When individuals attempt to communicate meanings, they have to choose that symbol or set of symbols that they feel will function most effectively to convey their *intended meaning* (these symbols may be in the form of words, facial expression, gestures, posture, use of space, and so on). Similarly, the person to whom these symbols are directed must choose to concentrate on the symbols that combine to represent what he or she believes is the sender's intended meaning. The person who chooses symbols and puts them in the form of a code is the encoder, and the person who attempts to decipher the meaning(s) of these symbols is the decoder. When the encoder and decoder are functioning with optimum effectiveness and efficiency, the transmitted and perceived meanings will be virtually identical, and the process of exchanging these meanings will take a minimum amount of time.

Many factors may serve to impair the effectiveness and efficiency with which meanings are encoded and decoded. Such disparate factors as the encoder/decoder attention span, intelligence, linguistic skills, cultural conditioning, and even educational level may have a major impact on the encoder or decoder or both. In this section, however, we are going to concentrate on three types of encoder/decoder variables that have consistently had a very disruptive impact on the quality of small-group communication: (1) status differences, (2) closed-mindedness, and (3) ego-involvement.

To begin, we must recognize that both encoders and decoders must deal with varying symbols that typically do not have fixed and absolute meanings. For example, Winston Churchill's middle and index fingers raised in the form of a *V* meant one thing; the same gesture by a protestor against the Vietnam War meant quite another. When Martin Luther King and his black followers sang "We Shall Overcome," the meaning was hardly the same for members of the Southern Christian Leadership Conference and the Ku Klux Klan.

Status Differences To a very large extent, meaning is a function of perception. In the small group the way we view others, the way we behave, and the meanings we assign to the symbols used are often affected in dramatic ways by marked differences in status among group members. Indeed Shaw writes insightfully that "status differences exert a powerful influence upon the pattern and content of communications in the group. In general, more communications are directed toward the high-status member, and the content of such messages tends to be more positive than messages directed downward in the status hierarchy." [7]

Anyone who has observed the small group closely is probably aware of

[7] M. E. Shaw, *Group Dynamics: The Psychology of Small Group Behavior* (New York: McGraw-Hill, 1971), p. 243.

the disruptive potential of status differences at least at the intuitive level. Both ascribed and achieved status may significantly affect communicative interaction as early as the first minute of a group meeting. However, marked differences in achieved status may not evolve for some time. When differences in achieved status do evolve, they are often attributable to differences in the quality of ideas and guidance that one gives to the group as well as overall qualitative differences in participation.[8]

The level of one's own status is not as important as the *perceived difference between one's own status and that of other members of the group.* Alschuler theorizes that marked differences in status will result in cognitive dissonance—the discussant may experience dissonance or tension in the sense that his motivation to participate actively is blocked by members of higher status. The clear implication is that members will become more concerned with reducing dissonance than with achieving group objectives.[9]

Clearly perceived status differences can have a markedly disruptive impact on the quality and quantity of communication in the small group.[10] Perceived differences in status often result in the high-status members conforming more to the norms of the group than other group members. Many more contributions tend to be directed to high-status than to low-status members. Finally, contributions directed to high-status individuals tend to have a more positive content than those directed to low-status individuals.[11]

In short, marked differences in perceived status may negatively affect the quality of communication in the small group. Members are often inhibited in the presence of high-status individuals and reluctant to provide the clarifying and analytical type of feedback that is characteristic of effective discussion. Furthermore, status differences tend to result in an unbalanced interaction with the status of a discussant rather than the content of the discussion shaping the pattern and amount of interaction. Finally, status differences may result in a high level of conformity that can have a detrimental effect on the process of communication as well as on the group product.

Closed-mindedness Effective communication in the small group presupposes the ability of all discussants to be able to perceive as well as to convey subtle differences in meaning. Closed-minded individuals consis-

[8] M. H. Fisek and R. Ofshe, "The Process of Status Evolution," *Sociometry* 33 (1970): pp. 327–346. See also W. J. Doyle, "The Effects of Leader Achieved Status on Hierarchically Differentiated Group Performance," *Dissertation Abstracts International* 30 (7–A), 2747.

[9] L. R. Alschuler, "Status Equilibration, Reference Groups, and Social Fields," *General Systems* 18 (1973): 99–118.

[10] J. Berger, B. P. Cohen, and M. Zeldith, "Status Characteristics and Social Interaction," *American Sociological Review* 37 (1972): 253–255.

[11] Shaw, *Group Dynamics*, p. 281.

tently exhibit an inability to deal effectively with subtle shades of meaning. This is so because of the structure of their belief and value systems. Individuals with a distinctive belief system can typically be identified by their "cognitive style." Miller and Steinberg define cognitive style as the characteristic ways in which individuals structure their beliefs and attitudes about the world and as the ways they process and respond to incoming information.[12]

The cognitive style of closed-minded persons makes it difficult for them to deal realistically with the symbols and stimuli to which they must attach meaning. One study examined "possible differences in the amount of time required by high-dogmatic and low-dogmatic persons to identify the humorous aspect of a picture when the humor was based on a situation that violated a conventional, seldom-challenged belief. All participants in the study were shown a *Playboy*-type, centerfold picture, taken from *Harvard Lampoon's* parody of *Playboy*. The picture's humor lay in the nude girl's tanning pattern: she was tanned where one would normally expect her to be untanned, and untanned where one would expect her to be tanned. As Miller and Bacon predicted, the high-dogmatic person took significantly longer than their low-dogmatic counterparts to recognize just what was funny about the picture." [13]

A discussant's dominant beliefs and values are often crucial determinants of the nature of message that is encoded, and, perhaps more importantly, beliefs and values vitally affect the meanings that a discussant chooses to decode in any communicative exchange. Some knowledge about a discussant's belief on a given type of behavior or about a member of a group can be useful. Extensive knowledge about a discussant's belief system can be invaluable.

An individual's *belief system* represents the total universe of that person's beliefs about the physical world, the social world, and the self.[14] The concept of belief system is particularly relevant to the encoding and decoding activities that are central to small-group communication. Rokeach writes that "all information impinging upon the person from the outside must be processed or coded in such a way that it is either rejected or somehow fitted into the belief-disbelief system. We call this processing-coding activity thinking. Our guess is that it must be within some such context as the belief-disbelief system that thinking takes place." [15]

---

[12] G. R. Miller and M. Steinberg, *Between People: A New Analysis of Interpersonal Communication* (Chicago: Science Research Associates, 1975), p. 144.

[13] Ibid., pp. 155–156.

[14] M. Rokeach, *Beliefs, Attitudes, and Values* (San Francisco, Calif.: Jossey-Bass, 1968), p. 123. See M. Rokeach, *The Nature of Human Values* (New York: The Free Press, 1973), pp. 3–25, for a complete discussion of value systems and belief systems.

[15] M. Rokeach, *The Open and Closed Mind: Investigations into the Nature of Belief Systems and Personality Systems* (New York: Basic Books, 1960), p. 47.

138   If a communicator's belief system is composed of beliefs that are sufficiently extreme, the belief system may control the nature of the messages
that the individual can encode and decode. Indeed Leathers's research
on revolutionary reactionaries such as Robert Welch, Billy James Hargis,
and Carl McIntire suggests that the structure of their belief system controls
the content of their communication.[16] For example, the reactionaries believe that many of the major institutions in the United States are being
controlled by a Communist conspiracy. Their beliefs lead them to conclude, furthermore, not only that appearances are unreliable, but also that
reality is exactly the opposite of what it appears to be. Thus Dwight Eisen-
hower was almost universally perceived as a morally upright patriot—to
the reactionaries, this is strong evidence to support their belief that he was
a Communist dupe. Similarly, the national media repeatedly suggest that
reactionary organizations appeal to a very small percentage of Americans
—reactionaries take this as strong evidence to support their belief that
they have widespread popularity.

"But these people are extremists," you say. "Granted that their belief
systems may control the content of their communication, what does that
have to do with the communication of the average discussant?" The reader
may assume that the average discussant has the belief system that is characteristic of the open mind. Most of us would like to think that we have
open minds. In fact, in many discussions the discussants' own statements
suggest that their minds are more closed than open.

"What," you may ask, "are the defining characteristics of the closed
mind?" Rokeach puts the matter succinctly when he writes that "this leads
us to suggest a basic characteristic that defines the extent to which a person's system is open or closed; namely, the extent to which the person
can receive, evaluate, and act on relevant information received from outside on its own intrinsic merits, unencumbered by irrelevant factors in the
situation arising from within the person or from the outside." [17] Specifically, your mind is closed to the extent that (1) the things in which you
disbelieve are absolutely and consistently rejected, (2) there is almost complete isolation between those things in which you believe and disbelieve,
and (3) you are unable to distinguish between beliefs opposed to your
own.[18]

The closed or partially closed mind can have a stultifying effect on communicative interaction in the small group. Illustrations are plentiful, for
closed minds are not difficult to find in discussions. The following excerpt

[16] D. G. Leathers, "Belief-Disbelief Systems: The Communicative Vacuum of the Radical
Right," in *Explorations in Rhetorical Criticism*, ed. by C. J. Stewart, D. J. Ochs, and G. P.
Mohrmann (University Park, Pa.: The Pennsylvania State University Press, 1973), p. 131.

[17] Rokeach, *The Open and Closed Mind*, p. 57.

[18] D. G. Leathers, "Belief-Disbelief Systems: The Communicative Vacuum of the Radical
Right, p. 127.

is based on exchanges of members of a building committee for a local church:

LEW: I am committed to putting in pews and using laminated beams. That building consultant from Chicago wants stacking chairs, but his ideas are absolute hogwash.

HAROLD: Lew, don't you think we owe it to the congregation to examine the alternatives to pews and laminated beams?

LEW: No. You guys who don't go with the laminated beams and pews all think alike. You are yes men for the national office in Chicago.

Clearly, Lew has a closed mind on this subject. He absolutely rejects all views opposed to his (his disbeliefs), refuses to consider other beliefs, and is unable to distinguish between and among the various beliefs held by other members of the building committee.

Such a belief system makes for very inefficient communication in that other members must expend excessive energy in inducing Lew to become more flexible or they must work around him. Lew's encoding and decoding skills are impaired to such a degree that effective communication among members of the building committee is difficult.

There is no easy and universally useful method of dealing with the closed-minded discussant. However, the need to deal with this problem is apparent, for closed-minded behavior consistently has the effect of lowering the quality of small-group communication. Clearly, we must use some technique to deal with the communication problems associated with closed-mindedness.

We must recognize that most people attach a very negative value to closed-minded behavior; closed-mindedness is certainly not the "in" thing. Few people will persist in the more extreme forms of closed-minded behavior *if they are fully aware that other group members perceive them to be closed-minded. Frequently, however, group members are aware of neither their predisposition to be closed-minded nor the fact that other group members perceive them to be closed-minded.*

Let us use a simple analogy for purposes of illustration. The person who takes a glucose tolerance test and discovers that he or she is diabetic or prediabetic is apt to alter future eating habits. Similarly, we would maintain that the discussant who discovers that he or she is closed-minded or has a propensity for closed-minded behavior will make an attempt to alter his or her behavior.

Consequently, we would urge all members of your group to take a simple test that measures your tendencies to be closed-minded—the short form of the Dogmatism Test.[19] Please compute your scores, and discuss the implications of the scores with your fellow group members.

---

[19] V. C. Troldahl and F. A. Powell, "A Short-Form Dogmatism Scale for use in Field Studies," *Social Forces* 44 (1965): 211–214.

140   **Ego-Involvement**   Ego-involvement is the third encoder-decoder variable that may have a major impact on the quality of small-group communication. Of course, ego-involvement and closed-mindedness are conceptually related; the individual who is highly ego-involved on a wide range of issues will tend to be more closed-minded than his or her counterpart with low ego-involvement. These two concepts do differ in specificity and focus, however. Closed-mindedness is a measure of one's beliefs with regard to the world and reality in general. In contrast, ego-involvement is a measure of the intensity of one's attitudes on a specific issue or issues. Because one's position on issues is apt to change frequently, ego-involvement is a more volatile concept than closed-mindedness.

Ego-involvement is the arousal, singly or in combination, of the individual's commitments or stands in the context of appropriate situations, be they interpersonal relations or a judgment task in the actual life of an experiment.[20] As a discussant's ego-involvement on a specific issue increases, his or her flexibility and the flexibility of those with whom he or she attempts to communicate tends to decrease.

The degree of one's ego-involvement on a given issue is measured by the number of positions that an individual finds objectionable or unacceptable—this is known as the latitude of rejection. The original procedure for measuring ego-involvement was rather cumbersome and was modified by Leathers in two projects he directed as a political consultant. Let's assume that I am trying to determine your ego-involvement on whether we should have full diplomatic relations with Cuba. I would ask you to consider the following six options: (1) absolutely should, (2) probably should, (3) possibly should, (4) possibly should not, (5) probably should not, and (6) absolutely should not. I would ask you to circle all the options or positions that you found objectionable. If you circled 2, your ego-involvement would equal 2, 3 would equal 3, and so on. In short, the more alternatives you reject, the higher your ego-involvement on any issue.

If you are in a group with one or more highly ego-involved individuals, their high ego-involvement is not apt to disrupt communication when you agree with their position. It is when you disagree that ego-involvement becomes a particular problem. Please note that (1) a discussant's felt discrepancy between his or her stand and your own is significantly greater when he or she is ego-involved, (2) the ego-involved discussant is much less apt to change his or her position to agree with yours than a discussant with low ego-involvement, and (3) discussants will reach some degree of perceived group agreement with greater frequency with other group

---

[20] C. W. Sherif, M. Sherif, and R. E. Nebergall, *Attitude and Attitude Change* (Philadelphia: Saunders, 1965), p. 65.

members of low ego-involvement than with group members who are highly **141**
ego-involved.[21]

The risks of taking a stand opposing that of a highly ego-involved individual are substantial. For example, in my consulting work for a mayoral candidate in a major city, my field research indicated that there was a wide range of opinions among city voters as to how the next mayor should deal with "hippies." More important, the voters were highly ego-involved on this issue. Consequently, my advice to the candidate was to

> avoid speaking about "hippies" as such, but an overt appeal to "valley youth" with exciting ways of involving them in city government would have immense appeal for the parents. Most Valley people are against hippies or have ambivalent feelings about them. Significantly, very few parents consider their own children to be hippies. The parents are probably hungry for constructive proposals to involve their own young people in socially desirable projects.

Mortensen highlights the real importance of ego-involvement as an encoding/decoding variable when he writes that "clearly, the concept of personal involvement is critical to an understanding of how individuals establish and then maintain simultaneous orientations toward all aspects of a communicative situation. High ego-involvement functions as the basis for judging all other aspects of the social situation. Hence, it affects not only resistance to change but also one's predisposition, impression of credibility, susceptibility to attitude change, and a host of matters affecting the outcomes of the encounter." [22]

Group Process Variables—the Consensus Climate As we indicated in Chapter 2, at least eight major forces interact in the small group to make small-group communication distinctive. Although these forces are not communication variables as such, they can have a major impact on communicative interaction in the small group. These intragroup forces are group process variables. They function to affect group communication as a direct result of the development of a clearly identifiable set of pressures, rewards, and punishments that are *internal* to the group.

In broadest perspective the group process variables often interact in such a way as to create one of two climates in which small-group communication takes place—the consensus climate and the conflict climate. Neither in its extreme form is conducive to good group communication.

Uniformity pressures play a major role in creating the consensus climate. Is there a student of the small group whose curiosity is so dead that he or she has not heard of the Asch experiments? In one typical experiment Asch asks students to compare the length of one vertical line with three

[21] K. K. Sereno and C. D. Mortensen, "The Effects of Ego-involved Attitudes on Conflict Negotiation in Dyads," *Speech Monographs* 26 (1969): 12.
[22] C. D. Mortensen, *Communication: The Study of Human Interaction* (New York: McGraw-Hill, 1972), pp. 166–167.

142   other lines. Asch surrounds the "naïve subject" with his own "plants," who make unanimous but incorrect judgments about the length of the lines. Asch notes that three-quarters of the naïve subjects yielded to the unanimous judgment of the "plants" on at least one trial and that one-third of the naïve subjects agreed with the "plants" on at least half of the trials.[23]

The uniformity variable is active in a group when members experience pressure to bring their attitudes, beliefs, values, and behavior in line with the prevailing standard in the group in order to achieve consensus. Some people will agree to almost anything if trusted members of their peer group tell them something.

The uniformity variable will not always work and not on all people, however. Cartwright and Zander note that uniformity pressures are most apt to force an individual to accept the group's opinion when the following conditions are met: (1) the quality of evidence provided by other group members is compelling, (2) the stimulus being judged is ambiguous, (3) the subject's confidence in the correctness of his or her own perception is low, (4) the discrepancy between the individual's and the group's opinion is large but not too large, and (5) the individual knows that other members of the group are aware that his or her opinion differs from theirs.[24] Moreover, individuals whose opinions are relatively close to the group's and individuals who like group members are much more likely to conform.[25]

Clearly, uniformity pressures may have the effect of producing group thought control with the serious diminution of independent, critical thinking that such thought control suggests. Not surprisingly, Irving Janis has come up with the provocative concept of groupthink.

Groupthink results from a special type of uniformity pressure. According to Janis, groupthink refers to a "mode of thinking that people engage in when they are deeply involved in a cohesive in-group, when the members' strivings for unanimity override their motivation to realistically appraise alternative courses of action." [26] It is characterized by an ineffective type of communicative interaction in groups that leads to defective decision making.

Ultimately, groupthink may have been a major factor in leading groups to make decisions that resulted in fiascoes on the international scene. De-

[23] S. E. Asch, "Effects of Group Pressure Upon the Modification and Distortion of Judgments," in *Groups, Leadership and Men,* ed. by H. Guetzkow (Pittsburgh: Carnegie Press, 1951).

[24] D. Cartwright and A. Zander, *Group Dynamics: Research and Theory,* third edition (New York: Harper and Row, 1968), p. 140.

[25] T. R. Tirney, "A Study of Conformity Behavior," *Dissertation Abstracts International,* 1971, Vol. 32 (4-A), 2196.

[26] I. L. Janis, *Victims of Groupthink: A Psychological Study of Foreign-Policy Decisions and Fiascoes* (Boston: Houghton Mifflin Company, 1972), p. 9.

cisions leading to Pearl Harbor, our involvement in the North Korean and Vietnam wars, and the Bay of Pigs may have been materially affected by the groupthink phenomenon.

Whether the decision makers were Franklin Roosevelt and Admiral Kimmel, Harry Truman and Dean Acheson, Lyndon Johnson and Walt Rostow, or John Kennedy and Dean Rusk, Janis believes that these impressive minds were affected by the phenomenon of groupthink. As Janis writes:

> the concept of groupthink pinpoints an entirely different source of trouble, residing neither in the individual nor in the organizational setting. Over and beyond all the familiar sources of human error is a powerful source of defective judgment that arises in cohesive groups—the concurrence-seeking tendency, which fosters over-optimism, lack of vigilance, and sloganistic thinking about the weakness and immorality of out-groups. This tendency can take its toll even when the decision-makers are conscientious statesmen trying to make the best possible decisions for their country and for all mankind.[27]

A number of the intragroup forces described in Chapter 2 must interact to produce the conditions necessary for groupthink to take place. The groupthink phenomenon combines strong pressures to uniformity with a high level of cohesiveness. In addition, group members typically feel a strong sense of interdependency while being keenly aware that other members of the group are observing their actions carefully. The need for compatibility is great whereas the particular needs of the group leader are such as to inhibit dissent. Even the small size of the group may contribute to a feeling that only this in-group is apprised of all the facts.

An outside observer can determine whether the consensus climate associated with groupthink exists by looking for the presence of some or all of the following symptoms: (1) a shared illusion of invulnerability by group members, which often results in excessively risky decisions; (2) collective efforts to rationalize the group's decision and to discount the thinking of dissidents; (3) an unquestioned belief in the group's inherent morality; (4) direct conformity pressure brought to bear on dissenting members to bring their opinions into line with those of the majority; (5) self-censorship by individuals of doubts they may have about the wisdom of the group's decisions; (6) a shared illusion of unanimity about judgments that conform to the majority view; and (7) the emergence of self-appointed mindguards, who protect others in the group from information that

---

[27] Ibid., p. 13. Former Secretary of State Dean Rusk has appeared as a guest lecturer for the past several years in a seminar taught by one of the authors. Because Janis alleges that Rusk was one of the victims of the groupthink phenomenon, Rusk was asked to discuss the concept in the seminar. He indicated that Janis has raised some extremely important questions about intragroup forces that may affect decision making in the small group. Although Rusk has reservations about some of the assumptions made to develop the concept of groupthink and about some of the examples used to attempt to validate it, he indicated that he is currently doing some of his own research on problems of decision making in the consensus climate.

144   might lead the group to question the effectiveness and morality of their decisions.[28]

Irving Janis draws his examples of groupthink from the conference tables of internationally known decision makers. There is little reason to think, however, that the groupthink phenomenon afflicts only very famous and influential groups. Our experience leads us to conclude that groups at a wide range of levels must deal frequently with the communication problems that are inherent in the consensus climate associated with groupthink.

Group Process Variables—the Conflict Climate   Ironically, when intragroup forces are not working to produce consensus, they are often working to produce conflict. From the standpoint of high-quality communication, the conflict climate can be just as undesirable as the censensus climate.

Not all conflict is undesirable, of course. Conflict may serve some very useful functions, such as increased concentration, the refinement and clarification of the discussants' thinking, the synthesis of ideas, and even increased mutual respect as the result of ideational struggle and evolution in the group.

Conflict becomes undesirable when it may be characterized as destructive. Deutsch defines a conflict as destructive if it has destructive consequences wherein "the participants in it are dissatisfied with the outcomes and all feel they have lost as a result of the conflict."[29]

What is it about the nature of group interaction that increases the probability that destructive conflict may occur? The same set of intragroup forces that interact to produce the consensus climate may interact to produce the conflict climate. The intragroup forces of social influence, interdependency, and leadership often become particularly important factors in the development of the conflict climate.

In the first place, when we interact in groups, we are aware that others are watching us. This realization often triggers a type of display behavior that makes the barnyard rooster look like an introvert. Some individuals in groups act in ways designed to inflate their own self-image and deflate the image of others. Much like a golf-playing friend of mine, these individuals seem to undergo a metamorphosis when in the presence of a group of people. My friend is the model of civility and decorum when playing

---

[28] Ibid., pp. 198–199. S. Milgram, *Obedience to Authority* (New York: Harper and Row, 1974), p. 113, in his fascinating book examines a variable closely related to conformity pressure that can contribute to the consensus climate. Whereas conformity refers to going along with peers of one's own status who "have no special right to direct his behavior," obedience refers to the actions of an individual complying with the orders of a superior or a figure of authority.

[29] M. Deutsch, "Conflicts: Productive and Destructive," in *Conflict Resolution Through Communication*, ed. by F. E. Jandt (New York: Harper and Row, 1973), p. 158.

alone or with me. When playing with a group (particularly if his wife is watching), he often becomes argumentative and defensive, curses frequently while throwing his clubs in the air, and suggests that the only suitable outcome is for him to look good ("Damn, Leathers, this is intolerable; with all these people here, I simply must break 90 today").

Secondly, positions that are expressed in the intimate environment of the small group are very difficult to recant. If I announce to members of a group that I am for free love, my commitment to that position will grow simply by virtue of the fact that I have made my position explicit with the group. In the eyes of many discussants, such public commitments carry the attendant responsibility of attacking positions that conflict with them.

Thirdly, many individuals view a small group as a vehicle to be used to sharpen and satisfy their competitive instincts. The group member sees himself gaining only if other members are losing. Such competitive behavior within the group (1) tends to produce communication between conflicting parties that is unreliable and impoverished; (2) stimulates the view that the solution to the conflict is the type that is imposed on other group members by superior force, deception, or cleverness; and (3) leads to a suspicious and hostile attitude that maximizes, rather than minimizes, differences among group members.[30]

Finally, two or more group members often get locked in a leadership struggle that produces destructive conflict. The potential for such conflict is greater when the aspiring leaders operate from a hidden agenda (they deny their interest in becoming leaders but work covertly to take over the group's leadership). In such cases, the conflict is destructive by definition because any outcome other than becoming group leader is unsatisfactory.

Although there is no perfect technique for handling destructive conflict, it is important to deal with it before the conflict becomes very bitter and group communication disintegrates totally. The "nominal group process" is perhaps the most promising technique that may be employed in the early stages of group deliberation before the conflict becomes deep-seated. The "nominal group process" prevents premature closure to the alternatives available to the group and provides substantial tolerance for conflict and even incompatible ideas. The nominal group has this potential because group members spend the first ten to twenty minutes of a meeting silently deliberating and writing out their ideas. Then each individual provides one idea from his list, which is written on a flip chart in the full view of other members. This round robin listing of ideas continues until the members have no further ideas. General discussion then ensues, which is followed by silent voting (a rank ordering of the ideas or rating).[31]

[30] Ibid., pp. 161–162.
[31] A. Van de Ven and A. L. Delbecq, "Nominal Versus Interacting Group Processes for Committee Decision-Making Effectiveness," *Academy of Management Journal* 14 (1971): 203–207.

Techniques for Dealing with Sources of Communicative Disruption

This chapter has been designed to describe those message, encoder-decoder, and group process variables that can function in such a way as to lower significantly the quality of communication in the small group. Special emphasis has been given to illustrating and explaining the disruptive effects of such variables. Those students, managers, technical specialists, and others who have been exposed to this material agree that it significantly increases their potential to be effective small-group communicators. Almost invariably, however, they ask *what corrective actions they should take to deal with the type of communication problems they typically encounter.*

The Techniques Test for Resolving Small-Group Communication Problems has been designed specifically to meet this need. No technique will work in all situations, of course, and many factors may either enhance or reduce the effectiveness of a technique in a given instance. Nonetheless, existing research does allow us to make some fairly precise judgments about the relative effectiveness of a given technique for dealing with a given communication problem.

In the test that follows, you are asked to make judgments about the relative value of the techniques for dealing with the individual communication problems that are described. Please rank-order the five possible techniques for each communication problem, giving a 1 to the best technique and a 5 to the worst.

Communication Problem 1. You are in a group where one of the group members continues to use extremely abstract language ("I believe our chief competitor suffers from a cognitive occlusion"). In dealing with communication problem, you should

____1. Disregard the discussant's abstract language to avoid conflict.

____2. Ask the discussant if he has ever experienced a cognitive occlusion.

____3. Attempt to eliminate such abstractions by negatively reinforcing the discussant who uses them.

____4. Ask the discussant to define what he means by providing a concrete example.

____5. Hand the offending discussant a dictionary.

Communication Problem 2. At least one of the group members insists on expressing his or her views indirectly through implicit inferences ("Well, it seems to me that the question of whether we should do business with Farquardt becomes more complicated when you know where he lives"). In dealing with this communication problem, you should

_____1. Drive out to see where Farquardt lives.

_____2. Wait until after the discussion and check this line of reasoning to see if it is valid.

_____3. Ask the discussant to state what assumptions he is making about Farquardt.

_____4. Try to exert group pressure to sharpen the discussant's thinking.

_____5. Positively reinforce those discussants who do make their assumptions explicit.

Communication Problem 3. One of the group members insists on making statements which he or she probably thinks are humorous ("Certainly I am not suggesting that Johnson dyes his hair—it is just turning orange naturally"). In dealing with this communication problem, you should

_____1. Question the discussant about the intent of his or her statement.

_____2. Treat yourself to a real belly laugh.

_____3. Give the discussant a copy of _Mad_ magazine.

_____4. Ask yourself whether the comment is relevant.

_____5. Try to move the discussion immediately back to the task at hand.

Communication Problem 4. Lather consistently expresses himself in an incongruent manner. He often yawns while telling group members how utterly absorbing he finds the discussion to be. At other times, he gets a totally confused look on his face while assuring one of the group members that the meaning of their contribution is very clear. In dealing with this communication problem, you should

_____1. Disregard Lather.

———2. Accuse him of being insincere.

———3. Flash Lather a confused expression.

———4. Wait for five minutes before seeking clarification.

———5. Rely on the nonverbal content of Lather's contribution as the true indicator of his meaning.

Communication Problem 5. Gordy Lather has a much higher ascribed status than any other member of the group. He makes no attempt to identify with the other members of the group, and the great differences in status are making for ineffective and inefficient communication. In dealing with this communication problem, you should

———1. Attempt to elevate the status of other group members with premeditated compliments.

———2. Make it so unpleasant for Lather that he withdraws from the group.

———3. Suggest that group members engage in role playing to illustrate the effects of a status differential.

———4. Work to increase your achieved status as a counterbalancing force against Lather's high ascribed status.

———5. Make Lather the group leader.

Communication Problem 6. Gordy Lather exhibits the characteristics of a closed mind—that is to say, that he is highly dogmatic. He is absolutely convinced of the correctness of his own opinions, absolutely rejects all opposing opinions, and lumps together all of his opponents as light thinkers. In dealing with this communication problem, you should

———1. Devote five separate group sessions to sensitivity training in order to open up Lather's mind.

———2. Suggest pointedly that some group members are becoming dogmatic.

———3. Have group members remind Lather that much of his thinking is deviant.

_____4. Have all members take the Dogmatism Test and discuss the implications of their scores.

_____5. Try to ostracize Lather because he is a troublemaker.

Communication Problem 7.   One member of your group seems highly ego-involved on one of the peripheral issues the group is discussing. Not only is this member strongly committed to his or her own position on the issue, he or she consistently rejects all alternatives that group members present. In dealing with this communication problem, you should

_____1. Suggest that the discussant join an extremist group.

_____2. Make your opposition to his or her views explicit so that the discussion can zero in on the issues.

_____3. Discuss central issues before moving on to the peripheral issue.

_____4. Ask the discussant for some facts.

_____5. Recess the meeting.

Communication Problem 8.   This group seems to be experiencing the "groupthink" phenomenon. The group is very cohesive, and strong uniformity pressures exist. As a result, group members are not appraising ideas critically but simply accepting anything the leader likes. In dealing with this communication problem, you should

_____1. Call in an objective consultant who will lead the group in a vigorous discussion of those intragroup forces that are inhibiting critical thinking in the group.

_____2. Add a "devil's advocate" to the group who will force members to defend their positions.

_____3. Change leaders.

_____4. Ostracize the "yes-men" in the group.

_____5. Change the seating arrangement.

150   **Communication Problem 9.**   This group is experiencing destructive conflict. Two of the members are locked in a leadership struggle, and members are beginning to choose sides. Because of the level of conflict, the group is producing few ideas, and communication has virtually ceased. In dealing with this communication problem, you should

_____1. Take a cold shower.

_____2. Ride out the storm.

_____3. Suggest that "nominal grouping" be used.

_____4. Suggest that the group choose a leader.

_____5. Move immediately to get more information that is relevant to the group's task.

Scoring the test is simple. Begin by checking the proper ranking for each communication problem (see keyed answers, which follow shortly). Compare your rankings with the "keyed" ranking for each communication problem. Then compute a "difference score" for each set of rankings. If your ranking deviated from the keyed ranking by over one point, multiply the difference by two. For example, note how the scores for communication problem 1 would be computed.

Keyed Ranking	Your Ranking	Difference
3	3	0
4	4	0
2	5	6
1	2	1
5	1	8
	Total Points =	15

Add up your computed scores for each of the nine communication problems to determine your total score on the test.

A perfect score on the Techniques Test for Resolving Small-Group Communication Problems would be 0. The higher your point total, the lower the quality of your performance on the test. Although we are still gathering data on expected performance on the test, you may use the following guidelines as a rule of thumb. If you got 40 or below, your performance was excellent; between 40 and 50, your performance was average; and above 50, your performance was poor.

If your performance was average to poor, you should read this chapter again and make a diligent attempt to master the concepts presented. Whatever your score, the test provides you with much valuable information that **151** you can use to help improve the quality of communication in groups in which you participate.

ANSWERS FOR TEST

Communication Problem 1: 3, 4, 2, 1, 5
Communication Problem 2: 5, 4, 1, 3, 2
Communication Problem 3: 2, 4, 5, 3, 1
Communication Problem 4: 5, 4, 2, 3, 1
Communication Problem 5: 3, 5, 1, 2, 4
Communication Problem 6: 2, 3, 4, 1, 5
Communication Problem 7: 5, 3, 1, 2, 4
Communication Problem 8: 1, 2, 3, 5, 4
Communication Problem 9: 5, 4, 1, 3, 2

SUPPLEMENTARY READING

Back, K. W.; Bunker, S.; and Dunnagar, C. B. "Barriers to Communication and Measurement of Semantic Space." *Sociometry* 25 (1972): 347–356.

Berger, J.; Cohen, B. P.; and Zelditch, M. "Status Characteristics and Social Interaction." *American Sociological Review* 37 (1972): 241–255.

Cheney, J.; Harford, T.; and Solomon, L. "The Effects of Communication Threats and Promises upon the Bargaining Process." *Journal of Conflict Resolution* 16 (1972): 99–107.

Hare, A. P.; Borgatta, E. F.; and Bales, R. F., eds. *Small Groups: Studies in Social Interaction.* New York: Alfred A. Knopf, 1966. Chapter 6.

Narrell, M.; Bowers, J. W.; and Bascal, J. P. "Another Stab at 'Meaning': Concreteness, Iconicity, and Conventionality."*Speech Monographs* 40 (1973): 199–207.

Leathers, D. G. "Testing for Determinant Interaction in the Small Group Communication Process." *Speech Monographs* 38 (1971): 182–189.

Wallach, M. A., and Mabli, J. "Information versus Conformity in the Effects of Group Discussion on Risk Taking." *Journal of Personality and Social Psychology* 14 (1970): 149–156.

Wih, R. E., and Sen, S. K. "Conformity Influence in Small Groups: A Probabilistic Measure." *Journal of Social Psychology* 86 (1971): 45–54.

QUESTIONS AND EXERCISES

1. Identify those factors in your group that lowered the quality of communication. Why did they lower the quality of communication?
2. We identified four message variables that have proved to be particularly disruptive. Can you think of other message variables that you have observed to be disruptive? Why were they disruptive?
3. Do you feel that the members of your group have equal status? Identify the members with the highest status and the lowest status. What effects have their status differences had on their communication and on

152   the communication of other members of your group? What should the
group do about perceived status differences among members?

4. At any point in your group meetings, would you say that either a consensus or conflict climate prevailed? What forces helped create that climate? Did the group take any action to deal with the undesirable effects
of either a consensus climate or a conflict climate? What were the
steps? Were they successful?

5. What is the nominal group technique? Why is it labelled a "nominal"
group technique?

6. After each individual in your group takes the Techniques Test for Resolving Small-Group Communication Problems and *before* you check
the keyed answers, take the test again as a group. As a group, you must
decide on the ranking of the options for each of the nine communication problems. Groups typically get better scores on the test than individuals. Why? Was your group score better or worse than the individual scores? Discuss the results with the members of your group.

7. Prepare a paper analyzing the Techniques Test for Resolving Small-
Group Communication Problems. Indicate what you believe the
strengths and weaknesses of the test to be and why. Also indicate what
changes you would make in the test, illustrate your proposed changes,
and provide a rationale for the changes.

8 The Functions of Nonverbal Communication in the Small Group

T he functional importance of nonverbal communication is difficult to exaggerate. In many social situations the exchange of meanings is accomplished almost solely by nonverbal behaviors. We place heavy reliance on nonverbal communication for good reason. To communicate effectively, we must be able to assess accurately the true feelings, intentions, and motivations of those with whom we communicate. These internal states of the communicator are frequently concealed or intentionally distorted. When this is the case, nonverbal cues are the best source of reliable information. Frequently, they are the only source of such information.

People at all levels of society are now exhibiting an intense curiosity about the nonverbal means of communication. At least intuitively, they sense that it is important, but often they are not sure why. Too frequently attempts to satisfy this curiosity lack specificity or direction. They do not identify the specific functions of the different nonverbal communication systems and do not specify how the communicator may develop his capacity to use these systems effectively and efficiently.

To begin this chapter, we demonstrate the functional importance of nonverbal communication generally and in the small group in particular. The chapter identifies and illustrates the functions of the nonverbal communication systems that are particularly important in the small group. More specifically, the purposes of this chapter are (1) to describe and contrast the potential of the nonverbal systems for exchanging different types of meaning in the small group, (2) to increase the reader's sensitivity to the

154   different types of nonverbal cues that are detectable in the small group, and (3) to help develop the reader's capacity to make effective and efficient use of such cues.

The Functional Importance of Nonverbal Communication

IN HUMAN COMMUNICATION

Viewed from a broad perspective, nonverbal communication is functionally important to the individual for six major reasons: (1) nonverbal, not verbal, factors are the major determinants of meaning in the interpersonal context; (2) feelings and emotions are more accurately exchanged by nonverbal than verbal means; (3) the nonverbal portion of communication conveys meanings and intentions that are relatively free of deception, distortion, and confusion; (4) nonverbal cues serve a metacommunicative function that is indispensable in attaining high quality communication; (5) nonverbal cues represent a much more efficient means of communication than verbal cues; and (6) nonverbal cues represent the most suitable vehicle for suggestion.[1]

Researchers consistently find that nonverbal cues are the dominant source of meaning in communicative interaction. For example, Argyle "found that with initially equated signals the non-verbal messages outweighed the verbal ones by at least 5 to 1, and where they were in conflict the verbal messages were virtually disregarded." [2] Careful consideration of the types of communication situations we typically encounter should confirm the validity of such findings. Think of the last time you asked someone for a date or underwent a job interview. You had a vested interest in determining the true feelings of the individuals with whom you were interacting and in determining their assessment of you. Did you rely primarily on nonverbal or verbal cues?

Clearly, we most frequently and accurately communicate our true feelings and emotions by nonverbal means. This is so because the messages conveyed nonverbally are often involuntary. Those messages that are not consciously controlled are apt to be very revealing. Judges and juries have

[1] D. G. Leathers, *Nonverbal Communication Systems* (Boston: Allyn and Bacon, 1976), pp. 4–7.

[2] M. Argyle, "The Syntaxes of Bodily Communication," *International Journal of Psycholinguistics* 2 (1973): 78. R. L. Birdwhistell, *Kinesics and Context* (Philadelphia: University of Pennsylvania Press, 1970), p. 158, claims that "probably no more than 30 to 35 per cent of the social meaning of a conversation or an interaction is carried by the words." A. Mehrabian, "Communication Without Words," *Psychology Today* 2 (1968): 51–52, estimates that 93 percent of the total impact of a message may be attributed to nonverbal factors.

long recognized the reliability of information provided by involuntary cues. One recent study of the decision-making behavior of American juries found that the jurors relied heavily on such cues.[3]

Because of the nature of nonverbal cues, they are typically free of deception and distortion. Nonverbal cues can, of course, be used for such purposes, but verbal messages are much more frequently used to dissemble or to deceive. Interrogation procedures employed by many top law enforcement agencies make use of this finding. Thus the suspect is often confronted with the unanticipated witness or surprise evidence. In such cases, the interrogators focus their attention on nonverbal, not verbal, reactions.

Whether a communicator is under extreme pressure or not, the meanings he or she communicates are often inconsistent. The confident verbal statement may be contradicted by an anxious facial expression or a nervous gesture. When an individual is faced with multiple meanings that are incompatible, he or she faces an important decoding decision. Will he or she rely on verbal or nonverbal cues as the most accurate indicator of feelings and emotions? When faced with such a choice, individuals typically rely on nonverbal cues. Such cues are apt to be most reliable.[4]

If given sufficient time and proper motivation, even the most inept communicator will convey his or her intended meaning. Unlimited time is a rare luxury, however. In our profit-conscious society, a premium is placed on efficient communication. Indeed a number of communication consultants command handsome fees because of their ability to improve communicative efficiency in organizational or other contexts. Such consultants recognize that the nonverbal media are inherently more efficient than verbal discourse.[5] This is particularly true in regulating communicative interaction. The raised eyebrow or the wandering gaze can control communicative interaction more directly and effectively than countless words.

Finally, nonverbal communication functions very effectively as a vehicle for suggestion. Often the social demands of a situation or the interpersonal needs of the participants require that we express ourselves indirectly. The most obvious example is the invitation to become intimate. To make a sexual overture to a minor by verbal means is to invite prosecution. To do so nonverbally is to absolve oneself of legal liability and perhaps minimize the risk of personal rejection.[6] The potential of using nonverbal communication for suggestion is not limited to the semantics of the sexual encounter, however. Frequently, we wish to signal another individual that we are becoming uncomfortably embarrassed, anxious, or even insecure. To do so

[3] "Experts Tell How Speech Affects Juries," *The Atlanta Constitution*, Thursday, December 18, 1975, p. 3-E.

[4] A. Mehrabian, *Silent Messages* (Belmont, Calif.: Wadsworth, 1971), p. 43.

[5] J. Reusch and W. Kees, *Nonverbal Communication* (Berkeley: University of California Press, 1956), p. 14.

[6] E. Goffman, *Behavior in Public Places* (London: Collier-Macmillan Ltd., 1963), p. 14.

verbally may trigger a spiraling exchange of hostile and defensive messages. To do so nonverbally may represent a face-saving technique of tangible benefit to all concerned parties.

The functional importance of nonverbal communication is undeniable. Indeed, when considered from the perspective just presented, "nonverbal communication has great functional significance in our society. In a great variety of situations a communicator can much more easily achieve his communicative purpose by the increased accuracy and efficiency with which nonverbal communication provides him." [7]

IN SMALL-GROUP COMMUNICATION

Nonverbal communication is particularly important in the small group because of the unique set of physical, psychological, and social forces that affect interaction. The dynamics of interaction place a premium on quick and accurate reading of significant communication cues. The stream of such cues is almost limitless and unceasing. It can overwhelm the unready; it can overpower the unsure; it can befuddle the untrained.

In such a demanding climate, nonverbal communication takes on added importance for the following reasons: (1) *physical proximity of group members,* (2) *channel availability,* (3) *regulatory requirements,* (4) *reality testing,* and (5) *corrective requirements.*

Members of small groups work in extremely close physical proximity. Often members are so close together that the distance that separates them is known as "personal distance" (one and a half to four feet). Such limited physical separation makes individuals uncomfortable in most other settings and indeed even in the small group may have marked effects on their behavior. Even the most distant members typically interact within the close phase of social distance (four to seven feet).

The close physical proximity has concrete implications for group members. Because they are so close to each other, members consistently convey and are exposed to a constellation of meanings that reveal more about their self-image, social identity, attitudes, and behavioral propensities than is revealed in almost any other type of communication situation. In one sense, group members are like the emperor who wore no clothes. They have little power to conceal what they might wish to conceal because they can be observed so easily and carefully. In contrast, the public speaker can use physical separation to control carefully his presentation of self. Feedback is very limited, so that the public speaker need not worry about the damaging and revealing information that is often part of instantaneous feedback. In addition, his physical separation from his audience assures him that the more subtle cues in his facial expressions and gestures will not be available for their critical interpretation.

[7] D. G. Leathers, *Nonverbal Communication Systems,* p. 4.

In contrast, in the small group the fund of intrapersonal and interpersonal information is almost limitless. This wealth of information can, of course, be either a source of great satisfaction or frustration.

Those group members who strive to identify the real person behind the mask and drop their own masks should be stimulated by such a communication environment. The manipulator should be wary because the sources for the involuntary transmission of meaning are multiple and the risks of exposure are great when interacting with trained and vigilant discussants. Because the members are in such close physical proximity, virtually all communication cues are within the physical purview of group members. The fact that many of these cues are nonverbal and that they would be undetectable were members separated by greater distances is very important. To be this proximate to other individuals is to increase substantially one's communication potential.

Secondly, such physical proximity provides group members with the opportunity to use all the nonverbal channels of communication. Each of the channels of nonverbal communication such as facial expression, vocal cues, or odor has boundaries or limits beyond which a channel cannot be employed or can only be employed with limited effectiveness. From the receiver's perspective, the boundaries for facial expression are physical. As distance between communicators increases, the limits of our eyesight force us to lose subtle but often important differences in the use of facial muscles. Such a loss of information may make the difference between detecting deception and missing it. Similarly, communication by vocal cues and odor has, respectively, acoustic and chemical boundaries. As distance increases, we may lose parts of the vocal cues that reveal much about the communicator's emotional state. The boundaries of odor are obvious.

Thirdly, nonverbal communication is particularly important in the small group because it serves an important regulatory function. Exchanges in the small group by their nature are fluid, spontaneous, interactive, and rarely governed by explicit rules to control the interaction. As such, exchanges in the small group are not easily initiated, sustained, or terminated. Few group members relish the role of self-appointed referee who tells another discussant when to stop or start. Indeed the effective and efficient regulation of interaction by verbal means is frequently very difficult. To respond to Bud's rambling monologue with "You may not know it, Bud, but you are through" is not really adequate. Similarly, to initiate a comment with "Shut up, Sherri, I want to talk" is not apt to improve interpersonal relationships or improve your leadership prospects. Nonetheless, the initiation, termination, and length of contributions must be regulated. As we shall point out, such regulatory functions are often performed best by eye behavior, gesture, or posture.

Fourth, nonverbal communication is important in the small group because it is an important vehicle for reality testing. If interpersonal relation-

158   ships are to be satisfying and productive, our own behavior must be based on an accurate assessment of the motivations and emotions of other discussants as well as their propensity to respond in given ways to our communicative efforts. If our assessment is inaccurate, our own behavior may be built on misconception at best and on delusion at worst. Our best guide to the way others perceive us and the situation and, consequently, our best guide to reality in the group is the nonverbal content of communicative interaction.

Finally, nonverbal communication in the small group is important because it provides us with realistic opportunities to correct or modify our own communication behavior. Verbal communication does not have the same potential. Often the verbal feedback we receive is intentionally qualified, distorted, or masked so as not to offend or antagonize us. We recall an occasion when a student stopped by to see us and asked for an honest evaluation of his term paper. Although we felt the paper was mediocre at best, we knew the student was highly motivated and conscientious and did not wish to discourage him. Hence we replied "the organization of the paper and the analysis might be improved but it does reflect some creativity." Without hesitating, the student replied, "I think you are giving me a bunch of bullshit." He accurately perceived that our verbal feedback was misleading and of limited corrective value. He also perceived that our inadvertent nonverbal feedback was a much more accurate indicator of our true feelings and, hence, of more value to him. During actual interaction in the small group, communicators must make almost instantaneous modifications in their messages to make sure that they are expressing themselves clearly, directly, and forcefully. To have the potential to make such modifications, they must have feedback of maximum corrective potential. Our research suggests that the enlightened discussant will rely heavily on nonverbal feedback.[8]

The Functions of the Nonverbal Communication Systems

PRIMARY SYSTEMS

Nonverbal communication is composed of three major systems, which, in turn, have their own subsystems.[9] Each system, and subsystem, commu-

---

[8] Idem, "The Process Effects of Incongruent Communication in the Small Group," paper presented at the convention of the International Communication Association, Portland, Oregon, April 16, 1976.

[9] Idem, *Nonverbal Communication Systems*, pp. 230–231. The different communication systems and subsystems that make up interpersonal communication are treated in detail in this volume: (1) verbal communication system, (2) visual communication system (kinesic, proxemic, and artifactual communication), (3) auditory communication system, and (4) invisible communication system (tactile, olfactory, and telepathic communication).

nicates different types of meanings and serves distinctive functions. Although each system serves important functions, the relative importance of a system in any given instance is heavily dependent on the type of communication situation. For example, in a heterosexual relationship, much is communicated by the distance that separates the interactants. In such a situation, proxemic communication is particularly important because the concerned parties have complete freedom of choice in their spatial behavior. In the small group, in contrast, proxemic communication has less potential because individuals seated around a table have very limited opportunity to modify their spatial orientations and relationships.

In the discussion that follows, therefore, we have divided nonverbal communication into primary and secondary systems. This classification is not to suggest that one system is intrinsically more important than another. It does suggest that in the small group some nonverbal systems may be used to communicate more meanings more effectively than others. In the small group the primary carriers of nonverbal meaning are facial expression, gesture, and posture.

Facial Communication   The face functions primarily as an affect display system. No other communication system serves this function so effectively or efficiently. The emotions communicated by facial expression can be consistently and accurately identified by the skillful discussant. If all facial expressions were an honest reflection of authentic emotions and if all discussants had equal skills in sending and receiving meanings by facial expression, the mastery of this medium of communication would be a relatively simple matter.

In fact, facial expressions are usually a reliable source of meaning, but in a number of situations they may not be. Whether the communicator intends to deceive by facial expression or not, untrained observers vary markedly in their capacity to decode facial meanings. Furthermore, we now know that such a capacity can often be developed to a remarkable degree. We conclude, therefore, that the group member should work actively to understand (1) what meanings the face can communicate, (2) how such meanings are apt to relate to the actual intentions and feelings of the communicator, and (3) how he or she can develop his capacity to encode and decode meanings via facial expression.

Recent research suggests that ten basic classes of meaning can be communicated reliably by facial expression: happiness, surprise, fear, anger, sadness, disgust, contempt, interest, bewilderment, and determination.[10] Although facial expressions sometimes combine different classes of meaning in the form of "facial blends," the reader should probably concentrate

---

[10] Ibid., p. 24. P. Ekman, W. V. Friesen, and P. Ellsworth, *Emotion in the Human Face: Guidelines for Research and an Integration of the Findings* (New York: Pergamon Press, 1972), pp. 57–65, maintain that the face is capable of communicating eight basic classes of meaning.

on these basic classes. Of course, the intensity of facial expressions varies. The individual expressing anger does not typically have a fit, and the individual expressing interest usually does not salivate while becoming bug-eyed. Surprise or contempt or bewilderment are frequently communicated facially, for example, but such expressions may be very subtle and detectable only by the alert and sensitive member.

Usually, these basic classes of facial meaning accurately reflect an individual's internal states. As such, they are important sources of information in the small group. In many cases, the receiver does not make effective use of such information, however. Lack of sustained eye contact is the most obvious reason. Failure to make effective use of one's decoding capacity is probably the more common reason. Facial expressions change very rapidly and are often subtle. At minimum, the receiver must be alert and concentrate.

Facial expressions are typically reliable indicators of the communicator's actual emotions, but not always. It is difficult to deceive with facial expression for a number of reasons. First, you can internally monitor your words as you speak and modify them to conceal your intent if you desire; you cannot monitor your own facial expressions in the same way because you cannot see them. Secondly, it is much easier to inhibit verbal than facial expression because the "facial expressions that are triggered during the experience of an emotion are involuntary (although they can be interfered with), and words are not." [11] Thirdly, it is much easier to use words rather than facial expressions as a medium of falsification. [12]

Nonetheless, facial expressions may, on occasion, be consciously controlled, and the individual must be alert to this fact. We may exert such control because of *cultural display rules* (for example, white males must not cry in public), *personal display rules* (one will not exhibit contempt to children), *vocational requirements* (the used-car salesmen must exhibit apparent surprise when the customer discovers that the odometer has been turned back), or the *need of the moment* (we lie or deceive to protect ourselves). [13]

Whatever the reason for controlling facial expression or, in some cases, "putting on a false face," the receiver should recognize that the sender is apt to use one of three techniques: (1) *qualifying*, (2) *modulating*, or (3) *falsifying*. The basic classes of facial meaning already identified are *qualified* when you add another facial expression to the original to modify the impact. For example, a look of anger immediately accompanied by a look of bewilderment may say to you that I am very upset by what you did but I don't really want to believe that you did it. Facial meaning is *modulated*

[11] P. Ekman and W. V. Friesen. *Unmasking the Face* (Englewood Cliffs, N.J.: Prentice-Hall, 1975), p. 136.
[12] Ibid.
[13] Ibid., pp. 138–139.

when you change the intensity of the expression to communicate stronger or weaker feelings than you are actually experiencing. For example, you may communicate slight sadness facially when you feel abject grief because you think it socially unacceptable to prostrate yourself on the casket. Finally, when *falsifying*, "you show a feeling when you have none (*simulate*); or you show nothing when indeed you do feel a particular way (*neutralize*); or you cover a felt emotion with the appearance of an emotion you do not feel (*mask*)." [14]

In some cases these techniques of facial management may serve a useful purpose. When you feel utter contempt for another group member, neutralizing or masking may be a suitable short-term expedient. In the long run, however, group members must be able to identify consistently the type of facial meaning communicated when it is an authentic reflection of the communicator's feelings and, just as importantly, recognize attempts to mislead through facial management that may serve to block the long-term goals of the group and assure undesirable interpersonal outcomes.

The obvious question at this point is, How does the small-group member detect attempts to use facial expression to deceive? To begin, one must learn to focus attention on the face of the individual who is trying to communicate. More specifically, one should concentrate on the lip and mouth area, the timing of the facial expression, and the location of the facial expression vis-à-vis the verbal utterance and be alert for microexpressions.

The person who is consciously attempting to manage facial expressions will focus his or her efforts on the lip and mouth area. He or she will do so because involuntary movement in this area is apt to reveal deception.

The timing of the facial expression is particularly important. Facial expressions are apt to have a spontaneous quality when they are accurately reflecting the communicator's true emotions and intentions. There "is no hard and fast general rule to tell you what the onset, duration, and offset are for each of the emotions. . . . If you watch carefully, you will know when the timing is off, and this can be crucial in spotting deception clues." [15]

The location of the facial expression in the communicational stream is often helpful in detecting deception. The person who flashes an angry facial expression two full seconds after the utterance is not apt to be very believable. Indeed ministers, politicians, and other public figures who must greet long lines of people may frequently fall into this trap. Can you recall the time when a public figure has expressed overwhelming pleasure in seeing you and, then, only very belatedly flashed his ingratiating smile?

Finally, deceivers often quickly flash involuntary microexpressions, which may last only between one-fifth to one twenty-fifth of a second. Although they were previously thought to be undetectable to anyone who could not

[14] Ibid., p. 141.
[15] Ibid., pp. 150–151.

match the eyesight of Superman, recent evidence suggests that a number of microexpressions are detectable by the unaided eye. When they are detected, they frequently provide very reliable clues to the felt emotion of the communicator.[16]

The individual capacity to transmit meanings by facial expression differs substantially; this is true whether one is trying to communicate honestly or deceitfully. Similarly, the capacity to identify meanings conveyed by facial expression accurately also differs markedly. In our own research, scores on tests of encoding and decoding performance using facial expression ranged from 100 percent to 30 percent.[17]

Perhaps more importantly, we now have evidence to suggest that we can markedly improve our ability to communicate by facial expression. Izard cites research that suggests we may improve this capacity by as much as 51 percent with minimal improvement around 5.1 percent.[18]

With this potential for improvement, it is imperative that we work to develop this important communication capacity. We believe that the most effective training technique is the Facial Meaning Sensitivity Test. This forty-picture test is designed to measure both your ability to perceive meanings conveyed by facial expression and your ability to convey such meanings by facial expressions. This test has been used extensively in the classroom, in consulting in government and the private sector, and recently with children with various types of perceptual disabilities. The evidence suggests that diligent use of this test and related training devices will substantially increase your effectiveness in facial communication.[19]

Secondly, we suggest that you study the video tape of a discussion group of which you have been a member. Play and replay the video tape; use slow-motion replay if necessary. Ask yourself how many classes of meaning you communicated by facial expression and what meanings you could identify in the facial expressions of others. By discussing your analysis of the video tape with other groups, you should get some idea of how proficiently you are using facial expression.

Finally, we suggest that you make diligent use of the training pictures provided at the end of this chapter. Nothing is as valuable as the practice in actual discussions. In actual discussion, however, you cannot stop the interaction at a critical point to give a facial expression the type of careful thought and study that you think it deserves.

[16] Ibid., pp. 151–152.

[17] D. G. Leathers, "The Facial Meaning Sensitivity Test," paper presented at the convention of the Southern Speech Communication Association, Richmond, Virginia, April 1974.

[18] C. E. Izard, *The Face of Emotion* (New York: Appleton-Century-Crofts, 1971), p. 218.

[19] D. G. Leathers, *Nonverbal Communication Systems* (Boston: Allyn and Bacon), pp. 26–32, describes the development of the Facial Meaning Sensitivity Test (which features the forty photographs of the Loren Lewis series) and illustrates how the test is taken and how to interpret results.

Gestural Communication Gestural communication is particularly important in the small group because of the close physical proximity of group members. This proximity assures that virtually every gesture can be perceived. The effective communicator will identify those gestures that convey consensually shared meanings and determine what those meanings are.

There can be little doubt that, in the aggregate, gestures represent an important form of nonverbal communication. Indeed Goffman writes that body idiom "is a conventionalized discourse. We can see that it is, in addition, a normative one. That is, there is typically an obligation to convey certain information when in the presence of others and an obligation not to convey other impressions, just as there is an expectation that others will present themselves in certain ways." [20]

A gesture refers to the movement of some specific part or parts of the body. In human communication, generally, a communicator's gestures are reliable indicators as to the *intensity* of his or her feeling. In the small group specifically, gestures serve two functions of major importance: (1) they are reliable cues as to a communicator's behavioral predispositions— that is, cooperative, defensive, or hostile behaviors, for example, are apt to follow certain types of gestures; (2) they function to regulate interaction among groups members.

Although one should be cautious about assigning invariant meanings to a single gesture, there is a good deal of evidence to suggest that gesture-clusters and gesture-patterns are valid sources of meaning. *The sender often uses them to signal how he or she wants the receiver to behave whereas the receiver can often use them to anticipate how the sender is apt to behave.*

The ability to sense how a discussant is *about* to behave and to sense an opportune moment to take the offensive is particularly important in decision-making groups seeking consensus. Negotiation is a specialized form of decision making in the small group, and it is in negotiating sessions that Nierenberg and Calero have carefully studied the functions of gesture. Their study of the video tapes from many negotiating sessions reveals that the skillful negotiator is an expert in both the use and interpretation of gestures. They write that "frequently a postmortem on video-recorded negotiations that have failed reveals that a demand, request, or offer was made at a time or in such a manner as to cause the other persons to become defensive. From this point on concessions, agreements, or other forms of cooperation become more difficult. Failing to recognize early signs of disagreement, discomfort, or discontent will usually lead to a more complicated situation in which agreement on any issue will prove to be almost painful." [21]

[20] *Behavior in Public Places,* p. 35.
[21] G. I. Nierenberg and H. H. Calero. *How to Read a Person Like a Book* (New York: Pocket Book, 1973), p. 50.

There are a number of important types of gestures that communicate a discussant's attitudes and feelings at the moment of the gesture. They also suggest rather accurately how that individual is apt to respond to suggestions, directives, demands, and so on at that particular point in the discussion. Of the major types of gestures, the following are particularly important: (1) openness, (2) evaluation, (3) confidence, (4) self-control, (5) defensiveness, (6) suspicion and secretiveness, and (7) nervousness. In a broad sense, the first three types of gestures might be viewed as positive; and the last three, as negative.

Communicating a sense of openness in the small group is very important. It signals other discussants that you are making a real effort to convey your feelings honestly. Gestures of openness are apt to trigger the same type of gestures from others in the group. In a sense, gestures that communicate openness are the nonverbal equivalent of words that are self-disclosing. Both forms of communication have the effect of eliminating or diminishing behavior that is calculated to withhold or distort personal information.

Openness gestures not only stimulate interaction in the group, but they also help to shape an environment in which group members can reach a consensus. Significantly, a persistent pattern of openness gestures is often a signal to interactants that the group should move directly to reach agreement. At such times, individuals often "unbutton their coats, uncross their legs, and move up toward the edge of the chair and closer to the desk or table that separates them from their opposer. This gesture-cluster is in most instances accompanied by verbal language that communicates a possible agreement, solution, or generally a positive expression of working together. . . ." [22]

Open hands, the unbuttoning of coats or loosening of ties, and the general relaxation of limb discipline often communicate openness. In contrast, crossed arms, crossed legs, and related gestures often communicate inaccessibility and defensiveness. When considered in context, such gestures can be reliable indicators of current feelings and behavioral predispositions. One should be cautious about using such cues to make more global generalizations, however. Shortly after one of the best-selling books on nonverbal communication came out, one of a professor's very attractive female graduate students stopped him in a hallway. "Isn't this new nonverbal book wonderful?" she said. "It tells you so much about how people will behave." He could not help noticing that she was standing with arms folded over her chest as they conversed and replied "It certainly is interesting, but I think we should be cautious about believing all of the sweeping generalizations. For example, the author says that girls who stand with arms folded over their chests are frigid. I don't think that this is necessarily true. Do you?" Flinging her arms away from her chest and turning red in

[22] Ibid., p. 46.

the face, she replied forcefully, "No, I certainly don't. I get your point."

Evaluation gestures take a number of forms. Such gestures suggest that an individual is actively involved in processing incoming information and in weighing the action of his or her fellow discussants. Stroking the chin or cheek are characteristic evaluation gestures. The deliberate manipulation of pipe and glasses are also important.[23] Timing is probably the key to identifying evaluation gestures. The thoughtful response is apt to be delayed; and the gestures, rather slow and methodical.

Confidence gestures may be identified in two ways. First, one should watch for gestures that would tend to contradict a feeling of confidence. Secondly, one should watch for gestures that are characteristically associated with the confident person. Thus a "confident person is likely to talk without hand-to-face gestures like covering the mouth and nose-and-head-scratching, so in reading gestures for confidence, one should watch for a doubt or other negative gesture that would contradict the feeling that is being projected."[24] Among the most representative of confidence gestures are steepling (the individual joins fingertips on both hands to form a "church steeple"), hands jointed together at the back with chin thrust upward, feet on the table, and leaning back with both hands supporting the head.[25]

Gestures used to communicate self-control can be quite revealing. Such gestures certainly imply that the individual is making an effort to curb an impulsive reaction or to prevent a nondeliberative and possibly irrational response. If justified, such gestures suggest that something untoward is happening in the group, and the alert discussant will make an effort to determine what that is. The clenched fist and lip biting are characteristic gestures of self-control.

Of the seemingly negative types of gestures, defensiveness gestures are very important. They take many forms, but *often they suggest a literal attempt to block out unpleasant ideas and/or individuals.* If you have seen the baseball umpire retreat from the infuriated manager, you will recognize that crossed arms are a traditional gesture of defensiveness. Finally, in extreme cases, the discussant may turn his chair around so that the chair-back faces the discussants and then straddle that chair. Any of these gestures should alert discussants to the fact that something is making this discussant defensive.[26]

Gestures of suspicion and secretiveness are also readily identifiable because they tend to be very distinctive. Slight but slow and methodical rubbing of one's nose and turning one's body at least partially away from the object of suspicion are good examples.[27] In one of our laboratory experi-

[23] Ibid., pp. 59–64.
[24] Ibid., p. 93.
[25] Ibid., pp. 95–103.
[26] Ibid., pp. 47–57.
[27] Ibid., pp. 67–71.

ments we had a "plant" violate the expectations of unsuspecting discussants by addressing them with ambiguous messages that raised questions about the plant's sincerity. After receiving one such ambiguous message, a discussant moved his chair so that it was facing *away* from the plant at about a 45-degree angle.

Finally, nervousness gestures are communicated in many ways, although some nervousness gestures are difficult to detect. Fidgeting, tugging at one's clothing, and jingling money in one's pockets are representative examples. *Hand-to-face gestures are perhaps the most significant.* When you see a discussant tug on his ear or partially cover his mouth while speaking, it is usually a sign of nervousness.[28] The frequency of such gestures may be a good measure of the level of tension in the group. We have observed that when the level of tension in a group is becoming very high, the members are frequently talking in hushed tones; often their voices become almost inaudible. Such nervousness cues, when frequent, may be communicating an important type of meaning. They suggest that the group is experiencing or is about to experience a serious interpersonal problem.

The seven types of gestures discussed so far are similar in that they may reveal much about the communicator's internal state and about his tendency to behave in a certain way. Such gestures may have the indirect effect of regulating interaction in the group. That is not the primary function of this type of gesture, however. Other gestures serve the regulatory function.

Regulation is a particularly important function in the small group. Regulation of interaction may be undertaken either by the addressor (sender) or the addressee (receiver). Hand movement and eye behavior, as well as vocal inflection, are most frequently and effectively used to regulate interaction.

To regulate behavior, the addressor usually looks at the addressee at the end of completed thoughts; if the addressee does make eye contact or nods, the addressor assumes the addressee is decoding and continues speaking. Because some addressors have a tendency to look at addressees only when they desire a response, the act of establishing eye contact in itself is often a meaningful signal.

Wiener, Devoe, Rubinow, and Geller note that the addressee may use one of four types of addressee regulators in responding: (1) addressee moves his eyes upward without speaking (meaning = the addressee is thinking and the addressor should wait); (2) addressee maintains a blank look without speaking (meaning = addressee is confused and the addressor should attempt clarification); (3) addressee maintains eye contact with a slow, rhythmic head nod (meaning = addressee understands and the addressor may continue speaking); and (4) the addressee maintains eye con-

---

[28] Ibid., pp. 106–112.

tact and smiles (meaning = the addressee understands but has nothing to add).[29]

Significantly, many subtle gestures in the form of eye behavior and hand movements are detectable only in the small group because of the close physical proximity of discussants. Hence, in the small group, such gestural cues are particularly rich in communicative significance.

Postural Communication   Whereas gestures are often used to signal behavioral predispositions and to regulate interaction in the small group, posture functions to define the nature of relationships that may endure for a considerable period of time. Posture often functions symbolically to communicate what one sees as the type of relationship with other discussants that is expected or even demanded because of one's position. Thus Scheflen writes perceptively that "people may also exchange behaviors of an aggressive, dominating, or antagonistic nature. They may clash about territorial violations or transgression of rights, threaten each other, or even come to blows. But more often, they exchange only displays or representations of dominance-submissive behavior. . . ."[30]

Mehrabian maintains that we use posture to communicate varying degrees of immediacy, power, and responsiveness. Immediacy or closeness to another individual signals degree of liking or disliking whereas our perception of high power over others is usually reflected in an expansive posture that connotes superior status on the part of the communicator. Finally, one communicates responsiveness by the amount of bodily movement in the form of postural and gestural changes; the person with a relatively fixed and rigid postural orientation can be fairly described as unresponsive.[31]

To communicate the basic types of meaning by posture, one may assume any of three basic postures: type 1 (inclusive or noninclusive)—one places the body in such a way as to either invite or block interaction with others; type 2 (vis-à-vis or parallel)—the vis-à-vis postural orientation is used to communicate intimate feelings to a single individual whereas the parallel orientation signals a desire to communicate to the entire group; type 3 (congruent or incongruent)—assuming a postural orientation similar to, or congruent with, the person with whom one is communicating suggests agreement and possibly the perception of a status equal whereas an incongruent posture may suggest disagreement and disapproval.[32] It is, of

[29] M. Wiener, S. Devoe, S. Rubinow, and J. Geller, "Nonverbal Behavior and Nonverbal Communication," *Psychological Review* 79 (1972): 208. For an excellent article on the communicative functions of the hands, see P. Ekman and W. V. Friesen, "Hand Movements," *Journal of Communication* 22 (1972): 353–358.

[30] A. E. Scheflen, *Body Language and the Social Order* (Englewood Cliffs, N.J.: Prentice-Hall, 1972), p. 23.

[31] *Silent Messages*, pp. 113–118.

[32] A. E. Scheflen, "The Significance of Posture in Communication Systems," *Psychiatry* 27 (1964): 326–329.

course, very important to be alert for such postural orientations as one important source of meaning in the small group.

SECONDARY SYSTEMS

Facial, gestural, and postural communication are primary sources of meaning in the small group because of the functions they serve and because members of a small group have repeated opportunities to make optimum use of these nonverbal media. In contrast, the proxemic, vocalic, and artifactual systems of communication are identified as secondary systems because the small-group environment places severe limitations on how and how effectively they can be used.

Proxemic Communication   Proxemic communication is the use of space and spatial relationships to communicate meaning. Although proxemic communication plays a very important role in human interaction generally, it serves rather limited functions in the small group. This is so because most group discussions are held around a table. Spatial relationships are, therefore, fixed and not easily manipulated. For example, one cannot adjust the distance between oneself and others from public to intimate because the more or less fixed distance for communicative interaction in the small group is "social distance."

Although the *actual* distance separating discussants remains relatively fixed, the perception of space in the proximate environment may change drastically over time. We do know that individuals isolated in work groups for substantial periods of time will begin to exhibit territorial behavior with very pronounced features. At first, individuals will demarcate fixed geographical areas and highly personal objects as theirs, but with the passage of time they begin to lay claim to the more mobile and less personal objects.[33]

Indeed the concept of territory is much more important in the small group than either space or distance. According to Goffman, each of us conceives of "territories of self," which have changeable boundaries but boundaries that we do not want violated. Of the eight territories of self, use space (that space immediately surrounding us, which we must have to perform personal functions such as lighting a cigarette, gesturing, or removing the contents of a briefcase) and possessional territory (that area in which we place ourselves and our possessions such as gloves and handbags) are particularly important.[34]

Violations of a discussant's territorial expectations frequently do occur. The most common and frequent territorial violations are (1) closer placement of one's body to another individual than one's status allows, (2) use

---

[33] I. Altman and W. Haythorn, "The Ecology of Isolated Groups," *Behavioral Science* 12 (1967): 169–182.

[34] E. Goffman, *Relation in Public* (New York: Harper and Row, 1971), pp. 32–38.

of one's body and hands to touch and defile the sheath and possessions of another, (3) the use of the penetrating gaze to transgress or circumvent societal expectations, and (4) the use of the voice to intrude upon someone's auditory preserve.[35]

Discussants typically react to such territorial violations in a tense and antagonistic manner. Withdrawal from the discussion and sometimes physical withdrawal from the room often follow. At the very least, inappropriate proxemic behavior will complicate a communicator's task because it diverts attention from the meanings he or she is attempting to communicate. In some cases, it can severely impair interpersonal relationships because the "violated" discussant often deeply resents the violation of his or her proxemic expectations.

Some of the author's students have been conducting a series of experiments in the library at the University of Georgia. Using concealed cameras, they record the reactions of students whose proxemic expectations they violated. Frequently, such students make a concerted effort to defend their use space and possessional territory by the use of books, clothing, and even elbows and knees to demarcate their personal territory. When such tactics fail, the violated students often exhibit a loss of self-confidence and seem uncertain. One aggressive student reversed the trend, however. When an attractive female "plant" violated his proxemic expectations by staring at him and moving into close, intimate distance, he simply smiled at the plant and placed a hand on her knee. She beat a hasty retreat from the library.

Vocalic Communication   Like proxemic communication, vocalic communication is of secondary importance in the small group. This is so because it is difficult to use the full communicative potential of the voice in the intimate atmosphere of the small group. Certainly, the voice may be used in such a way as to affect the way other discussants perceive the communicator's personality and to communicate basic emotions. Effective public speakers frequently use the voice for this purpose, but the vocal dynamics of a Billy Graham in the small group are more apt to be perceived as pneumatic excess rather than charismatic expression.

Nonetheless, the group member must be aware of the fact that a "dull voice" is often equated with a "dull person" in the small group, just as the speaker with little variation in pitch and rate is apt to be perceived as introverted and withdrawn. Although one's vocal characteristics do shape one's perceived personality in the small group, we do not believe this function to be of major importance. The nature of an individual's vocal cues in the small group appear to serve two primary functions: (1) they serve as an important supplemental source of information along with facial expressions, gesture, and posture, and so on, which the receiver can use to help determine the communicator's true feelings, and (2) they serve to

---

[35] Ibid., pp. 44–48.

indicate the intensity of the communicator's feelings at a given moment.[36]

Artifactual Communication Artifactual communication (communication by appearance) functions in an important but secondary way in the small group. Unlike facial expression, gesture, and posture, which are frequently and quickly altered as a response to intragroup pressures and a response to communication cues being exchanged, artifactual communication is a relatively fixed and inflexible medium.

Nonetheless, artifactual communication is important. The appearance of the discussants tends to place limits on the type of communicative interaction that is acceptable. More specifically, our "visible self functions to communicate a constellation of meanings which define who we are and what we are apt to become in the eyes of others. In interpersonal communication the appearance of the participants establishes their social identity." [37]

Moreover, our social identity carries with it the responsibility to communicate in a manner that is consistent with the expectation of those for whom that identity has meaning. The communicative interaction in a group composed of a priest, a policeman, a nurse, a person in the military, and a left-wing demonstrator would be predictable in one sense. When acting in his or her official capacities and attired in the uniform of his or her profession, each discussant would be expected to behave in specified ways. Although each individual might violate the expectations in many ways, the fact that his or her appearance defines very distinctive behavioral expectations is important. In a sense, the more role-bound one's appearance, the more limited are one's communicative flexibility and potential in the small group.

Although extreme, our example emphasizes the fact that appearance does shape social identity to a large degree and that social identity may significantly affect our ability to communicate in the small group. In fact:

> Once established our social identity—as perceived by others, and by us—places limits on how, when, and where we are expected to engage in interpersonal communication. Our social identity carries with it the implicit responsibility to communicate in such a way as to meet the expectations of those for whom that identity has meaning. When we violate those expectations, our communicative interaction with others is apt to become ineffective and inefficient.[38]

INTERACTION OF THE NONVERBAL COMMUNICATION SYSTEMS

Each of the nonverbal communication systems is properly identified with specific communication functions and different types of meanings.

---

[36] Leathers, *Nonverbal Communication Systems*, pp. 123–133.

[37] Ibid., p. 86. For development of the contention that clothes are a medium of communication that defines the wearer, see K. Gibbins and T. K. Gwynn, "A New Theory of Fashion Change: A Test of Some Predictions," *British Journal of Clinical and Social Psychology* 14 (1975): 1–9.

[38] Ibid., pp. 86–87.

Facial expressions, gestures, and postures are, consequently, reliable **171** sources of meaning in their own right. In the small group, however, these primary sources of meaning do not typically act in isolation. They typically interact. In those instances, we must consider the nonverbal sources of meaning in the aggregate. When they do interact, the obvious question is, What basic types of meaning are communicated?

We conducted a study designed to answer that question. Based on a content and factor analysis of the meaningful movements of discussants in problem-solving discussions, this research suggests that facial expression, gesture, and posture function together to communicate five basic classes of meaning. We identify these classes of meaning as (1) involvement, (2) feeling, (3) analysis, (4) control, and (5) flexibility. Each class of nonverbal meaning is, in turn, composed of specific types of meanings that are closely related to each other but basically dissimilar from the types in another class.

The degree to which a given discussant communicates involvement may vary, for example. Our research suggests that involvement is best represented by scales that measure the following communication qualities: interest/disinterest, attentive/unattentive, involved/withdrawn, and responsive/unresponsive. Similarly, feeling is best measured by pleased/displeased and friendly/hostile scales; analysis is best measured by deliberative/spontaneous and analytical/impulsive scales; control is best measured by the confident/uncertain and clear/confused scales; flexibility is best measured by the flexible/inflexible and the yielding/unyielding scales.[39]

Identifying and Interpreting Nonverbal Cues

To make maximum use of our communication potential, we must be able to identify quickly and interpret accurately meaningful cues in the small group. This chapter has been designed to provide us with the knowledge to undertake such a task effectively. To develop this potential fully, however, we believe that concentrated and repeated practice is necessary.

To test and expand your decoding capacity, we have developed the Visual Test of Nonverbal Cues in the Small Group.[40] This test consists of ten different photographs of five discussants seated around a conference table (*read directions on p. 192 before you start the test on p. 172*).

[39] Leathers, *Nonverbal Communication Systems,* p. 87.

[40] Seated around the table from left to right are Hope Pedrero (1) John Hocking (2), Dale Leathers (3), Deborah Weider-Hatfield (4), and Michael McGuire (5). The authors wish to thank the photographic subjects for the time, energy, and concentration that went into the photographing sessions used to develop the ten photographs in the test; in future references the five discussants will be referred to by number. Photographer Jim Morganthaller deserves special mention for his shrewd advice and his highly professional performance in shooting and developing the large number of photographs from which the final choice was made.

Group Communication Situation 1

THE VISUAL TEST OF NONVERBAL CUES IN THE SMALL GROUP

Group Communication Situation 1

In the space provided below, please write out your complete description of the nonverbal cues you can identify in the picture. Indicate what meanings are being communicated nonverbally, indicate what functions the nonverbal cues are serving or might serve, and explain how you would make use of these cues were you a member of this group.

THE VISUAL TEST OF NONVERBAL CUES IN THE SMALL GROUP

Group Communication Situation 2

In the space provided below, please write out your complete description of the nonverbal cues you can identify in the picture. Indicate what meanings are being communicated nonverbally, indicate what functions the nonverbal cues are serving or might serve, and explain how you would make use of these cues were you a member of this group.

175

THE VISUAL TEST OF NONVERBAL CUES IN THE SMALL GROUP

Group Communication Situation 3

In the space provided below, please write out your complete description of the nonverbal cues you can identify in the picture. Indicate what meanings are being communicated nonverbally, indicate what functions the nonverbal cues are serving or might serve, and explain how you would make use of these cues were you a member of this group.

_____

_____

_____

_____

_____

_____

_____

_____

_____

_____

_____

_____

THE VISUAL TEST OF NONVERBAL CUES IN THE SMALL GROUP

Group Communication Situation 4

In the space provided below, please write out your complete description of the nonverbal cues you can identify in the picture. Indicate what meanings are being communicated nonverbally, indicate what functions the nonverbal cues are serving or might serve, and explain how you would make use of these cues were you a member of this group.

_____

_____

_____

_____

_____

_____

_____

_____

_____

_____

_____

_____

_____

Group Communication Situation 5

THE VISUAL TEST OF NONVERBAL CUES IN THE SMALL GROUP

Group Communication Situation 5

In the space provided below, please write out your complete description of the nonverbal cues you can identify in the picture. Indicate what meanings are being communicated nonverbally, indicate what functions the nonverbal cues are serving or might serve, and explain how you would make use of these cues were you a member of this group.

_____

_____

_____

_____

_____

_____

_____

_____

_____

_____

_____

_____

_____

THE VISUAL TEST OF NONVERBAL CUES IN THE SMALL GROUP

Group Communication Situation 6

In the space provided below, please write out your complete description of the nonverbal cues you can identify in the picture. Indicate what meanings are being communicated nonverbally, indicate what functions the nonverbal cues are serving or might serve, and explain how you would make use of these cues were you a member of this group.

_____

_____

_____

_____

_____

_____

_____

_____

_____

_____

_____

_____

_____

THE VISUAL TEST OF NONVERBAL CUES IN THE SMALL GROUP

Group Communication Situation 7

In the space provided below, please write out your complete description of the nonverbal cues you can identify in the picture. Indicate what meanings are being communicated nonverbally, indicate what functions the nonverbal cues are serving or might serve, and explain how you would make use of these cues were you a member of this group.

THE VISUAL TEST OF NONVERBAL CUES IN THE SMALL GROUP

Group Communication Situation 8

In the space provided below, please write out your complete description of the nonverbal cues you can identify in the picture. Indicate what meanings are being communicated nonverbally, indicate what functions the nonverbal cues are serving or might serve, and explain how you would make use of these cues were you a member of this group.

_____

_____

_____

_____

_____

_____

_____

_____

_____

_____

_____

_____

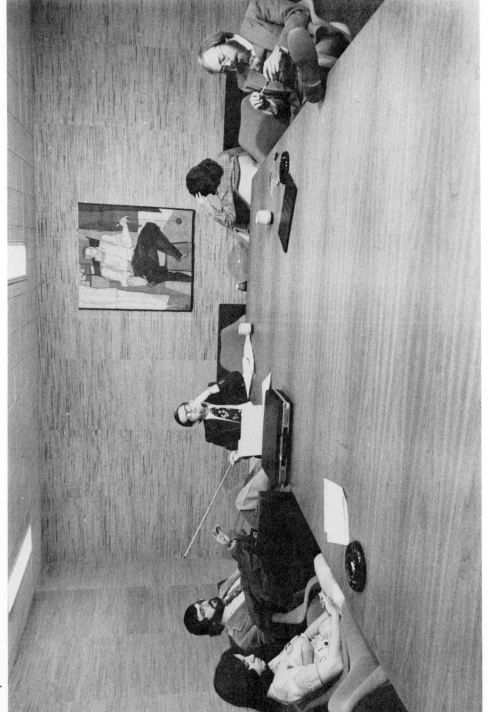

THE VISUAL TEST OF NONVERBAL CUES IN THE SMALL GROUP

Group Communication Situation 9

In the space provided below, please write out your complete description of the nonverbal cues you can identify in the picture. Indicate what meanings are being communicated nonverbally, indicate what functions the nonverbal cues are serving or might serve, and explain how you would make use of these cues were you a member of this group.

189

THE VISUAL TEST OF NONVERBAL CUES IN THE SMALL GROUP

Group Communication Situation 10

In the space provided below, please write out your complete description of the nonverbal cues you can identify in the picture. Indicate what meanings are being communicated nonverbally, indicate what functions the nonverbal cues are serving or might serve, and explain how you would make use of these cues were you a member of this group.

table. Each photograph was carefully posed to feature an identifiable and meaningful set of nonverbal cues. These cues are geared directly to the content of the chapter you have just read.

As you study each of the ten photographs, attempt to determine what meaning or set of meanings is being communicated. In some cases, facial expressions may be the significant source of meaning; in others, gesture, posture, or the use of the space may be the key. Remember also that the nonverbal cues can provide you with different types of information. They may reveal what emotions the discussants are experiencing, how they are *about to respond,* the way they *perceive relationships* in the group, how *interaction* in the group *is being regulated,* or many other things.

Study each photograph carefully. Then in the space provided below the photograph write out your description of the meanings you believe are being communicated nonverbally, indicate what functions the non-verbal cues are serving or might serve, and explain how you would make use of these cues were you a member of this group.

In photographs 3 and 4 you should assume that discussant 3 is in the process of making a comment. In photograph 6 assume that the other discussants are responding to a comment made by discussant 5.

Use the test "key" that follows to determine your total score on the Visual Test of Nonverbal Cues in the Small Group. Wherever you were able to identify one of the keyed "meanings" for a given communication situation, give yourself two points. The labels used in the test key may be different from yours. Nonetheless, give yourself two points whenever you believe that the meaning(s) in the test key and the meaning(s) you identified are a reasonably close match.

Total up the points you earned on the test. Please use the following guidelines to judge the quality of your performance on the test:

Excellent = 100–90
Good = 90–80
Average = 80–70
Poor = 70 and below

Test Key *(turn to p. 172 and begin test; return to this test key when you finish the test)*

Communication Situation 1: This photograph was designed to focus on gestural cues that reveal the feelings and emotions of the discussants as well as their behavioral predispositions. Discussant 1 is anxious and attempting to maintain self-control (clenched hands). Discussant 2 is exhibiting openness (open coat and palm) as well as interest and confidence. Similarly, discussant 3 is exhibiting openness to ideas being presented (coat) but shows some surprise or displeasure (facial expression). Discussant 4 is suspicious (nose scratching and eye behavior) and may be a bit defensive (note left arm). Discussant 5 is confident (hand in vest) and open (note open arms and legs as well as coat).

Communication Situation 2: This photograph focuses on territorial violation. Discussant 2's "territory of self" is being violated by the penetrating eye behavior of 1 and 3. The physical territory, or use space, of discussant 5 is being violated by 4. Discussant 1 is making a gesture of evaluation and disapproval whereas 3 is communicating both interest and disbelief. Discussant 4 is literally blocking out 5 while reflecting disinterest. Discussant 5 appears to be showing self-control as well as defensiveness (note blocking motion of right elbow).

Communication Situation 3: This photograph highlights the nonverbal feedback of the other discussants to the contribution being made by 3. Discussant 1 is uncertain and seeking help from other group members (note facial expression and upturned palms). Discussant 2 is confused. Discussant 3 seems disinterested to the point of boredom. Discussant 4 is interested and attentive whereas 5 seems to be attempting to exercise self-control over a hostile impulse (note facial expression, tightly clasped pencil in right hand, and knuckles of the left hand).

Communication Situation 4: This photograph also highlights nonverbal feedback to a different and more positive contribution being made by 3. Discussant 1 is uncertain and seeking clarification or help. Discussant 2 is interested but a bit confused. Discussant 3 communicates interest and involvement (note bodily lean). Discussant 4 is displeased to the point of being contemptuous of 3 whereas 5 is interested and responsive (note overall bodily orientation and fairly expansive hand gesture).

Communication Situation 5: This photograph is designed to show a group locked in conflict. A direct move to seek consensus at this point is not apt to be successful, and even more serious interpersonal problems seem imminent. Discussant 1 is angry but exhibiting self-control (note clenched fists and facial expression) whereas 2 is enraged. Discussant 3 is defensive to the point of outright intimidation (note closed gestures via crossed legs, buttoned coat, and constricted bodily orientation; tentative hand gesture; and worried facial expression). Discussants 4 and 5 are clearly unreceptive to the ideas of 1 and 2 because of their closed and defensive gestures (note closed arms over chest).

Communication Situation 6: This photograph illustrates how gestural cues may be used to regulate interaction in the small group; in this case, the cues should regulate and guide 5 in any additional comment he may make. Discussant 1 is using an evaluation gesture while signaling 5 that she requires further time to process his message (note facial expression). Discussant 2 is confused and needs clarification; 3 is gesturing "A-Ok," which means he understands 5's message, probably approves, and thinks 5 should proceed. Discussant 4 is communicating understanding and approval, but has nothing to add; 5 is clearly interested and involved and making a point both verbally and nonverbally (note the use of the pipe as a medium of accentuation).

Communication Situation 7: This photograph illustrates how the postures of the discussants may be used to communicate perceived relationships. Discussants 1 and 2 clearly like each other and are exhibiting mutual approval (touching and virtually identical postures are frequently used to communicate such meanings) as well as a high degree of immediacy; 3 is communicating defensiveness and unresponsiveness (crossed arms and constricted posture), withdrawal (closed eyes), and low perceived status (notice that he has very little use space with his folder closed in front of him whereas 4 and 5 have much use space with their papers spread out expansively in front of them). Discussants 4 and 5 are confident (4 with arms crossed behind head and upturned chin and 5 with hands hooked in vest) and high status (note large amount of use space and the mugs in front of them).

Communication Situation 8: This photograph features a variety of nonverbal cues that communicate different types of meaning. Discussant 1 is communicating anger and self-control. The photograph also reveals how 2 and 5 view their mutual relationship: 5 has higher perceived status and is more confident than 2 (note that 5's "steeple" is much higher than 2's whereas the eye behavior of 2 suggests that he is suspicious of 5 or intimidated by him). Discussant 3 shows extreme disinterest and has probably tuned out the rest of the group.

Communication Situation 9: This photograph is designed to show how a sociofugal spatial orientation affects communication and perceptions in the group—the distance and physical barriers that separate the discussants create a number of problems. Discussant 1 is uninterested, uninvolved, and probably lacks confidence (note downcast eyes). Discussant 2 has literally blocked 1 out of the discussion with the barrier of briefcase and coat and is faced with the unenviable task of attempting to communicate with a nongroup. Discussant 3 is withdrawn and lost in evaluation (note the aimless and ironic use of a pointer that points to nothing). Discussant 4 is totally withdrawn and has literally blocked all possible nonverbal cues. Discussant 5 is disinterested and withdrawn, and his exaggerated claim to use space suggests a contemptuous attitude toward the group (note how he has spread out his pipe-smoking paraphernalia; pipe cleaning is not a signal that communicative interaction in the group is effective).

Communication Situation 10: This picture is designed to illustrate the sociopetal use of space in the small group. Overall, the picture communicates a sense of great immediacy and involvement. Discussant 1 seems to be evaluating whereas 2 and 3 are clearly interested and involved; 3 may be the highest status person in the group because of his central seating position; 4 is pleased and attentive, and 5 is evaluating. In contrast to photograph 9, where the discussants are apt to perceive each other as cold, impersonal, uninvolved, and even introverted because of their spatial orientation, discussants in photograph 10 are apt to like each other and view the situation as warm and conducive to interaction and are apt to be more disclosing.

SUPPLEMENTARY READING

Cuceloglu, D. "Facial Code in Affective Communication." *Comparative Group Studies* 3 (1975): 395–407.
Ekman, P., and Friesen, W. V. "Detecting Deception from the Body or Face." *Journal of Personality and Social Psychology* 29 (1974): 288–298.
———— *Unmasking the Face*. Englewood Cliffs, N.J.: Prentice-Hall, 1975.
Izard, C. E. *The Face of Emotion*. New York: Appleton-Century-Crofts, 1971.
Leathers, D. G. *Nonverbal Communication Systems*. Boston: Allyn and Bacon, 1976. Chapters 2, 3, 5, and 6.
Scheflen, A. E. *Body Language and the Social Order*. Englewood Cliffs, N.J.: Prentice-Hall, 1972. Chapters 1, 2, 3, and 10.
Speer, D. "Nonverbal Communication of Affective Information." *Comparative Group Studies* 3 (1972): 409–423.

QUESTIONS AND EXERCISES

1. Nonverbal communication is particularly important in the small group for at least five reasons. Of the five, which do you think is most important? Why?
2. Compare and contrast the major functions served by facial, gestural, and postural communication. Of the three types of nonverbal communication, which do you believe you use most skillfully? Why? Give concrete examples of how you used facial expression, gestures, and posture effectively. Also give examples of how you used these types of nonverbal communication ineffectively.
3. Has anyone in your group used facial expressions to falsify? Discuss this question with your group. Did the group member(s) falsify by simu-

196
lating, neutralizing, or masking? What were the effects of such falsification on group interaction?

4. Was the interaction in your group characterized by positive or negative gestures? Why?

5. In your group meetings have you made any attempts to regulate interaction by the use of addressee regulators? If so, what gestures did you use? Were they effective? If not, what gestures might you have used to regulate interactions?

6. As a group, prepare your own version of the Visual Test of Nonverbal Cues in the Small Group. Decide what nonverbal cues you wish to use and why, take pictures of group members using these cues, and check out your test on friends and associates to determine if your friends reliably attach the same meanings to the nonverbal cues that you intended. Prepare a paper on this experience that emphasizes the value of "your" test and what you learned about nonverbal communication in the small group.

7. Have three video tapes made of the meetings you hold during the term. Present a one-hour analysis of these video tapes to the class. In that analysis you should (1) identify the nonverbal cues that were used to exchange meaning, (2) indicate whether the nonverbal cues contributed to or helped block the attainment of groups goals, and (3) indicate how the nonverbal cues might have been used more effectively.

Part 4
THE QUALITY
OF GROUP
OUTCOMES

9 The Identification and Measurement of Interpersonal Outcomes

I nterpersonal relationships are demanding. An overriding sense of euphoria may change instantly to despair. This is so because interpersonal relationships are associated with action and reaction, with expectation and frustration, and with agreement and conflict. Such relationships are frequently perilous because the interactants can rely on neither rules nor precedents to guide their behavior.

Sustaining interpersonal relationships often requires concentration; beginning them frequently produces perspiration. If you disagree, think of your own dating relationships. For many, the beginning is torture. For some, the response is bizarre. Consider the case of Les Franklin. Les, a part-time minister and graduate student, shared an apartment with a friend for a year. Les was an intelligent fellow, but he had a great fear of beginning interpersonal relationships. In dealing with his problem, he made his friend a most unusual offer. He emphasized that he wanted to call a girl for a date but did not know how to proceed. Moreover, he was gripped by a very real sense of anxiety and dread because he was unsure of the girl's expectations and could not anticipate her response to a phone call. Consequently, he moved to reduce the strain. He proposed that his friend serve as a ghostwriter who would prepare a complete "script" that he could use when phoning the girl.

Although Les's proposed strategy may have been a bit unusual, his fear of beginning an interpersonal relationship was not. He was anxious, uncertain, and hesitant in part because he recognized that he could exert only partial control over the desired relationship. Although he did not want to *share* control of the outcome, he realized that it was inevitable.

The shared control of outcomes helps distinguish interpersonal from noninterpersonal relationships. Thus the boss briefing his subordinates, the professor lecturing to his students, the judge addressing the defendant, and the drill sergeant issuing directives to army recruits are all examples of noninterpersonal relationships. One individual exerts an inequitable degree of control over the relationships.

As Miller and Steinberg point out, "In noninterpersonal relationships, most rules are articulated by a group of people who impose them on others. For instance, even the highest ranking military officers have little say about the nature of rules governing their relationships with enlisted men. . . . The only way effective communication can occur in such situations is for all parties to know the rules ahead of time or be willing to follow the lead of one who already knows them." [1]

In short, noninterpersonal relationships are characterized by *external* control of the interaction. Interpersonal relationships feature *internal* control. Indeed in interpersonal relationships "no one else, no other group of people, directly influences the rules that develop. The communicators are free to set up patterns that suit their own needs." [2]

This chapter focuses on the identification and measurement of interpersonal behavior in the small group. It is designed to identify those types of interpersonal behavior that have a particularly significant impact on the quality of interpersonal relationships. It illustrates how to measure the predispositions of group members to behave in certain ways as well as how to measure the actual behavior. Such measurement can yield very valuable information. This chapter also provides the group members with the potential to modify their interpersonal behavior(s) in ways that maximize the quality of interpersonal relationships in the group.

The single act of one member can be important. Usually, however, the interpersonal behavior of group members exhibits an identifiable pattern or style. For example, in groups where members consistently act in a cooperative fashion, meet mutual expectations, and disclose a considerable amount of personal information about themselves, we can see that such *trusting behaviors* represent a dominant style of interaction. If such trusting behaviors endure over a period of time and are representative of interaction during that period, we would define them as an *interpersonal outcome*. An *interpersonal outcome* consists of a *closely related set of interpersonal behaviors that are present in a group for a period of time that allow group members to develop a set of expectations and interaction patterns.*

[1] G. R. Miller and M. Steinberg, *Between People: A New Analysis of Interpersonal Communication* (Chicago: Science Research Associates, 1975), p. 55.
[2] Ibid., p. 56.

Interpersonal Outcomes

At first glance, it may seem that we are using the term *outcomes* in a paradoxical way. When we think of outcome, we often use it to describe the result(s) of human interaction rather than interaction itself. When we ask who won the basketball game or fight, who won the case in a divorce court, or if marital counseling was successful, we are asking about instrumental outcomes of interpersonal interaction.

These types of instrumental outcomes are undeniably important. Indeed the types of task outcomes associated with the small group will be discussed in detail in the next chapter. If you think for a moment, however, you will recognize that the outcomes of interpersonal relationships are not confined to such tangible products as the amount of money you collected or even the score of a basketball game.

Can you recall the time when you said, "My relations with that person will never be the same because I cannot trust him any longer"? Can you recall the time when you muttered, "That bastard manipulated me and used me for his own ends"? Can you recall saying, "I can't wait to work with those people again because they empathize with me"? If you can recall such situations, you know that interaction with others produces interpersonal as well as task outcomes.

Only recently have scholars recognized the importance of interpersonal outcomes.[3] Definition and classification of the major types of interpersonal outcomes are difficult.[4] Even in one-on-one relationships, the perceptions of the two individuals involved are apt to differ drastically. What one person views as forthright and sensitive interpersonal behavior, another person may view as manipulative and nonempathic.

Completely objective criteria for judging the relative desirability of interpersonal behaviors do not exist. Nonetheless, some interpersonal behaviors are generally recognized as defective.[5]

---

[3] R. W. Pace and R. R. Boren, *The Human Transaction* (Glenview, Ill.: Scott, Foresman and Company, 1973), pp. 104–125.

[4] S. L. Tubbs and S. Moss, *Human Communication: An Interpersonal Perspective* (New York: Random House, 1974), p. 12.

[5] S. M. Jourard, *Personal Adjustment* (New York: The Macmillan Co., 1963), p. 285, identifies what he labels "Ineffective Interpersonal Behavior": (1) defective empathy—a failure to create an accurate imaginative picture in one's mind of the present subjective state of the person with whom one is interacting; (2) deviant socialization—relating to others in socially unacceptable ways; a male attempting to hold hands with a male would be an example; (3) irrational anxiety—once rejected for being spontaneous, one may fear subsequent attempts to be spontaneous; (4) defective knowledge of people in general—this is often related to one's own unwillingness to reveal anything about one's self; (5) faking and manipulating—"The confirmed 'phony' may, if he persists in masking his authentic feelings

Clearly, our relationships with others are often defective because we reveal too little about ourselves or because what is revealed is often calculated to present a misleading picture of the inner self. Many group members expend most of their energy trying to adjust their public identity in a way to make it compatible with what they perceive to be their own self-interests. In Goffman's words, they are primarily concerned with presentation of self.[6] Such individuals in "their first few communications with the leader and the group . . . are completing the sentence stem that reads, 'I am the kind of person who—.' Whether they portray themselves as cool, outraged, pathetic, or helpful, they are beginning the adjustment of their public identity to the particular setting and audience."[7]

The concept of a carefully calculated public identity is instructive. It suggests that group members must often deal with counterfeit emotions and motivations. Real and contrived motivation may appear to be indistinguishable. The perceptual problem is not a simple one. On occasion, a communicator's motivation is hidden not only from other group members but from himself. Figure 9.1 makes the point. Using the Johari window as his frame of reference (no pun intended), Zima claims that at any given moment our interpersonal relationships with others may be classified into one of four areas. In area 1, the communicator's true motivation is known both by him and others, whereas in area 2 our motivation is not known by us but is apparent to others. In area 3 our own motivation is clear to us but unknown by others. Finally, in area 4 our motivation is clear neither to us nor to those with whom we interact.

FIGURE 9.1
THE JOHARI WINDOW

	Known to Self	Not Known to Self
Known to Others	1. Area of Free Activity	2. Blind Area
Not Known to Others	3. Hidden or Avoided Area	4. Area of Unknown Potential

From J. P. Zima, "Self-Analysis in Inventory: An Interpersonal Communication Exercise," *Speech Teacher* 20 (1971): 109.

---

and purposes, eventually lose sight of them in himself. That is, in hiding his true feelings from others, he will ultimately hide them from himself and become increasingly 'self-alienated.' " See also S. M. Jourard, *Disclosing Man to Himself* (Princeton, N.J.: S. Van Nostrand, 1968), pp. 18–34, and David Johnson, *Reaching Out: Interpersonal Effectiveness and Self-Actualization* (Englewood Cliffs, N.J.: Prentice-Hall, 1972), pp. 1–7.

[6] E. Goffman, *The Presentation of Self in Everyday Life* (Garden City, N.Y.: Doubleday Anchor, 1959), pp. 17–76.

[7] R. D. Mann, *Interpersonal Styles and Group Development* (New York: John Wiley and Sons, 1967), p. 271.

Area 1 "is the region of free exchange between individuals." [8] The larger this area, the greater our potential for engaging in interpersonal communication that leads to satisfying interpersonal outcomes. For many individuals, however, areas 3 and 4 become home ground. Their potential for achieving satisfying interpersonal outcomes is limited.

In general, our ability to understand past behavior and predict future behavior is directly related to the amount of information we have about an individual's motivations and feelings. With such information, we can more readily determine how an individual may be predisposed to act.

Outside of the small group, interpersonal relationships often become reasonably predictable. Inside the small group, it is much more difficult to predict accurately how group members will interrelate and behave. This is so because the small group is a social system that exerts its own pressures on members; there are at least eight intragroup forces that may interact to modify the initial behavioral predispositions of a group member. Thus, as we emphasized in Chapter 2, the demands of the group as a social system may override the behavioral predispositions of the group members. The pressures to conform may control one's impulse to be assertive, the pressures of interdependency may control one's desire to take unilateral action, or the pressures associated with cohesiveness may control one's felt need to criticize another discussant.

Intragroup forces exert an undeniable influence on interpersonal behaviors in the small group. Aside from the obvious potential effects of personality differences, the different purposes for which groups are formed and the different situations in which they function can also be important.

In spite of the difficulties of predicting the exact nature of interpersonal behavior in the small group, a fairly stable pattern of interpersonal relationships is apt to evolve. Indeed we believe that certain types of interpersonal behavior in the small group characteristically lead to satisfying interpersonal outcomes. Although many more might be discussed, we are going to concentrate on four major classes of interpersonal behavior that are particularly important: (1) assertive behavior, (2) nonmanipulative behavior, (3) disclosing behavior, and (4) trusting behavior.

Process Effects of Interpersonal Behaviors

In Chapters 2 and 7 we described the small-group communication system and the major components that make up the system. We defined small-group communication as the process of exchanging consensually shared meanings. In addition, we emphasized that many factors affect the

[8] J. P. Zima, "Self-Analysis Inventory: An Interpersonal Communication Exercise," *The Speech Teacher* 20 (1971): 109.

process of exchanging meanings in ways that obscure or distort intended meanings. Any factors that materially affect the exchange of meanings in the small group (whether those factors are facilitative or disruptive) produce process effects.

Traditionally, we probably would think of process effects in terms of the impact of certain kinds of verbal messages. Thus a highly abstract message consistently results in confused, tense, and withdrawn feedback. These feedback qualities are process effects. However, we probably have not thought of the way(s) we present ourselves or the ways we relate to others and interrelate with others from this perspective. Nonetheless, interpersonal relationships often result in clear-cut process effects.

Frequently, interpersonal factors have a greater impact on the small-group communication process than the manifest verbal content of the message. Indeed interpersonal behaviors often affect the quality of communication in the small group. In a way, this is paradoxical because *the communication of individuals is often both an antecedent to and a consequence of certain types of interpersonal behavior.* For example, we know that communication that emphasizes cooperation and mutual disclosure is consistently associated with a high level of trust. At the same time, high levels of trust are consistently associated with relaxed, flexible, and objective communication in the small group.

ASSERTIVE BEHAVIOR

Nonassertiveness frequently results in serious interpersonal problems in the small group. To be nonassertive is often to be dominated, insecure, defensive, angry, and ineffective. Most students and teachers of small-group communication will readily recognize the problem.

Dominic Reticent, an outstanding student, is a good example of a nonassertive communicator. He seems to get lost in the group and withdraw. At the end of the term, he stops to see his instructor. He notes that he was very frustrated because his participation in his group was virtually nonexistent. He emphasizes that he was highly motivated to participate. However, whenever he felt the urge to speak, another group member beat him to the punch or cut him off. He admits that during a sixty-minute group presentation in class he made only one brief contribution, but he emphasizes that the quality of his listening was truly superior.

Dominic's extended state of nonassertiveness represents a very undesirable type of interpersonal behavior. By definition it makes him an ineffective communicator. To be nonassertive is to suspend many vitally important communicative functions. At minimum, nonassertiveness precludes *critical* interaction in the small group. Moreover, the nonassertive member creates perceptual problems. Those who attempt to communicate with him have a very difficult decoding task. His lack of assertiveness makes his true emotions and feelings obscure at best and undecipherable at worst.

Nonassertiveness is a common condition in small groups. The condition is particularly serious when accepted submissively. In fact, "the world contains many people who don't recognize their own strengths or who have learned to act in inferior ways because they believe themselves to be inferior. They find it impossible to express emotions like anger or tenderness; and hold their own desires inside themselves. Because they possess no control of their own lives, they become increasingly unsure. They accept the state of *unassertiveness.*" [9]

Unassertiveness in interpersonal relationships is rather easy to recognize. The unassertive discussant offers the few suggestions he does make in a very tentative manner; points are often made in a very indirect and verbose way; dishonest comments are often made to avoid a critical reaction or to avoid a reaction that would necessarily involve the nonassertive member in communicative interaction.[10]

You may wonder whether your own interpersonal behavior is typically nonassertive or assertive. If so, consider the following questions: (1) Do you have trouble maintaining conversations in social situations? (2) When a member of your group makes an unreasonable request, are you able to refuse? (3) Can you criticize a member of your group? (4) Do you openly express your inner feelings? (5) Would you rather repress your feelings than risk conflict in the group? (6) Do you find it difficult to deal with a subordinate? [11]

If your answer is yes to these questions, your behavior in the small group is apt to be nonassertive. If your answer is no, you have the potential to be appropriately assertive.

Assertion training has currently become a major training tool for improving the quality of interpersonal relationships. Such training could have been very beneficial to the major figures in the Watergate conspiracy. Mitchell, Erlichman, Haldeman, and even President Nixon displayed a disturbing tendency to say an equivocal yes to unethical and illegal activities when they should have said no unequivocally. To study the record of Watergate is most illuminating. It dramatically reveals a group of men with a carefully cultivated public image of assertiveness who were controlled in private by a fateful and a fatal state of perpetual nonassertiveness.

NONMANIPULATIVE BEHAVIOR

"Modern man is a manipulator. . . . He is a used car salesman talking us into an automobile we wouldn't otherwise buy and a responsible father

[9] H. Fensterheim and J. Baer, *Don't Say Yes When You Want to Say No* (New York: Dell, 1975), p. 17.
[10] Ibid., p. 38.
[11] Ibid., p. 50.

omnisciently deciding on the college and career for his son. He is the learned professor drily retailing subject matter with no opinions of his own. . . . He is the minister preaching in platitudes lest he offend important parishioners, the aging parent embracing illness as a tool to manipulate the waning attention of busy sons and daughters, and the politician who promises everything except new taxes." [12]

There can be little doubt that manipulation takes place in interpersonal relationships. Most likely, you have manipulated and been manipulated. We are not so cynical, however, as to suggest that manipulation is the predominant style in our interactions with others. Clearly, both manipulative and nonmanipulative styles are employed in our society. Indeed the style in a given situation or group may change from manipulative to nonmanipulative in a very short time.

The question then is not whether manipulation occurs. The questions are (1) What kind of communication is manipulative? and (2) What are the process effects of manipulative behavior in the small group?

Christie and Geis define manipulation as a means to get someone to do something he would not otherwise have done: "In the simplest cases the manipulation derives direct benefit at the other's expense." [13] As in all interpersonal relationships, the interactants share control of the outcomes. In the manipulative relationship, however, the manipulator seeks an inequitable degree of control over interpersonal outcomes.

To gain his objective, the manipulator typically employs a number of "manipulative communication patterns." Manipulative Communication features the concealment of one's own expectations as to desired interpersonal outcomes and insincere but concerted efforts to meet the expectations of those with whom one interacts. The manipulator's expectations typically remain unexpressed; the manipulator will not say what he wants. The manipulator strives to give the appearance of shaping his own behavior to meet the expectations of those with whom he communicates, but he often intentionally distorts the expectations of others so that he can meet them without blocking the attainment of his own, hidden goals. [14]

Surely, we can each recall examples of manipulative communication from our relationships. Consider the case of Bruce Valentino. Valentino was a handsome Ph.D. student of shallow convictions who specialized in manipulating a group of eager young ladies who persistently and aggressively sought his attention and affection. He took pains to conceal his own expectations while manipulating the expectations of "his girls" (each of the girls was convinced that Bruce would marry her, an expectation that Bruce carefully nourished in public while making derogatory remarks about the

---

[12] E. L. Shostrom, *Man, the Manipulator* (New York: Bantam, 1968), p. xi.

[13] R. Christie and F. L. Geis, *Studies in Machiavellianism* (New York: Academic Press, 1970), p. 106.

[14] Shostrom, *Man, the Manipulator*, pp. 48–50.

girls in private). In contrast to the girls, Bruce had two limited objectives: (1) to dine at the most expensive restaurants in the city at the girls' expense; and (2) to take virtual possession of the expensive cars which the girls invariably drove—on more than one occasion he used one girl's car to date another girl. Bruce skillfully modified the girls' expectation of marriage by blocking the expectation(s). He kept reasserting that his unselfish devotion to his Ph.D. studies precluded long-term relationships. The girls kept standing in line, and Bruce kept manipulating them until he decided to leave the Midwest and go to the Far West. At that point, one of the girls literally gave him her car and followed him west six months later after resigning from an excellent job.

Like Bruce, the successful manipulator exhibits a relative lack of affect in interpersonal relationships, an indifference to conventional morality, and a low ideological commitment (twelve years after his interaction with "his girls," Bruce still does not have his Ph.D. and, in fact, is engaged in an endeavor wholly unrelated to the subject to which he professed an unbreakable commitment).[15]

In many cases, the manipulated do perceive that they are being manipulated, however. When this is the case, there are typically undesirable consequences for both the manipulator and the manipulated. At the very least, the potential for developing mutual trust may be permanently lost. Moreover, the potential for reprisal is very real. When manipulation occurs in a small group, the reactions to it often divert attention from the group's primary objective(s) and result in a climate of antagonism, hostility, and conflict that assures undesirable interpersonal outcomes for all concerned. Of course, if manipulative communication is undertaken by only one member in a group, it may produce an uncomfortable but manageable impact on interpersonal relationships. If manipulation becomes the predominant style of interaction in the group, however, it may produce process effects that lower the quality of group communication for an extended period of time.

To put manipulative behavior in perspective, however, we would not argue that it always produces undesirable effects. As a means to a worthwhile end, manipulation may even seem praiseworthy to some. So much depends on one's perspective and the situation. Certainly, Lyndon Johnson was the consummate manipulator of men in his private meetings with influential senators:

> Face to face, behind office doors, Johnson could strike a different pose, a different form of behavior and argument. He would try to make each senator feel that his support in some particular matter was the critical element that would affect the well-being of the nation, the Senate, and the party leader; and would serve the practical and political interests of the senator.[16]

[15] Christie and Geis, *Studies in Machiavellianism*, pp. 3–4.
[16] D. Kearns, "Who Was Lyndon Baines Johnson?" *Atlantic Monthly* 237 (1976): p. 47.

When they were used to win support for his unpopular Vietnam policy, many Americans probably viewed Johnson's manipulative skills as deplorable. When used to win passage of his unprecedented program of civil rights legislation, the same skills were probably viewed more charitably.

As he cultivated his relationship with Roy Wilkins of the NAACP, Johnson changed the form of address in letters to Wilkins noticeably—from "To Roy Wilkins, from Lyndon Johnson" to "Dear Roy, My best, Lyndon" to "My Esteemed Friend" and, finally, to "your friend and admirer, Lyndon." Conversely, as Johnson's attempts to influence Wilbur Mills became progressively less successful, the mode of address also changed: (1) "To my friend and colleague Wilbur, from your good friend and greatest admirer. Lyndon"; (2) "to Wilbur Mills from Lyndon Johnson"; (3) "To Mr. Chairman from Mr. President." [17]

You, the reader, must be the ultimate judge of the desirability of manipulative behavior. As we can see, many factors might affect such a judgment.

DISCLOSING BEHAVIOR

Communication is very difficult when we have little information about the person with whom we attempt to communicate. Not only are we forced to guess about the person's intentions, expectations, and motivations, but we are apt to know little about the individual's belief and value systems that have such a vital impact on the way he or she encodes and decodes messages. It is almost impossible to adapt our communication to a person's needs if we do not know what those needs are.

Communication among adults often has a guarded and even stilted quality to it. This is so because adults have been conditioned to be on guard. They are hesitant to disclose personal information about themselves because they know that others may use it to exploit them. Because of the lack of self-disclosure, adult communication often seems both superficial and artificial.

In contrast, communication among children is often delightful because of its open, spontaneous, and honest nature. Communication of this type provides us with the ultimate model of self-disclosure. Children typically reveal much about themselves because they have not yet become cynical enough to fear the consequences of revealing intimate details about their innermost thoughts and their own behavior. For this reason, communication with children is typically very satisfying.

Contrast, if you will, the willingness of children and their parents to reveal personal things about themselves. A child is completely comfortable in reporting in public that he has to "pee," that his sister is in the "crapper," or that mommy and daddy were making love on the carpet in front

[17] Ibid., p. 52.

of the television last night. Calculate the chances that either mom or dad would disclose the same information.

Similarly, the truly inspired teacher of the elementary grades has the ability to stimulate much self-disclosure on the part of students in part because of his or her willingness to be self-disclosing. The mother of one of the authors taught first-graders for over forty years and is still teaching kindergarten while in her seventies. If there is one key to her success as a teacher, it is her ability to stimulate her students to be self-disclosing while she, in turn, is self-disclosing.

At this point, the reader may wonder precisely what we mean by self-disclosing communication. According to Pearce and Sharp, self-disclosure occurs when one person voluntarily tells another person things about himself or herself that the other is unlikely to know or to discover from other sources. In contrast, nondisclosing communication includes lying (a misleading presentation of self), concealment (intentionally refusing to present information about one's self), and various types of defensive behaviors.[18]

As a major type of interpersonal behavior, self-disclosure serves many functions in the small group. Three functions seem particularly important: (1) *self-disclosure can improve one's self-concept,* (2) *self-disclosure can fulfill the needs of group members,* and (3) *self-disclosure can improve the quality of communication.*[19]

Individuals who are more self-disclosing tend to have a more positive self-concept. It is not entirely clear, of course, whether self-disclosure contributes to a positive self-concept or whether a positive self-concept tends to promote self-disclosure. Most likely, there is a reciprocal effect here. In any event, two conclusions seem justified. An individual with a positive self-concept is less likely to behave in disruptive ways in the interpersonal environment of the small group. Secondly, we now have empirical evidence that suggests that the act of self-disclosure helps to build a positive self-concept.[20]

Self-disclosure also functions to satisfy individual needs. Americans are constantly reminded of their need to eliminate tensions. Physiological relief is but an aspirin or laxative tablet away. Psychological relief is a more complicated matter. For many, self-disclosure may be a good part of the answer. It provides relief because it is a cathartic experience. Tubbs and Baird put the matter succinctly when they write:

> Since many of our personal and emotional problems can result in pathological behavior when "bottled up" inside for long periods of time, the act of

[18] W. B. Pearce and S. M. Sharp, "Self-Disclosing Communication," *Journal of Communication* 32 (1973): 415.

[19] S. L. Tubbs and J. W. Baird, *The Open Person: Self-Disclosure and Personal Growth* (Columbus, Ohio: Charles E. Merrill, 1976), p. 11.

[20] Ibid., p. 12.

self-disclosure can be therapeutic. The guilt that often accompanies conceal-ment is minimized by sharing the problem with another. The therapeutic value of the traditional Catholic confessional is based on the premise that self-disclos-ing one's wrongdoings will relieve one of the guilt feelings often surrounding such behavior. My aunt has often remarked that "Going to confession is like seeing a psychiatrist." [21]

Any interpersonal behavior that controls or dissipates debilitating tensions must be taken seriously.

Finally, self-disclosure may improve the quality of communicative inter-action.[22] The primary reason is simple. High-quality communication is heavily dependent on our ability to perceive accurately the motivations and intentions of those with whom we communicate. The more self-disclosing we are, the more accurately others may perceive our basic moti-vations and intentions. Surely, those who understand more clearly how we view the world are much less apt to misinterpret either our general moti-vation or the specific messages we transmit.

Understanding the central functions of self-disclosure is not enough, however. We must recognize that the act of self-disclosure may vary along three primary dimensions: (1) *breadth or amount of information disclosed,* (2) *depth or intimacy of information disclosed,* and (3) *duration or time spent disclosing a particular type of information.* These three dimensions of self-disclosure are interrelated in the sense that an increase in one may result in a decrease in another. For example, we know that there is an in-verse relationship between intimacy and the amount of self-disclosure. The more intimate the subject, the less information an individual is apt to disclose.[23]

In effect, the amount, intimacy, and duration of self-disclosure provide an operational definition of any single act of self-disclosure. In addition, we must recognize that these dimensions or components of the self-disclosing act are affected by such factors as the sex, age, cultural conditioning, and the perceived relationship(s) of the discloser and disclosee.[24]

We do not know exactly why individuals often vary drastically in their willingness to engage in self-disclosing communication. The fact that males

[21] Ibid.

[22] Ibid., p. 11.

[23] P. C. Cozby, "Self-Disclosure: A Literature Review," *Psychological Bulletin* 79 (1973): 75.

[24] R. G. Weigel, V. M. Weigel, and P. C. Chadwick, "Reported and Projected Self-Dis-closure," *Psychological Reports* 24 (1969): 283–287. Cozby, "Self-Disclosure: A Literature Review," p. 76, reviews the impact of factors such as sex, face, and cultural conditioning on self-disclosure. Tubbs and Baird, *The Open Person: Self-Disclosure and Personal Growth,* p. 9, draw our attention to the important distinction between self-disclosing and self-revealing behavior. Self-disclosure is typically an intentional act whereas self-revealing be-havior, which is often manifested via nonverbal cues, is inadvertent and unintentional.

are much less apt to be self-disclosing than females is probably very significant, however. In our society it is simply not appropriate for males to reveal their innermost thoughts and feelings. For example, the male who cries in public is thought to be an emotional weakling. In short, males are conditioned to be nondisclosing.

In addition, self-disclosing communication, whether for males or females, can be a high risk endeavor. The ultimate act of self-disclosure is to tell another person that you love him or her. To reveal such personal information is to run the risk of rejection. It is our hypothesis that the person who is poker-faced, rigid, unresponsive, and nondisclosing in interpersonal relationships assumes this style because he or she has exaggerated fears of the ridicule and/or rejection that may result from self-disclosure. Nondisclosure is a form of self-protection but one for which we pay a high price. Ironically, the failure to engage in self-disclosing communication is often one of the major contributors to undesirable interpersonal outcomes.

There can be little doubt that disclosing behavior can improve the quality of interpersonal relationships. Delia suggests that the "result of such a quality [self-disclosure] in a person's interactions, of course, is a wide range of information concerning the subjective perspectives of others. One's attitude toward self-disclosure is, hence, not likely to affect the degree of his interactions with others so much as the quality of intensity of those interactions." [25] In broadest perspective, we now know that there is a strong positive relationship between the amount of self-disclosing communication in a group and the level of cohesiveness.[26] This finding is particularly important when we recognize that cohesiveness is frequently cited as the most desirable interpersonal outcome that may result from the interaction of group members.

For this and other reasons, we believe that self-disclosure is frequently a highly desirable type of interpersonal behavior in the small group. Neither continuous nor unrestrained self-disclosure is always valuable, however. At least one authority feels that our need to know about others must be balanced by our need (and theirs) for privacy on sensitive matters. Too much self-disclosure may expose us to the "tyranny of openness." This tyranny is defined by the uncomfortable and unsatisfying condition where no one is allowed to have a private thought.[27] To divest an individual of the "masks" he uses to create a counterfeit public identity may be titillating and useful in some cases. However, to promote self-disclosure to divest the same person of his or her last defense against hidden insecurities and felt weaknesses may simply be sadistic.

[25] J. G. Delia, "Attitude Toward the Disclosure of Self Attributions and the Complexity of Interpersonal Constructs," *Speech Monographs* 41 (1974): 361–362.

[26] D. L. Johnson and L. R. Ridener, "Self-Disclosure, Participation, and Perceived Cohesiveness in Small Group Interaction," *Psychological Reports* 35 (1974): 361–362.

[27] Cozby, "Self-Disclosure: A Literature Review," *Psychological Bulletin*, p. 88.

TRUSTING BEHAVIOR

Being assertive and self-disclosing while being nonmanipulative is very important. These behaviors certainly play a major role in shaping interpersonal relationships in the small group. Nonetheless, observation of hundreds of groups in the classroom and laboratory has convinced us that another type of behavior is of overriding importance in affecting the quality of interpersonal relationships and outcomes. That factor is interpersonal trust.

In the past few years, many researchers have come to recognize the paramount importance of interpersonal trust. Tubbs and Moss maintain that a high level of trust is a necessary condition for effective communicative interaction. They conclude that "total effectiveness requires a positive and trusting psychological climate. When a human relationship is clouded by mistrust, numerous opportunities arise for distorting or discrediting even the most skillfully constructed messages." [28] Sereno and Bodaken go even further:

> That trust is the most important relationship established between humans can be seen by looking at the works of poets, novelists, and philosophers, theologians, psychiatrists, and others who attempt to describe the human condition. The development of trust or its opposite, suspicion, is one of the vital outcomes of intimate interpersonal communication; the presence or absence of trust can easily strengthen or destroy a relationship. [29]

If you consider your relationships with others, the truth of these assertions will probably be obvious. The authors knew a young man (Gordy Lather) who devised a detailed and creative strategy for beginning a relationship with a young lady (Sherri). Lather called Sherri, posing as an internationally known expert in communication and offered her a fellowship to work with him. Because he was based in another city a thousand miles away, the "expert" agreed to fly in and brief Sherri at the airport. To Sherri's surprise, she was met at the airport, not by the famous professor but by Gordy Lather; Lather explained that the professor's plane had been diverted to Denver by bad weather. Lather noted also that he was one of the professor's former students and thus the professor had asked him to meet Sherri when his plane was diverted. As planned, Lather's elaborate story worked in the sense that he began a generally pleasurable dating relationship with Sherri. Eventually, it was terminated with considerable pain to both parties, however. Sherri's parting words to Lather seem most in-

---

[28] Tubbs and Moss, *Human Communication: An Interpersonal Perspective*, p. 12.
[29] K. K. Sereno and E. M. Bodaken, *Trans-Per Understanding Human Communication* (Boston: Houghton Mifflin, 1975), pp. 191–192.

structive: "While I am flattered by what you did and I am strongly attracted to you, I find it impossible to really trust you."

Most of us have at least a subjective notion of what interpersonal trust is. The current research literature on the subject employs a number of different definitions for trust, however. Interestingly enough, trust has recently been defined as the willingness of the communicators to disclose highly intimate information about themselves.[30] Although the willingness to be self-disclosing may contribute to a state of trust or even, on occasion, be a necessary condition to build trust, in itself it does not adequately define interpersonal trust.

Interpersonal trust is *that relationship that exists when the interactants base their behavior on the expectation and prediction that each will act in mutually beneficial ways as they strive to achieve objectives that involve some degree of risk.*[31] Pearce emphasizes that an individual experiencing a cognitive state of trust expects the person whom he or she trusts to avoid those behaviors that will result in unacceptably negative outcomes for the trusting person.[32]

Trust is affected by at least two main factors: (1) the basic image that one brings to the group and (2) one's behavior within the group. The former is an external factor and of only incidental concern in a chapter on interpersonal relationships.[33] We are primarily interested, however, in those intragroup behaviors that can be identified as trusting and with their effects on the small-group communication process.

Trusting behavior does exhibit a number of clear-cut qualities. The group member who engages in trusting behavior and expects the trusting behavior to be reciprocated will (1) be cooperative, (2) make his or her expectations clear, (3) emphasize that his or her behavior is contingent on a suitable response from the trusted party, (4) leave a number of options open, (5) indicate explicitly how he or she will deal with a violation of his or her trust, and (6) behave in a predictable manner.

There is no foolproof set of steps that one can take to build interpersonal trust. Nonetheless, there are some guidelines that one can follow. First, one person must act in such a manner that he or she runs at least

[30] C. W. Ellison and I. J. Firestone, "Development of Interpersonal Trust as a Function of Self-Esteem, Target Status, and Target Style," *Journal of Personality and Social Psychology* 29 (1974): 660–661. A. Tolor, M. Cramer, D. D'Amico, and M. M. O'Mara, "The Effects of Self-Concept, Trust, and Imagined Positive or Negative Self-Disclosures on Psychological Space," *Journal of Psychology* 89 (1975): 9–24, also define trust as the amount of personal information one person has revealed to another.

[31] K. Giffin, "Interpersonal Trust in Small Group Communication," *Quarterly Journal of Speech* 53 (1967): 225, defines trust as the reliance upon the communicative behavior of another person in order to achieve desired but uncertain objectives in a risky situation.

[32] W. B. Pearce, "Trust in Interpersonal Communication," *Speech Monographs* 41 (1974): 242.

[33] Ibid., p. 241.

the risk of personal loss. Secondly, the person responding to the act(s) of another must choose "the alternative in which he forgoes a personal gain and the first person does not incur a loss." [34]

More specifically, we are apt to enhance our chances of building trusting relationships by following these guidelines: (1) act in ways that are compatible with societal rules, traditions, and expectations; (2) act in ways that meet the interpersonal expectations of group members; (3) act in ways that exhibit as much concern for the goals of the other persons as our own; (4) make enforceable promises to those with whom we are interacting; and (5) provide those with whom we are interacting with credible evidence that we trust them. [35]

The question of how trust is built or destroyed in the small group is undeniably important. However, until recently, emphasis has been placed on those factors that affect trust rather than on the impact of a change in level of trust on communicative interaction in the group.

Focusing on the process effects of trust destruction, Leathers conducted an experiment in which trust was intentionally destroyed. A "selected subject" was conditioned to trust a "plant" who engaged in trusting behaviors described earlier. During the trust-building phase of the laboratory discussions, the selected subject was reinforced by the plant with statements such as "You are right—I agree with you completely" and "I like that idea so much I wish you'd expand on it. Will you?" During the final half of the discussion, the plant began violating the selected subject by violating his expectations, acting in an unpredictable way, and negatively reinforcing him. He said things such as "Are you serious in taking such an absurd position?" and "You are wrong. Dead wrong." The process effects of this trust destruction were measured by using the procedure described in Chapter 2.

As trust was destroyed, the quality of communication in the group deteriorated markedly. In particular, the communication of the selected subject became extremely tense, inflexible, and personal. The following is a sample of the communicative interaction between the selected subject and the trust-destroying plant:

PLANT: You are wrong. Dead wrong.

SUBJECT: [He suddenly begins to rub his hands together very vigorously, his neck muscles begin to constrict, and his eyes appear to open very wide. Meanwhile, the other discussants begin to squirm in their seats while they avert their eyes from the selected subject and the plant.] Oh, you think so huh. OK, you think that way. Why? You think I'm wrong; I don't think so. Why can't you recognize that ethnic studies

[34] R. L. Swinth, "The Establishment of the Trust Relationship," *Journal of Conflict Resolution* 11 (1967): 336.
[35] K. Giffin and R. E. Barnes, *Trusting Me, Trusting You* (Columbus, Ohio: Charles E. Merrill, 1976), pp. 53–58.

centers just give right-wingers more ammunition to claim that whites and blacks are different. I am convinced that that is the way it is. [He is exhibiting inflexibility.] Man, you are a strange cat. Oh wow, you can't be real. Are you kidding me? You are nothing but a white racist. [He is becoming personal—attacking the plant.] [36]

Prentice's follow-up research used the same methodology. He found that *not only did the communication of the trusting individual deteriorate as his or her trust was destroyed but that the communication of all other group members was negatively affected.* As his or her trust was destroyed, the communication of the selected subject became increasingly incomprehensible, inconsistent, absolute, inflexible, and antagonistic. Interestingly, the communication of the other members of the group became more incomprehensible, abstract, subjective, certain, and antagonistic. Moreover, the nonfluency of the selected subject increased by 64 percent and that of the other group members by 71 percent.[37]

In short, trusting and distrusting behaviors have a major impact on interpersonal relationships in the small group.[38] The destruction of trust results in a consistent and even dramatic drop in the quality of group communication. Few could deny that sustaining a high level of trust among group members is one of the most desirable interpersonal outcomes for everyone in the group or that sustaining a climate of distrust is one of the most undesirable interpersonal outcomes.

Measuring Interpersonal Outcomes

By this time, the reader may agree that assertiveness, nonmanipulation, self-disclosure, and trust are behaviors that are very important in establishing satisfying interpersonal relationships in the small group. He or she might agree further that such types or classes of interpersonal behavior become interpersonal outcomes when they persist over time and dominate interaction in the group.

To recognize the importance of such interpersonal behavior is not enough, however. We must be able to measure the group members' predispositions to behave in a certain way as well as their actual behavior.

---

[36] D. G. Leathers, "The Process Effects of Trust-Destroying Behavior in the Small Group," *Speech Monographs* 37 (1970): 187.

[37] D. S. Prentice, "The Process Effects of Trust Destruction in the Small Group," Ph.D. dissertation, UCLA, 1972.

[38] M. E. Tomassoni, "The Effects of Interpersonal Trust on Communication: A Critical Review with the Formulation of Untested Hypotheses," M.A. thesis, University of Georgia, 1974, explores in depth the attempts to define interpersonal trust and measure its effects on behavior in clinical, organizational, family, educational, and political situations. The sheer volume of the studies of interpersonal trust helps to attest to its importance.

Through such measurement we not only can predict that a given type of interpersonal outcome is apt to result, but we can also pinpoint the nature of the interpersonal outcomes that do result.

The basic message of this chapter is that group members should strive to achieve assertive, nonmanipulative, disclosing, and trusting interpersonal outcomes while working actively to avoid outcomes that feature nonassertion, manipulation, nondisclosure, and distrust.

First, how do we identify assertive behavior and outcomes? Assertive communication typically is associated with one or more of the following phrases or with phrases that convey basically the same meaning: "I like what you said" or "I don't like what you said"; "I like what you did" or "I don't like what you did"; "I want you to..." or "I don't want you to..."[39] To determine whether your group is engaging in behavior that is leading to a nonassertive outcome, we suggest that you take the following steps: (1) select representative ten-minute samples from the tape recordings of your group meetings; (2) listen to the taped segments carefully; (3) at the conclusion of each ten-minute segment, rate the behavior as a unit by applying the scales in Figure 9.2; and (4) discuss the implications of the ratings with particular emphasis on those behaviors that were strikingly assertive or nonassertive.

Please study the scales in Figure 9.2 before you begin. These scales were developed by John and Sue Baird to emphasize behavior that they have found to be appropriately assertive. For example, the sensitively assertive person will exhibit empathy for the position or plight of others in the group. At the same time, however, he or she will use the pronoun *I* to express his or her feelings directly; his or her comments will focus directly on the *behaviors* of other discussants that he or she finds acceptable or unacceptable; he or she will be honest in his opinions, will offer no apologies or excuses for his or her own behavior, and finally will use the direct eye contact, postural immediacy, and the firm tone of voice that are characteristic of assertive behavior.

Once you have determined the *actual level* of assertiveness in your group by applying the scales in Figure 9.2, compare it with the *ideal level*. Discuss what steps your group might take to close the gap, if a gap does exist.

Next we must know how to measure the predisposition to engage in manipulative behavior as well as how to measure actual manipulative behavior. The probability that you and your fellow group members will engage in manipulative (or nonmanipulative) behavior can be rather accurately measured by a new test. Please consider each of the items in Figure 9.3, and place a number in the blank that comes closest to reflecting your own feelings. The number 7 = strong agreement, and 1 = strong disagreement whereas 4 = neither agreement nor disagreement. Please use any

---

[39] Fensterheim and Baer, *Don't Say Yes When You Want to Say No,* p. 71.

FIGURE 9.2
EVALUATING ASSERTIVE BEHAVIOR

Asserter _____

Assertee _____

Assessor _____

Place   number on the scale (7 = Good; 1 = Poor)

                 Poor   Fair   Good

Use of empathy

Use of I-message

Focusing on behavior

Being honest

Avoiding excuses,
apologies, alibis

Good eye contact

Good posture

Assertive tone of voice

Overall evaluation of
assertive behavior

Reprinted with permission of Sue and John Baird.

FIGURE 9.3
THE MACH IV TEST

_____ 1. The best way to handle people is to tell them what they want to hear.

_____ 2. When you ask someone to do something for you, it is best to give the real reasons for wanting it rather than giving reasons which might carry more weight.

_____ 3. Anyone who completely trusts anyone else is asking for trouble.

_____ 4. It is hard to get ahead without cutting corners here and there.

_____ 5. Honesty is the best policy in all cases.

_____ 6. It is safest to assume that all people have a vicious streak and it will come out when they are given a chance.

———— 7. Never tell anyone the real reason you did something unless it is useful to do so.

———— 8. One should take action only when sure it is morally right.

———— 9. It is wise to flatter important people.

————10. All in all, it is better to be humble and honest than important and dishonest.

————11. Barnum was very wrong when he said there's a sucker born every minute.

————12. People suffering from incurable diseases should have the choice of being put painlessly to death.

————13. It is possible to be good in all respects.

————14. Most people are basically good and kind.

————15. There is no excuse for lying to someone else.

————16. Most men forget more easily the death of their father than the loss of their property.

————17. Most people who get ahead in the world lead clean, moral lives.

————18. Generally speaking, men won't work hard unless they're forced to do so.

————19. The biggest difference between most criminals and other people is that criminals are stupid enough to get caught.

————20. Most men are brave.

Reprinted from R. Christie and F. L. Geis. *Studies in Machiavellianism,* New York: Academic Press, 1970), pp. 17–18.

This test is easy to score if you realize that the following items represent manipulative behavior: 1, 3, 4, 6, 7, 9, 12, 16, 18, and 19. The other ten items represent nonmanipulative behavior. For each of the manipulative items give yourself the score in the blank. For the ten nonmanipulative items simply reverse the scoring procedure: Convert a 7 to a 1 and $6 = 2$; $5 = 3$; $4 = 4$; $3 = 5$; $2 = 6$; $1 = 7$. Now add up your twenty scores. If your score was 105 or above, you prefer manipulative behavior and you are apt to be manipulative. If your score was 90 or below, you prefer nonmanipulative behavior and are apt to be nonmanipulative.

number between 7 and 1 that most accurately reflects your feeling about an item.

If most of the group members have high Mach IV scores, you are apt to have a good deal of manipulative behavior, and a manipulative outcome is likely. At least twice during the time your group is meeting, members should listen to tapes of the meetings to see if they can identify instances of manipulative behavior. If a manipulative climate seems to prevail, the group should discuss what contributed to this climate and ways of dealing with it effectively.

Our analysis of interpersonal behavior in the group does not stop here, however. Now we must measure whether members of our group are predisposed to be disclosing or nondisclosing. To make this measurement, please have each member of your group take Jourard's Self-Disclosure Test.[40]

After the group has met for some time, listen to the tape recordings of the meetings. Make a list of all contributions that you consider to be either appropriately disclosing or nondisclosing. Which discussants were most disclosing? Which were most nondisclosing? Compare these results with scores on the Self-Disclosure Test to see if there is a relationship. Finally, discuss what might be done to raise the level of disclosure in your group if you believe this is a necessary step.

As we reported earlier, interpersonal trust is perhaps the most important of all behaviors in the small group. Although it is important, it is difficult to measure. The most precise way to measure the level of trust between two people is to record the choices they make in a game-playing situation.[41] Although the Prisoner's Dilemma is a creative and precise means of measuring trust, it hardly reflects reality as we are apt to find it in a group.

The short form of the Rotter Interpersonal Trust Test is perhaps the most practical way to measure the predisposition of group members to engage in trusting behavior.[42] To measure trusting (or distrusting) behavior as such, we suggest a very simple procedure. Use the scale that follows:

Completely Trust — 7 6 5 4 3 2 1 — Completely Distrust

Then, considering the other group members as a unit, rate them on this scale after the first meeting, a meeting midway in your series of meetings, and after the last meeting. If your ratings change by over one point toward distrust, you may conclude that you have experienced a distrusting outcome. Using the same procedure, apply the scale just given to the individual members of the group, and have them follow the same procedure. If the ratings are consistently on the right or left side of the scale, discuss the reasons for the trusting or distrusting outcome.

In this chapter we have concentrated on interpersonal behaviors that may lead to one of four major types of interpersonal outcomes. If our anal-

[40] S. M. Jourard, *Self-Disclosure: An Experimental Analysis of the Transparent Self* (New York: Wiley-Interscience, 1971), pp. 199–200.

[41] Leathers, "The Process Effects of Trust-Destroying Behavior in the Small Group," pp. 182–184.

[42] K. Chun and J. B. Campbell, "Dimensionality of the Rotter Interpersonal Trust Scale," *Psychological Reports* 35 (1974): 1062–1063.

ysis stopped here, the desirability of assertive, nonmanipulative, disclosing, and trusting patterns in interpersonal relationships would be obvious. We would maintain, moreover, that such interpersonal outcomes are highly desirable for two additional reasons. They facilitate high-quality communication in the small group, *and* they tend to maximize the satisfaction that group members derive from engaging in such communication.

In the next chapter we concentrate on the task outcomes that result from interaction in groups. We will learn that positive interpersonal relationships may not be a sufficient condition to produce high-quality task outcomes, but they may be a necessary condition.

SUPPLEMENTARY READING

Giffin, K., and Barnes, R. E. *Trusting Me, Trusting You.* Columbus, Ohio: Charles E. Merrill, 1976. Chapter 5.

Miller, G. R., and Steinberg, M. *Between People: A New Analysis of Interpersonal Communication.* Chicago: Science Research Associates, 1975. Chapters 1, 6, and 7.

Pace, R. W., and Boren, R. R. *The Human Transaction.* Glenview, Ill.: Scott, Foresman, 1973. Chapter 4.

Prentice, D. S. "The Effect of Trust-Destroying Communication on Verbal Fluency in the Small Group." *Speech Monographs* 42 (1975): 262–270.

Stewart, J., and D'Angelo, G. *Together: Communicating Interpersonally.* Reading, Mass.: Addison-Wesley, 1975). Chapter 5.

Tubbs, S. L., and Baird, J. W. *The Open Person: Self-Disclosure and Personal Growth.* Columbus, Ohio: Charles E. Merrill, 1976. Chapter 2.

QUESTIONS AND EXERCISES

1. Why is it more difficult to communicate effectively with a nonassertive individual?
2. Did you feel you were being manipulated at any time during your group meetings? Give examples and discuss with your group.
3. What basic functions may self-disclosure serve in the small group? Did self-disclosure serve any of these functions in your group? If so, give examples and discuss.
4. What is the "tyranny of openness"? Did your group maintain a reasonable balance between the need for self-disclosure and the need for privacy? Discuss.
5. Have you ever met a person who behaved like Bruce Valentino (see pp. 206–207) or Gordy Lather (see p. 212)? Prepare a paper in which you describe the best way of responding to someone like Valentino *or* Lather.
6. Listen carefully to the tapes of your group meetings, and make a list of all behaviors that seemed to lower the level of interpersonal trust. Then prepare a paper in which you indicate how the members of your group should have responded to the instances of trust-destroying behavior.

10 The Identification and Measurement of Task Outcomes

Groups meet for various purposes. In study groups, workshops, staff meetings, and round tables, the group is used primarily as a vehicle for presenting or exchanging information. In committees, conferences, and boards and councils, by comparison, groups are used to make decisions and to develop products. When groups are used in this way, the assumption typically made is that the group product will be qualitatively superior to anything the individual members could achieve solely by their own efforts.

There is now a good deal of evidence to support this assumption. When functioning with reasonable effectiveness, groups make decisions superior to those of individuals. As Maier points out, a group possesses important assets as a decision-making vehicle. Groups typically (1) have a greater sum total of knowledge and information, (2) employ a great number of approaches to a problem, (3) promote acceptance of decisions through the nature of participation in decision making; and (4) the group members are apt to have a better comprehension of the decision(s).[1] Nonetheless, as we emphasized in Chapter 2 and 7, there are a number of intragroup forces that may function to eliminate these initial advantages that a group possesses.[2]

In their impressive book, Johnson and Johnson conclude that groups

---

[1] N. R. F. Maier, *Problem Solving and Creativity in Individuals and Groups* (Belmont, Calif.: Brooks/Cole, 1970), p. 433.
[2] Ibid., pp. 432–433.

make decisions superior to those of individuals because the presence of other members (social influence) stimulates higher quality work, the resources of members are pooled, the greater number of people in a group increase the chance that a person of superior ability will help to shape the decision, errors made by chance are likely to cancel out, blind spots are frequently discovered by a group, discussion stimulates more ideas, and there is intragroup pressure to make risky decisions when justified.[3]

Groups are not apt to make better decisions and produce higher quality solutions, however, unless the quality of interaction in the group is high. Consider the fact that there is often a disturbing disparity between a group's potential productivity and a group's actual productivity. In fact, we must recognize that[4]

$$\text{Actual Productivity} = \frac{\text{Potential Productivity Minus}}{\text{Losses Due to Faulty Process}}$$

Much of this book has been designed to identify those factors that can disrupt the small-group communication process and to demonstrate the effects of these factors on the process. Although quality of communication is not the only factor that shapes actual productivity, it is typically a major factor; in many instances, it is the factor of overriding importance. Indeed this book has been designed to develop the thesis that *quality of communication in the small group is a major determinant of the quality of group product.* As we shall demonstrate in this chapter, we now have laboratory evidence that shows that the actual productivity of groups drops significantly with a deterioration in the quality of communication.

Many people are concerned almost exclusively with what a group can produce. They express little interest in or concern for the feelings of the group members. Their motto is that strong task pressure forces a group to get the job done. We believe that this is a myopic and restrictive view. It does, however, draw attention to the importance of productivity in our competitive society. No matter how many other desirable attributes a group may have, an unproductive group is not apt to endure.

This chapter focuses attention not only on those things a group can produce, but also on the behaviors geared directly to the development of group products. In particular, we identify those task behaviors and methods of decision making that produce task outcomes, contrast the potential of such methods, define the essential components of task outcomes, and demonstrate how the quality of such outcomes can be measured.

[3] D. W. Johnson and F. P. Johnson, *Joining Together: Group Theory and Group Skills* (Englewood Cliffs, N.J.: Prentice-Hall, 1975), p. 75.

[4] I. D. Steiner, *Group Process and Productivity* (New York: Academic Press, 1972), p. 9. The reader should note that Steiner views process in a much more general way than the authors of this book. For a detailed statement on the relationship between group process and the small-group communication system, see Chapter 2.

Task Behavior in the Small Group

In a broad sense, task behavior consists of anything group members do to achieve their objectives and goals. To reach such goals, the group member must assume many responsibilities. For example, Part 2 of this book (the two chapters on preparing for group interaction) describes and analyzes those task behaviors that are essential for effective decision making. Planning a discussion, securing and processing information, and selecting a suitable organizational format are all essential parts of "the process." As Bales has suggested, task behavior at minimum certainly includes the giving and seeking of information, opinions, and suggestions.[5]

Recently, many students of the small group have become preoccupied with decision making.[6] One might infer that decision making embraces the complete range of task behaviors in the small group. Such is not the case. Consider for the moment that all problem-solving groups make decisions, but not all decision-making groups solve problems. This is a distinction worth exploring because problem solving does require many of the same task behaviors as decision making, but it involves other behaviors as well.

DECISION MAKING AND PROBLEM SOLVING

We believe that decision making and problem solving can be distinguished from each other in at least three ways: (1) by the nature of the task behavior involved, (2) by the scope of the task behavior, and (3) by the stage in the discussion where such task behaviors typically occur.

Often groups meet *only* to decide among carefully prescribed alternatives. No problem-solving behavior as such is involved. The deliberations of an American jury is a good case in point. Before the jury meets behind closed doors, the judge carefully lays out the alternatives that the jurors may consider in their decision making: guilty of first-degree murder, guilty of second-degree murder, guilty of aggravated assault, or not guilty, for example. In such cases, the group must decide among alternatives that are fixed by forces outside the group. *Group members are not free to create their own alternatives.* Decision making "implies a given number of alternatives whereas in problem solving the alternative must be created. Thus

---

[5] R. F. Bales, *Personality and Interpersonal Behavior* (New York: Holt, Rinehart and Winston, 1970), pp. 91–97.

[6] See B. A. Fisher, *Small Group Decision Making: Communication and Group Process* (New York: McGraw-Hill, 1974), and D. Gouran, *Discussion: The Process of Group Decision Making* (New York: Harper and Row, 1974), for this type of orientation.

224   problem solving involves both choice behavior and the finding or creating of alternatives." [7]

Secondly, the scope of decision-making behavior is much broader than that of problem solving. Decision making involves the procedures the group will employ as well as the content of the discussion.[8] It involves the rules for gathering information as well as methods by which it will be evaluated. Although no precise estimate is available, one can safely assume that much more time is devoted to decision making than to problem solving in the small group.

Finally, decision making may, and typically does, occur during all stages of discussion. Problem solving, in contrast, should not begin until the nature and the magnitude of the problem have been carefully and completely defined. In untrained groups members often begin to offer solutions before they have the foggiest idea of the problem they are facing. Indeed one important decision a group may make is that no tangible problem is identifiable. Thus decisions must be made during every stage of discussion whereas solutions should be proposed and evaluated only during the final stages of deliberation. An effective group will make a multitude of decisions before choosing a preferred solution to the problem they are facing. It would be a bizarre group indeed that considered a multitude of solutions before making a single decision.

Since decision making is central to all task-oriented groups, it is apparent that the success of such groups is heavily dependent on the quality of the decision groups make. In many cases, the methods used to make decisions exert a controlling influence over the quality of the decisions.

METHODS OF GROUP DECISION MAKING

There are seven major methods that might be employed: (1) agreement (consensus) of the entire group, (2) majority vote, (3) decision by minority, (4) averaging of individual opinions of group members, (5) decision by the expert member, (6) decision by authority after discussion, and (7) decision by authority without discussion.[9]

The first method is typically the most effective. It makes maximum use of the inherent group assets and intragroup forces that are apt to produce a high-quality decision. This is so in large part because operationally "consensus means that all members can rephrase the decision to show that they understand it, that all members have had a chance to tell how they feel about the decision, and that those members who continue to disagree or

---

[7] Maier, *Problem Solving and Creativity in Individuals and Groups*, p. 445.

[8] Gouran, *Discussion: The Process of Group Decision-Making*, pp. 154–167, identifies both behavioral and procedural guidelines for effective decision making.

[9] Johnson and Johnson, *Joining Together*, p. 59.

have doubts, nevertheless, say publicly that they are willing to give the decision an experimental try for a period of time." [10]

Decision by majority vote is frequently employed. It combines the desirable features of both reasonable effectiveness and efficiency of decision making. Interaction preceding the vote is the critical element. It often takes a good deal of time to get majority support for an issue. Once achieved, however, members are more likely to work honestly and vigorously to implement the decision.

Decision by minority means simply that less than 50 percent of the group members support the decision. Although this method protects the group against the impasse that may result from the requirement of consensus or majority vote, it is not without risks. It provides subgroups with a variety of motivations—honorable, manipulative, obscure, and so on—with the opportunity to move the group to a decision with a minimum of support. Given the tendency of many group members to be reticent and withdrawn, a proposal of marginal utility may be railroaded through the group without the careful scrutiny that it deserves.

The fourth method of decision making requires no face-to-face interaction. The leader consults members individually to determine the preferred alternative among those being considered. The alternative that gets the most votes is the one that the "group" accepts. Although this method is very efficient, it is apt to lead to qualitatively deficient decisions because it does not require group evaluation of alternatives, and, in a five-person group, the chosen alternative might have the support of only two members.[11]

Decision by the expert member is a bit like taxation without representation. As with any decision-making group, members must assume responsibility for the decision(s) reached, but they often have little meaningful input into the decision-making process. It is efficient but can be arbitrary and capricious. If the "expert" is not really an expert or his motivation is less than wholesome, the decision may be irresponsible. This method is used frequently and can be illustrated by considering the actions of a faculty promotion committee.

Prof. I. M. Right is up for promotion. He is a brilliant young assistant professor with an abrasive personality and the unvarying conviction that all his opinions are right. The chairman of the promotion committee despises Right because Right once said that the chairman had a C+ mind and because the chairman knows that Right is, as usual, right about this assessment.

The promotion committee is composed of chairman Albert Pompous from Psychology, Forrest Hill from mortuary science, Robert Einstein from

10 Ibid., p. 60.
11 Ibid., p. 64.

mathematics, Marjorie Mead from anthropology, and Woodrow Hayes from physical education. As the meeting begins, Mead admits that she has not had time to read Right's file and will be forced to rely heavily on her colleagues' opinions. Einstein and Hayes quickly assert that they know nothing about sociology; so they cannot really appraise Right's record. At this point, Pompous moves in and asserts that he is an internationally recognized expert in social psychology; this is also Right's specialty. He notes that personally he has nothing against Right, but that he finds his record mediocre at best and that discussion of it would be a waste of time. Furthermore, he emphasizes that he is sure that his friends on the committee will not argue with him because he is the expert. Relieved that they do not have to put their ignorance on public display, Mead, Einstein, and Hayes quickly agree with Pompous, the self-proclaimed expert. Only Forrest Hill holds out, but he is brought quickly into line by conformity pressure. Right's recommended promotion is voted down unanimously.

The sixth method, decision making by authority, is different from decision making by expert.[12] Although the expert relies on the alleged superiority of his knowledge to control group members, the authority uses his superior power to exert dominant influence on the decision reached. In their extreme forms, both methods use the group as a facade. After all, a "group" decision is more apt to gain public respect and acceptance.

"The final method of decision making . . . is the one where the designated leader makes all the decisions without consulting the group members in any way. This method is quite common in organizations." [13] The group may be used as a rubber stamp but does not really function as a decision-making unit.

In retrospect only methods 1, 2, 3, 5, and 6 are *group* methods of decision making. Furthermore, in some forms, 5 and 6 are marginal because they may not involve face-to-face interaction of all the group members with actual evaluation of the alternatives before the group. At minimum, we believe these conditions must prevail if the decisions reached are to reflect the advantages of information processing and evaluation that group interaction can afford.

The validity of this conclusion is reflected in the finding that methods 1, 2, and 3 can be rank-ordered in terms of effectiveness (quality) and efficiency (time needed to reach decision). In order of the effectiveness of decisions they yield, the methods would be ranked method 1 = 1, method 2 = 2, and method 3 = 3. However, efficiency rankings are reversed because method 3 = 1, method 2 = 2, and method 1 = 3.[14]

To use the various methods of *group* decision making is to recognize that none of them represents a panacea. No single method is apt to work

---

[12] Ibid., pp. 64–65.
[13] Ibid., p. 79.
[14] Ibid., p. 79.

well unless the quality of small-group communication is high. Indeed in this book we emphasize that *group* methods of decision making are apt to be superior to methods of individual decision making *only when the small-group communication system functions effectively.*

We must recognize that the types of interacting groups described in this book often exhibit some or all of the following qualities: unstructured meetings, unfocused thinking, nonspecific conclusions, short problem focus, a task avoidance tendency, person-centered conflict, and "lack of closure" on decision or solutions.[15] When members of a small group cannot or will not work to deal effectively with communicative disruption in their small group, they may be well advised to use methods of decision making that are neither strictly "group" nor "individual" but hybrids. The essential question, however, is not whether interacting groups necessarily produce poor decisions. The essential question is whether the qualities identified previously are the inevitable result of group decision making or the avoidable result of ineffective communicative interaction within the small group.

If you feel that any of these methods of *group* decision making has some serious weakness for your situation, then you may be drawn to two new and intriguing methods of decision making—the nominal group technique (NGT) and the Delphi technique. They are hybrids in that they combine both individual and group decision-making techniques. They share the following features: (1) reliance on independent individual thinking for idea generation, (2) pooling of individual judgments, (3) separation of the idea-generation and evaluation stages, and (4) the use of mathematical voting procedures to reach decisions.[16]

Although both the nominal group technique and the Delphi technique may be profitably employed in a given situation, we believe that NGT may be most useful for the reader of this book. NGT is relatively easy to use. It consists of a carefully prescribed set of six steps: (1) silent generation of ideas in writing, (2) round robin recording of ideas, (3) serial discussion of ideas for clarification, (4) preliminary vote on item significance, (5) discussion of preliminary vote on item significance, and (6) final vote.[17] Secondly, NGT is, at least in part, a *group* technique of decision making.

NGT has now been rather carefully researched. The developers of NGT claim that the technique consistently produces desirable results. They emphasize that three measures have typically been used to compare the effectiveness of nominal and interacting groups: (1) the average number of unique ideas, (2) the average total number of ideas, and (3) the quality

[15] A. L. Delbecq, A. H. Van de Ven, and D. H. Gustafson, *Group Techniques for Program Planning: A Guide to Nominal Group and Delphi Processes* (Glenview, Ill.: Scott Foresman, 1975), p. 32.
[16] Ibid., p. 17.
[17] Ibid., pp. 44–67.

228 of ideas produced.[18] They conclude that in "terms of these three measure of performance, nominal groups have been found to be significantly superior to interacting groups in generating information relevant to a problem."[19]

METHODS OF CONFLICT MANAGEMENT

The discussion to this point assumes that the group is not operating in the type of conflict climate described in Chapter 2. When the group is locked in either task or interpersonal conflict, a number of different methods may be employed so that the group can actually reach a decision. Filley maintains that three major methods of conflict management may be used in the small group: (1) win-lose methods, (2) lose-lose methods, and (3) win-win methods.[20]

Win-lose methods are geared to the assumption that every group decision results in some winners and some losers. If you recall interacting in a group experiencing a lot of conflict, you know that this frequently happens. There are at least six types of win-lose methods. Someone may induce your compliance with a given decision because of the individual's favorable position in the group or simply coerce your acceptance of a decision by exerting mental or physical power. If these methods do not work, a subgroup may exercise minority rule by manipulating an authority figure in the group to force a decision through by virtue of sheer persistence and volume of vocal output. Finally, two commonly used win-lose methods are very similar. Those who voice a dissident opinion are either simply ignored or silenced by the use of majority rule.[21]

Some of the win-lose methods are more irritating than others. All, with the possible exception of majority rule, are apt to damage interpersonal relationships and lead to unsatisfactory outcomes. Our society is geared to reward winners, and those forced to bear the label of losers in the intimate atmosphere of the small group are not apt to do so without resentment or thoughts of retaliation.

The lose-lose methods of conflict management obviate the painful polarity between winners and losers because everyone loses to one degree or another. Lose-lose "methods are so named because neither side really accomplishes what it wants or, alternately, each side only gets part of what it wants. Lose-lose methods are based on the assumption that half a loaf

[18] Ibid., p. 16.
[19] Ibid.
[20] A. C. Filley, *Interpersonal Conflict Resolution* (Glencoe, Ill.: Scott Foresman, 1975), pp. 22–26. Conflict may focus on either task or interpersonal behavior within the small group. Because a great part of research on conflict has concentrated on task-oriented groups that are trying to make decisions, we chose to treat the subject in this chapter.
[21] Ibid., p. 22.

is better than none, and avoidance of conflict is preferable to personal confrontation on an issue."[22]

The four most commonly used lose-lose methods of conflict management are compromise, bribery, submitting an issue to a neutral third party, and the use of rules to regulate or eliminate conflict.[23] Compromise is, of course, often employed and is sometimes effective. If group members are not vigilant, however, the decisions that result from compromise are apt to be mediocre at best and capricious at worst.

Bribery may seem like an unreal and improbable method of conflict management, but it is frequently employed. It need not take the form of monetary bribery; psychological and even physical bribery may be even more effective. One of us vividly recalls the following interaction in a laboratory group that was locked in conflict. A male discussant asserted unequivocally that busts for the use of marijuana are absolutely necessary and should be continued. This comment was followed in just a couple of minutes by the remark of an extremely seductive girl sitting next to him. Smiling at him in a most familiar manner and placing her hand on his arm, she said, "I really think that we should legalize the use of marijuana. Don't you?" Without hesitating, the male discussant replied, "I definitely agree with you."

Submitting an issue to arbitration can be effective, but it means that the group has lost direct control over the decisions that result from such arbitration.

Finally, group members may choose to deal with conflict by relying on a set of rules that are externally imposed on the group; *Robert's Rules of Order* is a good example. Although such rules give a discussion an undeniable sense of direction and efficiency, they often serve to block the honest and spontaneous exchange of opinions that can make group decision qualitatively superior.

Win-win methods as the label implies are those methods of conflict management that result in decisions that are *not unacceptable to anyone in the group*. The two major win-win methods are consensus and integrative decision making.[24] Although it is difficult to produce decisions that are relatively acceptable to everyone in the group, there are compelling reasons for making the effort. We would suggest that such decisions are most likely to result when the interpersonal, task, and communicative behaviors in the group meet or come close to meeting the guidelines suggested in this book.

---

[22] Ibid., p. 23.

[23] Ibid., pp. 23–24.

[24] Ibid., pp. 26–27. Filley maintains that integrative decision making involves six steps: (1) review and adjustment of relational conditions, (2) review and adjustment of perceptions, (3) review and adjustment of attitudes, (4) problem definition, (5) search for solutions, and (6) consensus decision.

Measuring Task Outcomes

As we have suggested throughout this book, the evaluation of discussion is important in a number of ways. The discussion student should learn to judge group and individual performance, assessing achievement on the criteria of excellence. Awareness of the requirements for high-quality performance should help the learner improve his or her own participation. In nontraining or real groups, participants often wish to estimate the effectiveness of the group. Although they may not be accustomed to the use of rating scales or other paraphernalia of evaluation, they certainly should be capable of making judgments about the group's performance efficiency and production. They may, for instance, ask and answer such questions as, "How efficiently did this group use the time available, compared with other discussion groups of this kind?" Evaluation is important also in helping to explain effects; if a group fails to reach agreement, the explanation must be found in examination of earlier components, such as the following: Did intragroup forces function to create a conflict climate? Were interpersonal behaviors such that they resulted in the destruction of trust? Was the method of decision making inappropriate in that it polarized feelings and thinking in the group?

The most important evaluation of all is to decide the worth of the product or task outcome. In practice, the content and type of task outcomes vary dramatically. Committees may prepare a set of proposals that are simply passed on to others with superior power in the form of recommendations, or the committee may be empowered to implement a plan it develops. Conferences may produce anything from a vague and general statement of principles to a refined document that is legally binding for the parties, companies, or nations represented at the conference(s). Boards and councils may make clear-cut decisions on matters such as the retention, dismissal, or promotion of employees; or they may propose an elaborate solution to a problem of mutual concern to all the members.

Task outcomes, therefore, consist of the products of task-oriented groups and are the result of task behaviors that were undertaken to meet a set of goals or objectives. In contrast to interpersonal outcomes, the "goodness" of task outcomes is usually determined by factors that are external to the group (for example, will the solution really be effective in solving the problem, or is this a feasible undertaking?). The "goodness" or quality of interpersonal outcomes is based on the degree to which members found the group experience to be satisfying or unsatisfying.

Although group outcomes often differ markedly in substance and type, they share similar defining properties. Maier maintains that any group task outcome may be defined by the *quality* of the outcome and the degree of *acceptance* of the outcome by members of the group. Thus the "multiplication sign is used to indicate that if either the quality or acceptance dimension is zero, the decision is zero in effectiveness. Furthermore, if either is negative, the effectiveness will be negative but if both are negative, the effectiveness will be positive. Thus a solution that has negative quality (in that it is rejected) will have positive effectiveness, in that it will not be implemented." [25]

In addition to the vitally important dimensions of quality and acceptance, we maintain that a *group outcome* may be defined by the extent to which the (task) outcome was based on the *substance of the entire discussion* and the *extent of member satisfaction-commitment.*[26]

The task outcome may be evaluated at the close of discussion in groups that produce a well-defined solution at the end of deliberations. To concentrate evaluation exclusively on the final product is restrictive, however, in that groups make many decisions during different stages of group interaction. Such decisions may, in fact, be task outcomes that require evaluation.

Hence two types of evaluation are needed in the immediate discussion-training situation. First, during the discussion, there should be some kind of running record kept that indicates how performance is related to group productivity. Related running records should be supplied in connection with evaluating the group and the participants. Secondly, at the end of the discussion, there should be an estimate of outcome quality and member commitment-satisfaction.

These evaluations can perhaps best be made by observers who take no active part in the discussion. Our recent experience suggests the group members learn much by evaluating their own product, however. Each of the groups formed in our classes is required to do a one-hour analysis of their group at the end of the quarter. This oral analysis, which is presented to the class, has a two-part focus: (1) detailed evaluation of the quality of communicative interaction in the group with an attempt to determine

[25] Maier, *Problem Solving in Individuals and Groups*, p. 277. We recognize that the suitability of task behaviors and, ultimately, the quality of task outcomes may be heavily dependent on the nature of the task that a group undertakes. M. E. Shaw, *Group Dynamics: The Psychology of Small Group Behavior* (New York: McGraw-Hill, 1971), pp. 310–312, maintains that six independent dimensions may be used to describe the nature of a given group task: (1) difficulty, (2) solution multiplicity, (3) intrinsic interest, (4) cooperation requirements, (5) intellectual-manipulative requirements, and (6) population familiarity.

[26] We maintain that two types of satisfaction may be measured in the small group: satisfaction with interpersonal outcomes as described in the last chapter and satisfaction with task outcomes. B. Harris and J. H. Harvey, "Self-Attributed Choice as a Function of the Consequence of a Decision," *Journal of Personality and Social Psychology* 31 (1974): 1015–1019, found that satisfaction with fellow group members tends to drop in a group that produces inferior products.

what factors shaped the quality of this interaction and (2) detailed evaluation of the quality of product with in-depth discussion of the possible relationships between quality of communication and product.

This assignment has proved to be a very effective learning device. Although group members undertake evaluation of the process and product of their own group, such evaluation is not confined to the members themselves. In many cases, those actively involved cannot judge as objectively as can detached observers. Consequently, group members frequently use outside observers to evaluate their communication and product.

RUNNING RECORD OF PRODUCTIVE EFFICIENCY

During the discussion, observers might seek answers to questions such as these:

1. What proportion of the group's time was spent on matters unrelated to the problem for discussion?
2. To what extent were some members responsible for taking the group off on tangents?
3. To what extent did members help the leader keep the discussion on the track?
4. How adequately did the group analyze the problem?
5. How many different alternative solutions to the problem were proposed?
6. Which members were responsible for the alternatives proposed?
7. How thoroughly was each alternative solution discussed?
8. How much time was spent discussing each alternative?
9. Which members contributed most to discussion of each alternative?

Some of these questions can only be answered subjectively, and the evaluators may wish to take notes related to the questions while the discussion is in progress or while listening to tape recordings of group meetings. Others can be answered more objectively by tabulating proposals and responses on a chart designed especially for this purpose. One possibility for recording answers to some of these questions is the chart suggested in Figure 10.1. The student should practice designing his own running record chart for various purposes.

EVALUATION OF OUTCOME

At the end of the discussion, there should be a judgment of the group product, involving answers to such questions as these:

1. How good is the decision reached?
2. To what extent does the final decision represent the substance of the entire discussion?

FIGURE 10.1
RUNNING RECORD OF EFFICIENCY OF GROUP PRODUCTIVITY

	Number of Times Each Participant:				
Participants	Introduced topic unrelated to discussion	Helped leader keep on track	Proposed new solution to problem	Made contribution relevant to Proposal A	Made contribution relevant to Proposal B
Jim	I	I	I	IIII I	III
Fred	III			II	
Mary		II	I	IIII	I
Bert	I		I	IIII II	II
Ann		I	III	IIII	I

3. To what extent are members agreed on the decision?
4. To what extent are members satisfied with the decision?
5. To what extent are members committed to put the decision into effect?
6. To what extent are members committed to defend the decision in later talks with others?

It is obvious that an observer cannot answer all these questions with any certainty. It would be more satisfactory to ask the members whether they agree and to what extent they feel satisfied and committed, wherever this is possible. Where it is impossible, as it is in most situations other than training sessions, the evaluator must make the best estimate he can, based on his observation of member reactions. An example of rating scales for this purpose is presented in Figure 10.2.

QUALITY OF TASK OUTCOMES

Although it is important to evaluate the task outcome(s) on all of the dimensions cited in Figure 10.2, we believe that quality of product deserves particular attention. Frequently, the quality of a group's product is the primary criterion used to judge a group's success or failure. Because this is so, we should strive to use the most suitable and sensitive methods for measuring the quality of group product.

In fact, measures of the quality of group product abound, but rarely do they focus directly on the quality of ideas that comprise a group's task outcome. Many group productivity measures are deficient, not because they do not measure the group's product, but because groups are assigned

FIGURE 10.2
RATING SCALE FOR EVALUATING GROUP DECISION

QUALITY OF DECISION REACHED

5	4	3	2	1
Superior	Above Average	Average	Below Average	Poor

EXTENT TO WHICH DECISION WAS BASED ON SUBSTANCE OF ENTIRE DISCUSSION

5	4	3	2	1
Decision reflected substance to superior extent	Decision reflected substance to above average extent	Decision reflected substance to average extent	Decision only partially reflected substance	No relation between substance and decision

EXTENT OF MEMBER AGREEMENT

5	4	3	2	1
Apparently unanimous agreement	Some disagreement, but near consensus	Group divided, with majority for decision	Majority disagreed	Almost all disagreed

EXTENT OF MEMBER SATISFACTION-COMMITMENT

5	4	3	2	1
Almost all highly satisfied	Most members satisfied	More than half satisfied enough to support decision	Fewer than half satisfied enough to support decision	Almost no one committed to carry out decision

Directions: Check continuum at point representing your judgment.

to such trivial and insignificant tasks that the productivity measures are necessarily superficial and unenlightening.

In the laboratory, for example, groups have been assigned to such questionably significant tasks as discriminating between the angles of a series of lines, distinguishing between colored lights on a panel, differentiating between different signal light positions, functioning with members playing assumed roles, and communicating written messages through slots in a partition.[27]

[27] D. G. Leathers, "Quality of Group Communication as a Determinant of Group Product," *Speech Monographs* 39 (1972): 169.

For the types of decision-making groups discussed in this chapter, we believe that realistic measures of group productivity should focus on the ideational quality of the group's product. Surprisingly, Leathers's review of existing productivity measures found that none met the basic criteria set out.[28]

The Productivity Rating Instrument was developed as a response to an obvious need for such a measure. As illustrated in Figure 10.3, the PRI is

FIGURE 10.3
PRODUCTIVITY RATING INSTRUMENT

	+						−
	Effective			Effectiveness			Ineffective
Scale 1	3	2	1	0	1	2	3

Effectiveness = degree to which the ideas, which are part of the major decision or solution, help the group achieve the objective of developing a realistic solution.

	Feasible			Feasibility			Unfeasible
Scale 2	3	2	1	0	1	2	3

Feasibility = degree to which the major decision or solution reflects a picture of social reality that is consistent with relevant public attitudes.

	Creative			Creativity			Uncreative
Scale 3	3	2	1	0	1	2	3

Creativity = degree to which the major decision or solution reflects markedly original ideas not previously applied to the problem under discussion.

	Significant			Significance			Insignificant
Scale 4	3	2	1	0	1	2	3

Significance = degree to which the major decision or solution is based on relevant and significant information as opposed to nonrelevant and insignificant information.

	Comprehensive			Comprehensiveness			Noncomprehensive
Scale 5	3	2	1	0	1	2	3

Comprehensive = degree to which the group's major decision or solution reflects a response to all the dimensions of the problem under consideration.

Reprinted from Dale G. Leathers, "Quality of Group Communication as a Determinant of Group Product," *Speech Monographs* 39 (1972): 171.

[28] Ibid., p. 170.

very easy to use. A group member or outside observer simply studies the definitions of terms for each scale and then gives the group product a rating on each scale.

The use of the PRI can be illustrated by brief description of an experiment that is particularly relevant for this chapter. Leathers had long suspected, on the basis of observing many laboratory and classroom groups, that there was a direct relationship between the quality of communication in the small group and the quality of task outcome that resulted.

To test for this relationship, eighteen laboratory groups were formed; these groups were composed of undergraduates at UCLA. Each group was asked to discuss the following question: What, if anything, should be done about the greatly expanded use of drugs by college students? Unknown to the members of the groups, two "plants" were placed in each group. Six groups were selected as "communication disruption" groups; six, as "natural communication" groups; and six, as "communication facilitation" groups.

In the disruption groups, the "plants" engaged in a number of the communication behaviors described in Chapter 7. In this instance, the plants' behavior was designed to disrupt communicative interaction. For example, the plants introduced high-level abstractions (Well, J. Edgar Hoover took a strong stand against drugs, but don't you think he suffered from bureaucratic idiopathy?), irrelevant statements (My Uncle Harry is a pharmacist), and facetious comments (I use pot as an aphrodisiac—smoked pot this morning and seduced three guys on my way to school).[29]

In the natural communication groups, members were allowed to interact naturally with the expectation that the communication would be of average quality. In contrast, in the facilitated group, the plants did some of the following things to raise the quality of communication: (1) suggested that one discussant assume the procedural role of keeping a record of the ideas on which the group had reached consensus in order to avoid repetition and duplication of effort; (2) suggested that the group follow a set organizational format; (3) suggested that the group use brainstorming techniques in examining the drug problem in order to circumvent the inhibiting effects of premature, negative reinforcement; (4) encouraged discussants to provide a brief summary of particularly long and unwieldy contributions; (5) positively reinforced discussants who expressed themselves clearly, concisely, and relevantly; and (6) attempted to maintain thought continuity by encouraging discussants to establish the relationships between their contributions and the contribution that immediately preceded theirs.

As Figure 10.4 indicates, the quality of communication in the facilitated groups was, in fact, rated "high" whereas the quality in the natural groups was rated "average" and that in the disrupted groups was rated "low."

[29] Ibid., p. 167.

Trained judges were asked to measure the quality of task outcomes **237** (recommended solutions in this case) in the three different types of groups. Again Figure 10.4 demonstrates that there was a *direct positive relationship between the quality of communication and quality of the group product.*

In fact, the quality of the product in the groups experiencing high-quality communication was significantly higher on every scale of the PRI

FIGURE 10.4

TABLE I
MEAN RATINGS OF FEEDBACK RESPONSE IN GROUPS EXPOSED
TO THREE TYPES OF COMMUNICATION: FACILITATED, NATURAL, AND DISRUPTED

Feedback Dimension (Scale)	Quality of Communication			Mean Differences in Ratings*	
	High (Facilitated)	Medium (Natural)	Low (Disrupted)		
1. Deliberateness	4.70	3.68	3.39	√H–M(1.02)*	M–L(.29)
2. Relevancy	4.55	3.20	2.78	√H–M(1.35)*	M–L(.42)
3. Atomization	4.13	3.72	3.67	H–M(.41)	M–L(.05)
4. Fidelity	5.66	4.42	3.95	√H–M(1.24)*	M–L(.47)
5. Tension	4.73	4.67	2.76	√H–L(.06)	M–L(1.81)*
6. Ideation	5.15	4.55	3.85	√H–L(.60)	M–L(.70)*
7. Flexibility	4.18	3.52	3.30	√H–L(.66)*	M–L(.22)
8. Digression	3.92	3.76	4.08	H–L(.16)	M–L(.43)
9. Involvement	4.53	4.02	3.59	√H–L(.51)	M–L(.43)

* All differences between levels in quality of communication significant at .05 level. √ identifies a significant difference in quality of communication between groups exposed to facilitated and disrupted communication.

TABLE II
MEAN RATINGS OF QUALITY OF DECISION IN GROUPS EXPOSED
TO THREE TYPES OF COMMUNICATION: FACILITATED, NATURAL, AND DISRUPTED

Decision Dimension (Scale)	Quality of Decision			Mean Differences in Ratings*	
	High (Facilitated)	Medium (Natural)	Low (Disrupted)		
1. Effectiveness	6.14	3.21	1.79	√H–M(2.92)*	M–L(1.42)*
2. Feasibility	6.18	4.32	2.79	√H–M(1.86)*	M–L(1.53)*
3. Creativity	4.82	3.36	2.54	√H–M(1.46)*	M–L(.82)
4. Significance	6.10	3.75	2.46	√H–M(2.35)*	M–L(1.29)*
5. Comprehensiveness	5.60	3.86	1.89	√H–M(1.74)*	M–L(1.97)*

* All differences between levels in quality of decision (high, medium, and low), significant at .05 level. √ identifies a significant difference in quality of decision between groups exposed to facilitated and disrupted communication. The results in the two tables above are very easy to read if you use the following conversion system: $7 = +3$; $6 = +2$; $5 = +1$; $4 = 0$; $3 = -1$; $2 = -2$; $1 = -3$.

than in the groups experiencing low-quality communication. Thus, in the groups where quality of communication was high, the recommended solutions to the drug problem reflected superior effectiveness (scale 1), feasibility (scale 2), creativity (scale 3), significance (scale 4), and comprehensiveness (scale 5).

When the laboratory groups concluded their discussion, members were asked to provide a written description of the solution(s) their group had produced. The statements that follow are representative samples from the written statements that were turned in to the experimenter. If the group with high-quality communication really developed qualitatively superior products, you should be able to identify the groups that produced the following solutions. Simply indicate whether you believe the solution statements came from (1) high-quality communication groups, (2) average-quality communication groups, or (3) low-quality communication groups.

To aid you in measuring the quality of the solutions, please apply the five scales of the PRI to each of the solution statements. Which statement received the best rating? Which groups received the worst ratings?

Solution Statement 1

Education—Educate people
        Little kids
        Parents
        College students

Legalize—Have people register for controlled use of drugs
        Use British control of heroin

Solution Statement 2

The solutions we have suggested to solve these problems are (1) family love and caring for our fellow man, (2) education about different types of drugs, (3) lifting penalty for marijuana usage, (4) rehabilitation program for heroin and morphine users, (5) ex-users to go on lecture tour, (6) restrictions on pharmaceutical companies, (7) rid society of the casual attitude toward drugs, (8) try to bring different factions together to discuss remedies.

Solution Statement 3

The only real solution seems to be through education. "Propaganda" films and pamphlets in schools aren't going to do it. Give the people the truth about these drugs. Don't give lies that they know are not true. Then they will not believe any truths you give.

Solution Statement 4

To deal with the various facets of the drug problem we recommend: (1) supplying addicts with free rehabilitative drugs as in England; (2) change law to make marijuana a misdemeanor; (3) do additional research on marijuana on its long-term effects, if any; (4) mount a program to inform the public, which includes trips to institutions to observe and interact with suffering people; (5) take the profit factor out of the surreptitious sale and distribution of drugs with new laws; (6) medical research on rehabilitative drugs such as methedone; (7) create a "consumer's bureau" that provides detailed information about drugs and their effects; (8) use the media to publicize the problem and solicit volunteer help.[30]

Solutions 2 and 4 were produced by the groups that experienced high-quality communication whereas 1 and 3 came from groups where the rated quality of communication was low. After applying the PRI to each solution statement, we would rank-order the solution statements from best to worst in the following way: 4, 2, 1, and 3. You will probably agree at this point that solution statement 4 is more effective, feasible, creative, and comprehensive than 3 or the other two solution statements for that matter. (Scale 4 of the PRI is difficult to consider here because you do not have a full transcript of the discussions that produced the solution statements.)

When a group produces a product of inferior quality, the responsible group shoud ask why. We believe that many of the answers can be found by going back and analyzing the nature of the communicative interaction that led to that product. One of the main purposes of this book is to provide the reader with the knowledge and potential to increase materially the quality of communication in the groups in which they interact. We believe that group members who make diligent use of the communication concepts and techniques presented in this book will have a better chance of developing a qualitatively superior group product. To many members of decision-making groups, that is the ultimate reason for the use of a group.

SUPPLEMENTARY READING

Bishop, G. D., and Myers, D. G. "Informational Influence in Group Discussion." *Organizational Behavior and Human Performance* 12 (1974): 92–104.

Cohen, S. L., and Ruis, C. B. "Wary Shift or Risky Shift?" *Bulletin of the Psychonomic Society* 3 (1974): 214–216.

Cooper, M. R., and Ward, M. T. "Effects of Member Participation and Commitment in Group Decision Making on Influence, Satisfaction, and Decision Riskiness." *Journal of Applied Psychology* 59 (1974): 127–134.

Farris, D. R., and Sage, A. P. "Introduction and Survey of Group Decision Making with Applications to Worth Assessment." *I.E.E.E. Transactions on Systems, Man, and Cybernetics* 5 (1975): 346–358.

Harari, O., and Graham, W. K. "Tasks and Task Consequences as Factors in Individual and Group Brainstorming." *The Journal of Social Psychology* 95 (1975): 61–65.

Leathers, D. G. "Quality of Group Communication as a Determinant of Group Product." *Speech Monographs* 39 (1972): 166–173.

Shaw, M. E. *Group Dynamics: The Psychology of Small Group Behavior.* New York: McGraw-Hill, 1971. Chapter 9.

---

[30] Ibid. The solution statements reproduced here represent a part of this experiment not described in the cited article.

QUESTIONS AND EXERCISES

1. We indicate that Actual Productivity = Potential Productivity Minus Losses Due to Faulty Process. What does this mean? Can you identify examples of "faulty process" in your own group?
2. Identify the method(s) of group decision making that your group used. Which methods were most effective? Why? How did the method of decision making used affect the quality of the group's product(s)?
3. Identify the distinctive features of the nominal group technique. As a group, discuss the advantages and disadvantages of NGT. Would you use this method if your group were to start over? Why? Why not?
4. As a group, discuss the possible uses of the Productivity Rating Instrument. Indicate what scales you would add, delete, and/or modify to make it a better instrument. Defend your changes, and make a thirty-minute presentation on this subject to the class.
5. Choose a decision-making group in your community, and observe it for at least six weeks (it is easier to get permission to observe groups such as school boards, church and city councils, and the parks and recreation committee although decision-making groups in private corporations will often give permission to observe if confidentiality is assured). Identify the methods of group decision making used and the results produced. What steps should the group you observed take to improve decision making effectiveness? Offer your recommendations to the groups you have observed, and present an analysis of the group in class.

Part 5
LEADERSHIP

11 The Nature of Small-Group Leadership

Leadership behavior has fascinated students of the small group for decades. This fascination has grown as the small group has assumed increasing importance in our personal and professional lives. The national demand for leadership workshops and seminars continues to exceed the supply.

At the conceptual level, leadership is indeed a fascinating subject. At the applied level, our fascination frequently gives way to frustration. Such frustration may have many causes. However, it often begins with the agonizing realization that we know neither what behaviors will facilitate our emergence as leaders nor what behaviors are apt to assure us a continuing role as a leader of our group.

There is no foolproof method for attaining and retaining a leadership role in the small group. We are more apt to be successful if we operate from a realistic perspective, however. In the past, leadership research has concentrated on the personal qualities of the aspiring leader rather than on his behavior. At present, the "approach to quantifying leadership-as-person has given way to describing the functional roles that leaders perform. . . . The question previously asked was 'What are leaders personally like?' while the functional orientation has asked 'What is it that leaders do?' "[1]

We apply the functional perspective to our analysis of leadership behav-

---

[1] B. Schneider, "Relationships Between Various Critera of Leadership in Small Groups," *Journal of Social Psychology* 82 (1970): 253.

ior in this chapter and the next. This chapter identifies and illustrates those functions that are essential for effective leadership in the small group. Particular emphasis is given to the impact of leadership style on leadership functions.

Although this chapter concentrates on the most important functions of leadership, the next chapter identifies those leadership communication behaviors that are most suitable for performing the designated leadership functions. Because we believe that leadership communication behavior is a major determinant of the quality of group outcomes, it is important that such communication be of the highest possible quality.

Leadership, in general, means influencing others within a particular situation and social context in a way that induces them to interact, to be modified, to comply, to be directed, to move toward goal achievement. The person who influences may do so intentionally or without deliberate intent; and, if deliberately, his leadership attempt may be *direct,* open, obvious to all or *indirect,* subtle, suggestive, at least partially hidden. Persons influenced may be aware or unaware of the leadership source that induced them to change.

There is a prodigious amount of literature on leadership in general, and the student has doubtlessly been exposed to some of it in other contexts. Much of it has little direct bearing on the problems of leadership in discussion, and we can give it little attention here.

An important controversy has surrounded the question, Are there leaders and nonleaders, or is leadership situationally determined? Much energy has been expended in efforts to identify the traits of the leader. Is he physically stronger and larger, more intelligent, dominant, aggressive? Does he have certain personality characteristics? Research along these lines has not been overly fruitful, and there is now fairly general agreement that there are no persons who are natural, born leaders in every situation and others who are naturally followers. Rather, an individual seems to exercise leadership when his specific personal abilities, knowledge of a problem, and other qualifications interact fortuitously with a particular situation and with other persons who are predisposed to accept his influence on this problem, in this situation, at this moment. Perhaps this statement is too cautious, but it seems clear that almost every person may be a leader in some situations and a follower in others. When the situation changes, the leadership may also shift.

Studies of leadership have ranged over a wide assortment of situations and tasks, and probably, in part for this reason, many of the traits exhibited by leaders in one study have not shown up in others. Nevertheless, there probably are some generalized traits that tend to characterize those who provide leadership in social groups. In a thorough survey of the available studies, Stogdill found six factors associated with leadership in various situations:

1. *Capacity* (Intelligence, alertness, verbal facility, originality, judgment).
2. *Achievement* (scholarship, knowledge, athletic accomplishments).
3. *Responsibility* (dependability, initiative, persistence, aggressiveness, self-confidence, desire to excel).
4. *Participation* (activity, sociability, cooperation, adaptability, humor).
5. *Status* (socioeconomic position, popularity).
6. *Situation* (mental level, status, skills, needs and interests of followers, objectives to be achieved, etc.).[2]

Those who exercise leadership influence, Stogdill concludes, are those who have appropriate characteristics, including traits of personality, and who are in a situation where such influence is acceptable to the group: "Assuming potentiality for leadership, an individual's upward mobility would seem to depend to a considerable degree upon his being at the right place at the right time."[3] What the members consider acceptable is, in part, culturally determined and is also a function of the assigned task, the characteristics of the group members, and so on.

Hollander and Julian have reviewed the changing emphases in the study of leadership, moving toward recognizing the complex interactions of leader, followers, and situation. They call attention to four factors that have made the study of leadership a formidable problem. One has been the confusion between leader as person and leadership as process: "Leadership constitutes an influence relationship between two, or usually more, persons who depend upon one another for the attainment of certain mutual goals within a group situation." Another is that the relationship of leader and followers changes and builds over time "and involves an exchange or *transaction* . . ." A third is that a leader fulfills differential functions: initiator of structure, mediator, spokesman for the group to outsiders, decision maker, setter of goals and priorities, and so on. The leader's qualities that are effective are determined by the perceptions, expectancies, and satisfactions of the *followers*. A fourth complexity is to determine leader effectiveness in terms of the group's achievements. In the words of Hollander and Julian, "an approach to the study of leader effectiveness as a feature of the group's success, in system terms, offers a clear alternative to the older concern with what the leader did do or did not do."[4]

Our problem here is to examine leadership in small-group decision making and especially the interaction of leadership and communication. As Gouran suggests, leadership in this context "might be conceived as *those acts of communication (verbal and nonverbal) that facilitate the achieve-*

---

[2] Ralph M. Stogdill, *Handbook of Leadership: A Survey of Theory and Research* (New York: The Free Press, 1974), p. 63.

[3] Ibid., p. 82.

[4] Edwin P. Hollander and James W. Julian, "Contemporary Trends in the Analysis of Leadership Processes," in *Groups and Organizations,* ed. by Bernard L. Hinton and H. Reitz (Belmont, Calif.: Wadsworth, 1971), pp. 164–165.

246   *ment of group goals.*"[5] We are thus concerned, not with a single, designated leader, but with those persons who contribute influence affecting
group goal achievement. We must ask what the characteristics are of those
who make such contributions, what functions they are performing, and
what approaches or styles seem effective. The large number of variables
all interacting simultaneously will add to our caution in trying to explain
leadership influences.

In spite of the need for caution, we must say what we can about the
nature of leadership in the discussion situation specifically. Norman Maier
has underlined the great importance of leadership to decision-making
groups. He observed conformity pressures based on fear of disapproval
from the leader or boss and fear of disagreement with other participants.
From studying many discussion groups, he concluded that "disagreement
can lead either to hard feelings or to innovation, depending on the discussion leadership." He has also demonstrated that training for the leader
resulted in increased group satisfaction and a larger percentage of creative
solutions reached.[6]

The Assignment of Leadership

In discussion, it is wise to speak of leadership rather than the leader, so
as not to suggest that one person is always to direct whereas others are to
be pliable, yielding, and inert in terms of influencing the outcome of a
discussion. Leadership may shift during a discussion for various reasons,
and the responsibility for achieving results should be shared by the group
as a *whole*. Leadership should not be the exclusive possession of one member. At the same time, it is proper to speak of the designated leader. He
is a person who is assigned the primary responsibility for guiding the discussion. Most discussion groups have a designated leader: the chairman of
the board or committee, the mayor, the chief officer of a staff or department, the professional moderator of a public discussion, the appointed arbitrator of a labor-management negotiating conference. He may be designated as leader by the group members themselves, as when a chairman is
elected, or may preside because of his position, as when the mayor chairs
city council meetings. When the word *leader* is used alone in this book,
it usually refers to the person who is performing leadership functions at
the moment or to the designated leader.

The fact remains that leadership in a particular situation may or may
not be supplied by the designated leader. He is responsible for exercising

[5] Dennis S. Gouran, "Perspectives on the Study of Leadership: Its Present and Its Future," *Quarterly Journal of Speech* 60 (October 1974): 378.

[6] Norman R. F. Maier, *Problem-Solving Discussions and Conferences* (New York: McGraw-Hill, 1963), pp. 36–46 and pp. 244–246.

leadership, and, as long as he does so wisely and efficiently, his will probably be the strongest leadership influence. But leadership is not an all-or-nothing matter. Others will at times contribute to the total influence being exerted to guide the group. If the designated leader fails to function, others should and almost always do take over to supply the necessary influence. A group is in serious difficulty only when the designated leader fails and others also fail to apply the needed guidance. In other words, a group may perform productively and be temporarily without a specific person as leader, but it will flounder if it is even temporarily without leadership.

We must be specific in our labels. We can speak of the leader when referring to a designated leader or to one who is carrying leadership responsibility at the moment. We can refer to a leaderless discussion as one without a designated leader where leadership is shifting from person to person as one or another becomes central in influencing direction, decision, and so on or where the leadership functions have been divided up and assigned in advance to various members. Thus a leaderless discussion may be enjoying excellent leadership, but there is no single designated leader or appointed chairman. A leadershipless discussion, in contrast, is one in which no leadership is being exercised. Such a group is directionless and will almost certainly be low in task productivity and member satisfaction.

"Without leadership," as Gibb says, "there is no focus about which a number of individuals may cluster to form a group." At the same time, he suggests an important distinction between leadership and "domination or mere headship." In some situations the boss or authority figure can require acquiescence and regulate group activity and decision making simply by virtue of his or her role. Leadership, on the other hand, cannot be assigned as a right of proprietorship. It varies with the situation, with follower acceptance, with information possessed that propels a group toward a decision, and with other factors. A leader is not exercising leadership until he or she has followers in the specific situation of a moment.[7]

Leadership Functions

The *functions* approach to a study of small-group leadership asks what leadership does to influence group locomotion and goal achievement. Homans, in *The Human Group*, considers behavior in social situations more general than group discussion, but he is including discussion as one kind

[7] Cecil A. Gibb, "The Principles and Traits of Leadership," in *Small Groups: Studies in Social Interaction,* ed. by A. Paul Hare, E. F. Borgatta, and R. F. Bales, rev. ed. (New York: Alfred A. Knopf, 1965), pp. 87–95.

of activity engaged in by groups. "The job of the leader," he says, "is two-fold: (a) to attain the purposes of the group, and (b) in so doing to maintain a balance of incentives, both reward and punishment, sufficient to induce his followers to obey him." He refers to the necessity of maintaining the social system, not in a static state, but in a steadily changing state that retains this balance, a kind of "moving equilibrium." Students of discussion may not want to agree that the leader should induce his followers to "obey him," because discussion usually involves greater permissiveness than the concept of obedience suggests. Nevertheless, the basic duties visualized give insight into the essence of the leadership assignment.[8]

The leadership role as observed in many different group situations has been described in an extensive study by Hemphill. Leaders were found to perform five functions common to all the groups. They

1. Advanced the group's purposes.
2. Administered.
3. Inspired greater activity or set the pace.
4. Made members feel secure within the group.
5. Acted without regard to their own self-interest.[9]

Both Homans and Hemphill are concerned with social situations in general.

Stogdill, too, in his review of the leadership research, identified six functions associated with leadership by behavioral theorists:

1. Defining objectives and maintaining goal directions.
2. Providing means for goal attainment.
3. Providing and maintaining group structure.
4. Facilitating group action and interaction.
5. Maintaining group cohesiveness and member satisfaction.
6. Facilitating group task performance.[10]

A number of research studies have found two general kinds of leadership contributions: initiating structure and showing consideration for the persons involved. Bales has gone further by pointing to two kinds of specialized leaders within an interacting group: (1) a task-specialist, who is top person in giving ideas, making suggestions, and offering opinions; and (2) a social-emotional specialist, who is best liked, who promotes solidarity, and contributes to tension release.[11]

It must be emphasized that these two activities of dealing with the task

---

[8] George Homans, *The Human Group* (New York: Harcourt Brace Jovanovich, 1950), p. 423.

[9] See A. Paul Hare, *Handbook of Small Group Research* (New York: The Free Press, 1962), pp. 293–294.

[10] Stogdill, *Handbook of Leadership*, p. 30.

[11] Robert F. Bales, "The Equilibrium Problem in Small Groups," in *Small Groups: Studies in Social Interaction*, ed. by A. Paul Hare, E. F. Borgatta, and R. Bales, rev. ed. (New York: Alfred A. Knopf, 1965), p. 473.

and with persons are not unrelated. They are mutually interdependent. When the group is achieving, this fact may contribute to positive emotional feelings; and a warm, cohesive climate may make substantive achievement easier. No doubt, the opposite relationships also hold.

It should be emphasized, in addition, that a designated leader may have the skill to perform both these functions effectively. It is not necessary that two different champions emerge to promote intellectual and affective behavior. Although it is true some groups make conviviality their major concern to the detriment of work and others concentrate on achievement regardless of group harmony, the contribution of leadership is to balance these two requirements of group activity. Imbalance is caused when the leader is so eager to have a high-quality decision that he or she ignores the feelings of members or when he or she has such an emotional regard for the group that he or she cannot insist on rigorous standards of productivity.

In discussion there seems to be a third category of functions that is purely procedural. The leader in this regard is a kind of director of traffic and administrator of group activity. The procedural duties could serve either task achievement or social harmony but in any case would be trivial compared with the other two categories.

It is interesting to recognize in passing that many group members, when they talk of leadership, seem to be thinking primarily of procedural functions. Thus when some persons say they "like a strong, forceful leader who takes command and sees that the group moves forward," they mean only that they want him or her to preserve order, recognize only one speaker at a time, and bang the gavel for attention. If the leader begins to interfere with their right to say what they wish about the problem, they may change their minds about desiring strong, commanding leadership.

The wide range of duties performed by the designated leader in discussion or by several members sharing the leadership can be organized within these three broad categories of procedural, social, and task functions. All five of the general leadership functions described by Hemphill are represented directly in these divisions. The first, advancing the group's purposes, is common to task achievement and social harmony because most discussion groups seek both to be productive and to maintain the group. The second, administration, is approximately the same category we are calling procedural. The third, inspiring greater activity, is clearly a matter of task productivity, whereas the fourth, making members feel secure, concerns interpersonal relationships or group maintenance. The fifth function listed by Hemphill, acting without regard to self-interest, is again a general one cutting across all three of the others. Moreover, it is somewhat different in kind as well as in generality, for it raises questions directly about the leader's motives, dedication, and philosophies.

It is difficult and probably unnecessary to distinguish absolutely among task functions, social-emotional functions, procedural functions, and other contributions of leadership. It will be helpful, however, to look at some of the functions important to decision-making discussion.

SOCIAL FUNCTIONS

The social functions of leadership serve the purposes of promoting human relationships, developing group cohesiveness, maintaining the group as a cooperating unit, and in other ways helping members work together in a common cause.

Interaction is easier, naturally, in a group that is cohesive. Task productivity, too, is probably increased in many situations when an atmosphere has been created in which all members feel permitted to speak freely, fully, and frankly. One of the aims of leadership is to encourage interaction by helping to create a permissive climate.

A Michigan study of seventy-two conferences in business and government, cited by Collins and Guetzkow,[12] found the pleasantness of meetings and a positive affective atmosphere contributed to consensus. There is also some evidence that high influencers in the group who drive relentlessly toward task productivity may damage interpersonal relationships, perhaps by alienating others and giving them insufficient opportunity to participate.[13]

One of the unique values of group discussion is that the presence of others interacting orally apparently stimulates each person to think better than he or she does alone. Most members think of ideas that would not have occurred to them without this stimulus. Included within this larger phenomenon is the fact that the individual is roused to keener effort by his or her own contributions. Hence, if a member is silent, he or she is not experiencing a self-stimulus. By encouraging such a member to take an initial step, those contributing leadership may provide the group with later help it would otherwise be denied.

Triggering universal participation makes it more probable that real feelings, hidden purposes, and latent hostilities will be revealed. Bringing them into the open makes more likely the resolution of the disagreements they harbor. There is an old saying that "silence gives consent." In discussion, silence may mean unexpressed opposition, which will appear later as conflict or as obstacles to carrying out the group's decision. It is healthier for discussion when repressed feelings are brought out frankly. At least, leaders need to sense how persons are reacting. To do so is difficult in the case of silent members, who are often enigmas. If they can be encouraged to contribute something, they will almost always give some clue to their attitudes through tone of voice or facial expression, if not through the content of their comments.

[12] Barry E. Collins and Harold Guetzkow, *A Social Psychology of Group Processes for Decision-Making* (New York: John Wiley & Sons, 1964), pp. 109–111.
[13] Ibid., pp. 220–224.

Persons who contribute to the outcome are also more likely to be committed to its support. A member can help more enthusiastically to put a policy into effect if he or she was one of its architects. The silent participant may later be an opponent or at least a lukewarm supporter. The group needs the benefit of his or her help and should have the opportunity at the time to meet his or her objections and perhaps thereby improve the outcome.

Leaders encourage future contributions by responding to contributions with acceptance, not reacting with agreement or disagreement but indicating that the message is received, with appreciation that it was offered. Homans has stressed this point bluntly: "The leader must not take a moral stand and show approval or disapproval of what is being said. He must accept—utterly, or, as some say, he must create a permissive atmosphere." [14] If every time a low-status member who is participating infrequently makes a comment, a high who is also a high participator pounces upon the idea, the leader should gently come to the low's rescue. He or she may say, "Now, wait a minute. I'd like to hear more about that idea ..." The leader should not directly take issue with the high. What he or she does is show the low that the latter's ideas have worth (if they do), are welcome, and are being received. Note that the leader does not indicate whether he or she agrees with the low.

Norman Maier describes a "Risk Technique" for encouraging members to express opposition even in situations where the designated leader is the supervisor or boss. The leader wishing to hear complaints and objections to a proposal being considered by the company sets aside a special period within the discussion during which members are expected to talk about the *risks* that the proposed policy may introduce. In this period members feel less threatened by the situation because they are invited to express opposition, reservations, and doubts. Maier reports that criticisms often turn out to be due to misunderstandings and false assumptions, although they may result in modification of the policy. "The risk technique was developed," he says, "to aid the emotionally involved discussion leader in listening, accepting, and understanding." [15] It would also have the virtue of encouraging interaction from all participants in particularly threatening situations.

PROCEDURAL FUNCTIONS

The most critical procedural functions are related to the flow of communication during a discussion. The person "in charge" is assigned the responsibility of preserving order, preventing chaos, and keeping everyone

[14] Homans, *The Human Group*, p. 439.

[15] N. R. F. Maier, *Problem-Solving Discussions and Conferences* (New York: McGraw-Hill, 1963), pp. 171–177.

from talking at once. He or she achieves orderly talk by "directing the communication traffic" as if the words of members were automobiles hurrying by. He or she must see that only one person at a time talks; and when two or more persons are competing for attention, he or she is the one who must give the nod to the participant who may talk next.

The leader must protect the person speaking from interrupters and, in addition, remember who had asked earlier to speak. He or she can then return to those who were denied the floor earlier and ask if they still wish to contribute. As controller of communication exchange, the leader finds the assignment is to distribute speaking rights to all in a fair and comfortable manner.

At times, the leader will find it necessary to clarify what has been said or to remind members about the agenda agreed upon in order to make way for further communication. Otherwise, confusion and disorder may build up, and the talk may stop flowing. The leader has a larger responsibility in connection with the substance of the task where he or she must clarify the content of contributions, but the procedural aspects of clarification concern the statements he or she should make to keep the talk moving smoothly. Of course, there will be overlapping between the leader's procedural and task functions at this point, but it is not important that he or she be able to distinguish between them. A difficulty could occur, however, if two different persons were performing these two kinds of functions and they had a problem of coordination.

Guiding the communication flow is also critical for task achievement. The group must be encouraged to move from problem to outcome, to keep on the track. Such guidance must be indirect. The leader must suggest, not order; gently restrain, not scold; encourage, not drive; ask for cooperation, not manipulate, threaten, or dictate. To do so skillfully requires high-quality language usage and communication.

To guide the group's discussion of a problem, leaders must recognize when a contribution leads in an unproductive direction. One deflection, which is especially difficult to check, is the fascinating tangent. Every complex problem has many aspects, all interesting if members are thoroughly informed. The danger is that the group will become so absorbed in examining a fascinating aspect that no one, including the leader, recognizes for a time that this tangential material is leading away from a solution to the specific problem being discussed. The alert leader will see that the topic, although related, is not directly contributing to forward progress on the question at hand and will gracefully lead back to the planned pattern.

A similar deflection is the irrelevant fact or opinion. The designated leader must recognize it as unrelated, suggest that it may lead the group astray, and restore forward motion with a relevant question.

Part of guidance is to keep clearly before the group what is being discussed at the moment, so there will be no confusion about where they are and where they are heading. If a member's statement is unclear, it is the leader's responsibility to ask the member to restate it or to supply a clarification or to reword it more explicitly. Obviously, the leader must choose his or her words carefully. He or she should resist saying, "Is this what you're trying to say?" or "I'm going to restate that so it will be clear this time." Instead of scolding the participant for his or her failure, the leader could say, "Let me see if I understand you; you are saying that . . ."

A difficult part of the guidance function is to ask the right questions at the right time. In the words of Wendell Johnson, "The surest way to get a clear answer is to ask a clear question." In fact, the leader guides primarily by asking questions.

Perhaps the most common error is asking a question that is too broad. Because any number of answers can properly be given, the group is sent exploring in the direction determined by whatever aspect of the broad question the first member answering happened to choose. The direction pursued in this accidental manner may not coincide at all with what the leader had in mind. Hence he or she must stop members and pull them back when he or she could have avoided this necessity by asking a limited question in the first place.

Collins and Guetzkow report that "Chairmen of groups in high substantive conflict which ended in consensus did three times more seeking for information of an objective factual nature from members of their groups than did chairmen in groups which did not end in consensus." This result of questioning was not the same for groups in high affective, or interpersonal, conflict.[16]

The leader must decide how to ask questions to achieve many different purposes: to elicit additional information, to confirm understanding or agreement, to check on and pinpoint disagreement, to seek clarification, to resolve conflict, and so on. When seeking understanding for himself or herself and on behalf of the others, the leader must be the eager searcher with unsatiable curiosity and not the cross-examiner. He or she should communicate his or her eagerness to know and to share. He or she should invite explanation and must be careful not to talk down to members by pretending to ask a question when actually displaying the superiority of his or her own knowledge. A leader's tone and words should not imply, "I know the answer to this next question, but I am asking it to see if you dummies do." What he or she must do is demonstrate that he or she is one of the group's leading thinkers by the quality and eagerness of his or her questions.

Especially critical is the leader's skill in asking the follow-up question. By gently but persistently staying with a thread of thought, through asking

<hr>

[16] Collins and Guetzkow, *A Social Psychology of Group Processes for Decision-Making,* p. 113.

another question or two when the first one does not elicit a complete or clear response, the leader sets the example for thorough consideration of a complicated problem.

TASK FUNCTIONS

To watch an ineffective group is often frequently to recognize that group leadership is not performing the necessary task functions. Task functions that are necessary for a given group vary, and not all functions should receive equal emphasis. Furthermore, the leader(s) should frequently share task functions with other group members.

There is one task function that the leader must perform. He or she must be the group's watchdog and begin by identifying and defining the minimal set of task functions that must be performed. Throughout the discussion he or she must remain vigilant to see that they are performed.[17]

Once the meeting begins, we believe two leadership task functions are of primary importance: (1) guiding the group to select a method of group decision making that has the greatest potential for attaining group goals and (2) providing alternative methods of conflict management if the group should become locked in substantive conflict.

Other task functions that may vitally affect the group's success are treated in detail in Chapters 4 and 5. Although the group's leadership does not have the exclusive or even primary responsibility for securing and using information, it must function to see that these tasks are performed.

In retrospect, we should be cautious in our attempts to identify those social, procedural, and task functions that are associated with effective leadership. These functions cannot be separated in an absolute sense, and their relative importance depends on a number of factors. What functions should be performed will depend on the nature of the task, the situation, the purposes of the group, and other factors. In any situation there are likely to be both advantages and disadvantages in any possible leadership arrangement.

Styles of Leadership

The functional approach to leadership emphasizes what the leader actually does. In some groups there is a noticeable gap between what the leadership does and what should be done. Choice of leadership style is an important means of making actual and desired leadership behaviors congruent.

[17] L. E. This, *The Small Meeting Planner* (Houston, Texas: Gulf Publishing Co., 1972), pp. 146–163.

In many groups, members cannot exercise freedom of choice over leadership style. When such freedom of choice exists, it should be exercised with care. The choice frequently has a major impact on the quality of a group's outcomes.

Leadership styles have traditionally been defined by the amount of control exercised by a given leader or leaders. Thus the laissez-faire style of leadership is so permissive that members are given little if any direction. In contrast, the authoritarian style of leadership places control in a single leader and provides group members with little, if any, freedom of action. Neither of these styles has proved to be very effective, but there are many other leadership styles that fall within these extremes. Unfortunately, research on leadership styles has not featured a standardized set of labels. Consequently, research often uses different terms to describe closely related styles of leadership. For example, would you know the difference between democratic, follower-oriented, and participative styles—or between autocratic, restrictive, and directive? All these labels and many more have been used to identify leadership styles in the leadership literature.[18]

Whatever the label used, authorities agree that the style of guidance contributed by those exercising leadership is affected by orientation toward task and the persons involved. Oversimplifying a bit, Fiedler and other researchers have identified two "crucial clusters of leadership attitudes and behaviors . . . the critical, directive, autocratic, task-oriented versus the democratic, permissive, considerate, person-oriented type of leadership." [19]

Another fundamental distinction suggested by the research studies affects leadership style. Apparently, there are persons who are self-oriented and feel a need to have a place of importance in the center of a group's activities, whereas others are group-oriented and can work comfortably as part of the group, taking a follower role when this is helpful. Self-oriented persons tend to be authoritarian when in control, whereas the group-centered person can be more egalitarian.[20]

A similar dichotomy may exist among teachers leading classroom discussion. The teacher-centered group preferred by some may be more demanding and may elicit more student hostility or withdrawal. In contrast, learner-centered discussions may be more permissive and may produce greater interaction and positive feeling. Whether students learn more in one or the other seems to be a function of the teacher's goals and the type of examination.[21]

Thus styles of leadership are determined by the personalities of the individuals involved, by group preferences and even the culture or political

[18] R. M. Stogdill, *Handbook of Leadership*, p. 404.
[19] Fred E. Fiedler, "The Contingency Model: A Theory of Leadership Effectiveness," in *Group Processes*, ed. by Peter B. Smith (Baltimore: Penguin Books, 1970), p. 245.
[20] Hare, *Handbook of Small Group Research*, p. 293.
[21] Ibid., p. 317.

structure of the society, by the nature of the situation and the task, and by other factors. Although it is risky to offer generalizations about types of leadership in all the various circumstances, we should mention the styles that have been most often identified.

AUTHORITARIAN, LAISSEZ-FAIRE, AND DEMOCRATIC LEADERSHIP

One of the earliest studies of leadership styles was done by White and Lippitt on authoritarian, laissez-faire, and democratic leadership. They studied boys' club meetings and activities over a period of months. In one study, four trained, adult leaders shifted from group to group each six weeks, changing their leadership style with the shift. In the authoritarian version, all policy was determined by the leader. Techniques and activities were dictated by the leader one step at a time; thus the boys were uncertain about what would be permitted next. The leader determined as well the specific task assignment and companion for each boy. Remaining aloof from group activity except when demonstrating, the leader was dominant and was personal in his or her praise or criticism of member efforts.[22]

Although these club meetings involved many activities other than group discussion, there was a lot of social interaction and talk. The operational definition contrived to designate authoritarian leadership in these studies gives a good clue to the behavior characteristic of the autocratic leader in discussion. This kind of person tends to feel that ordinary members are limited in ability and cannot be trusted to manage without strict guidance and control. His or her leadership thus tends to be rigid and somewhat formal. He or she assigns the floor judiciously, discourages interruptions, expresses displeasure unless members wait for him or her to decide when to move forward, favors those who agree with him or her and is reluctant to recognize those disagreeing and in other ways dominates the talk and the entire decision-making procedure. Where the leader insists on maximum control, there is obviously minimum permissiveness. Members have little choice except submission to dictation. Such an arbitrary, autocratic dominator makes frequent direct influence attempts, retaliates by withholding privileges when members fail to agree, arbitrarily shuts off contributions that displease him or her, takes sides aggressively in conflicts, and in other ways operates as a combination emperor-oracle who has just received divine ordination.

The laissez-faire style granted the boys complete freedom to make group or individual decisions as they chose, with a minimum of leadership participation. The hands-off leader explained that he would answer questions

---

[22] R. White and R. Lippitt, "Leader Behavior and Member Reaction in Three 'Social Climates,'" in *Group Dynamics: Research and Theory*, ed. by Dorwin Cartwright and Alvin Zander, second ed. (New York: Harper and Row, 1960), pp. 527–553.

about activities and work companions when asked, but otherwise he took no part in the discussions of the work. He made no effort to appraise or regulate the course of events and commented on activities only when questioned.[23]

A discussion leader who behaved in this way would obviously fail to provide leadership, and thus we would be confronted with leadershipless discussion unless others filled the void. Actually, few such leaders can be observed. This category is worth defining primarily to fix the end of a continuum opposite autocratic leadership as a method of bracketing the democratic style. Designated leaders can be observed exhibiting some tendencies in the laissez-faire direction. Occasionally, a leader will not have done his or her homework and thus will not be well enough informed to provide effective guidance. Even less frequently, a member is designated chairman in a situation where the obvious and actual control is being exercised by a strong person who for some reason wants a puppet in ostensible control; under these conditions, the leader at times will resemble the laissez-faire style, remaining tentative and hesitant, exercising no control, permitting anything, preventing nothing, and supplying no direction or guidance until he or she receives the signal from the person who is the actual dominator.

The democratic style defined in the White-Lippitt study allowed members to decide policy through group discussion, with encouragement and assistance from the adult leader. Members could work with companions of their choice. The group divided up tasks and agreed on activity steps and objectives. The leader tried to be objective or fact-minded in praising or criticizing member achievement. His aim was to be a "regular group member in spirit without doing too much of the work."[24]

Democratic leadership style in discussion obviously lies between the extremes of autocracy and abdication. Members submit to some measure of control and guidance to provide some degree of order, efficiency, and forward locomotion. At the same time, there is a minimum of restraint and a maximum of permissiveness consistent with task productivity and good interpersonal relationships. In conflicts between the leader and the group, the democratic style of leadership requires that the group have its way.

The evidence from the studies summarized by White and Lippitt is revealing. Laissez-faire leadership was the lowest in quality; the least and poorest work was done under this style. Autocracy created much hostility and aggression, resulted in discontent including some dropping out of the groups, and encouraged submissive or dependent behavior. When interviewed, the boys tended to prefer the democratic leader. In this style, there was more group-mindedness and friendliness. Authoritarian leader-

[23] Ibid.
[24] Ibid.

ship produced somewhat greater quantities of work, indicating its efficiency, but work motivation was stronger under the democratic style, and there was more originality.

There is nothing very surprising in these results, but it is helpful to have this kind of confirming clues about leadership behavior. The autocrat is preferable to the do-nothing leader, for the latter invites chaos. At worst, he or she is not leading at all. The authoritarian leader is at least efficient, although at times he or she probably does not permit interaction to operate freely enough for discussion worthy of the name to occur.

Collaborating with Bradford in another study, Lippitt reported that a "hardboiled autocrat" caused resentment and stirred up incipient revolt; there was irritability and unwillingness to cooperate. The lowest morale of all in this study was brought on by the laissez-faire leader; no one knew what to do or to expect, and the result was absence of teamwork and the lowest productivity. The democratic leader, who shared decision making and explained the basis for his decisions, was met with enthusiasm; his group had the best teamwork and production in the study.[25] Fox also found positive leadership superior to negative leadership in promoting permissiveness, friendliness, and member satisfaction. Revealing, positive leadership took twice as long before consensus was reached or members felt that further talk would be fruitless.[26]

PERSONALITY CORRELATES OF AUTOCRATIC AND DEMOCRATIC LEADERSHIP

Rosenfeld and Plax searched for personality traits of persons preferring autocratic or democratic leadership. The autocratic leader tends to have an "object orientation ... lacking insight about self and others, manipulates others to his own end, without considering their feelings, or making any show of treating them as people." In contrast, they found the democratic leader "people oriented," with "insight into the motives and behaviors of himself and others, works toward the achievement of some goal with those he considers his equals, treating them as people, and always willing to share in both the rewards and punishments accrued." [27]

Their studies confirmed the Sargent and Miller findings that autocratic and democratic leaders have different communication behaviors. Authoritarian leaders offer more answers, ask fewer questions, communicate more

[25] L. P. Bradford and R. Lippitt, "Building a Democratic Work Group," *Personnel* 22 (1945): 142–152.

[26] William M. Fox, "Group Reaction to Two Types of Conference Leadership," *Human Relations* 10 (1957): 279–289.

[27] Lawrence B. Rosenfeld and Timothy G. Plax, "Personality Determinants of Autocratic and Democratic Leadership," *Speech Monographs* 42 (August 1975): 203–208.

negative reactions, are less concerned with having others participate, and affirm others less often.[28]

CHARISMATIC AND ORGANIZATIONAL LEADERSHIP

Levine describes four types of leaders whose behaviors differ according to cultural factors affecting interaction between leadership and membership. The first is the charismatic leader who has the ability to dramatize the group's goals and its solidarity through his or her own emotionality. Such colorful leaders may be rigid in their presentations, exaggerate chances of success, and overemphasize their individualistic role.

The organizational leader is Levine's second type. He or she is concerned with function, administration, and formal organization, underestimating the roles of discussion and thinking. Such a leader usually sacrifices the feelings of the members to efficiency, planning, and intense activity.

A third type is the intellectual or "expert" leader, who contributes perspective and objectivity, but is often inadequate in helping to carry out objectives in pragmatic ways.

Levine's fourth type is the informal leader, sometimes called an opinion leader, who is close to the followers and has acute sensitivity to grassroots feelings. He or she is able to work with the members "in a warm, flexible way," but often does not recognize himself or herself as leader. The important function of such an informal leader, Levine observes, lies in communication. Because he or she "is keenly sensitive to the various shades of other people's feelings and to subtle changes in their responses," the informal leader "is able to communicate to other leaders the desires of the members. . . ."[29]

PERMISSIVE LEADERSHIP

If we visualize a continuum with laissez-faire, or minimal-control, leadership at the left end, autocratic, or maximal-control, on the right end, and democratic leadership in the center, it is possible to suggest a style of leadership occurring to the left of democratic control and closer to the laissez-faire end. We could call this style *permissive leadership*. It would be characterized by even more freedom to speak up than is usual in the democratic style. The leader would be more a "director of traffic" than a

---

[28] Ibid. See also James F. Sargent and Gerald R. Miller, "Some Differences in Certain Communication Behaviors of Autocratic and Democratic Group Leaders," *Journal of Communication* 21 (1970): 233–252.

[29] Sol Levine, "Four Leadership Types: An Approach to Constructive Leadership," in *Small Group Communication: A Reader*, ed. by Robert S. Cathcart and Larry Samovar, second ed. (Dubuque, Iowa: William C. Brown, 1974), pp. 381–389.

	Laissez faire	Democratic control	Autocratic domination	
MINIMUM CONTROL				MAXIMUM CONTROL

guide. He or she would leave to members decisions about moving forward on substantive matters.

This style encourages spontaneity and may be appropriate where groups want to be especially creative. It may be desirable also in situations where members have low motivation to remain in the group, as in some extracurricular student activities or community improvement groups. No doubt there are other circumstances where extreme permissiveness and freedom of expression would be appropriate. Perhaps groups where interpersonal relationships are much more important than the task assignment, as in many social and recreational situations, would appreciate a permissive-leadership style.

SUPERVISORY LEADERSHIP

On this same continuum, to the right of center, we can probably identify a style of leadership that is more controlling than would be characteristic of democratic style but would stop far short of autocratic control. The supervisory style may be appealing where efficiency is crucial, as in some industrial work teams, and where opportunities for communication are limited.

Hare reports the results of studies comparing supervisory leaders, who do not "take part in the discussion but who see that the group finishes on time, with participatory leaders, who take part in the discussion and try to insure an equal chance for participation to all group members." Participatory style produced greater opinion change and higher satisfaction. The supervisory leader also had less influence on the group decision.[30]

Many other styles and types of leadership have been proposed and described, but those we have identified seem sufficient to suggest the basic differences. We can turn next to a somewhat different approach determined by the situation.

[30] Hare, *Handbook of Small Group Research,* p. 316.

Leadership and the Situation

Leadership contributions deemed effective in decision making will obviously vary with the situation. An urgent problem of great importance faced by a group where only one member has enough background information to understand the problem may call for firm, almost autocratic direction from that member. The same group, in other circumstances, may be willing to accept only democratic leadership. Thus the style of leadership and the traits of the person(s) considered appropriate for providing guidance will be different in various situations.

Fiedler has pursued more assiduously than any other researcher the question of leadership effectiveness in different situations and has developed a theory for explaining the kinds of leaders who are successful in various circumstances. His *contingency model* specifies that leadership effectiveness depends on the situation.

He and his colleagues first had leaders describe their most preferred and least preferred co-workers and then measured the difference perceived between the most and least preferred (this score is called "the assumed similarity between opposites," or ASo). They found that the leader who evaluates his or her least preferred co-worker favorably "tends to be more accepting, permissive, considerate and person-oriented" as leader. In contrast, the one who views his least preferred coworker unfavorably and who perceives a large difference between most and least preferred co-worker "tends to be directive, controlling, task-oriented and managing in his interactions."

When they tried to relate these scores with their success as leaders, however, the results were puzzling. Chosen leaders of such diverse groups as basketball teams, surveying teams, and company management groups sometimes had ASo scores that correlated positively with leadership effectiveness and sometimes negatively. The scores did not seem clearly related to leadership success until the researchers started to take into account the various situations. Reasoning that "a liked and trusted leader with high rank and a structured task is in a more favorable position that is a disliked and powerless leader with an ambiguous task," Fiedler found that "the relationship between leader attitudes and group performance is contingent upon the accurate classification of the group-task situation." [31]

Leaders rating their least preferred co-worker unfavorably were "man-

[31] Fiedler, "The Contingency Model," pp. 245–265.

aging, controlling, directive leaders" and were effective when the situation was either very favorable or very unfavorable; that is, when the task is highly structured and the leader well liked, directive, controlling behavior from the leader is appropriate and effective.

On the other hand, Fiedler reports, "considerate, permissive, accepting leaders obtain optimal group performance under situations intermediate in favorableness."

> These are situations in which (a) the task is structured, but the leader is disliked and must, therefore, be diplomatic; (b) the liked leader has an ambiguous, unstructured task and must, therefore, draw upon the creativity and cooperation of his members.[32]

Fiedler gives as an illustration the operation of a research team. In the early phases, when developing hypotheses and brainstorming ideas, the principal investigator can be democratic and permissive; all contributions are welcome. Later, however, when the tests are being given and data analyzed, the research director becomes managerial, controlling, even autocratic and does not allow a research assistant to be creative about instructing subjects or scoring tests! Fiedler observes:

> A similar situation is often found in business organization where the routine operation tends to be well structured and calls for a managing, directive leadership. The situation becomes suddenly unstructured when a crisis occurs. Under these conditions the number of discussions, meetings, and conferences increases sharply so as to give everyone an opportunity to express his views.[33]

Some Special Problems of Studying Leadership

It is important to emphasize one more time that analysis of leadership in small-group communication for decision making must be approached with caution. It is tempting to oversimplify the multitude of complex variables operating in an all-at-once fashion, and it may be helpful to suggest some of the special problems to be considered thoughtfully in trying to understand such a vital matter as leadership.

DEGREE OF CONTROL

What influence should a leader exert in discussion? How much power should he or she have? In democratic discussion groups, of course, power resides in the group. The leader will have whatever influence and power the group is willing to allow him or her, but this statement must be qualified. Temporarily, a designated leader may exercise more authority than

---

[32] Ibid., p. 253.
[33] Ibid., p. 264.

members approve of, and the group must expend time and effort to replace him or her or redistribute the leadership functions. A group may be lethargic, indifferent, or unalert and simply by default allow the leader more power than they really intend. Then, of course, there are groups where the designated leader is arbitrarily autocratic. Such is the case when a staff appears to "talk things over" but in reality is called together to be told by the boss what is to be done.

During an interactional discussion some leadership behaviors are related to talk about the substance of the problem and others to recognizing persons to speak, allotting time for each stage, and so on. The former could be called substantive control; and the latter, procedural. There is some evidence that many groups may want the designated leader to exercise firm procedural control even when they would not allow him or her to dominate the substantive contributions.

The individual leader must decide what his or her style of leadership will be. Where a group gives him or her wide latitude in the amount of control they will allow, the leader's dominance will be a function of his or her personal philosophy of leadership control, tempered no doubt by the way he or she sizes up what is appropriate under the circumstances.

EFFECTS OF CRISIS

Groups faced with crisis or urgency may accept firmer leadership and perhaps under some circumstances welcome autocratic control. Hamblin has hypothesized that influence becomes more centralized under crisis conditions; that is, that those high in influence will become even more influential and that a group tends to turn to a different leader if he or she falters under the emergency conditions. In a creative study, Hamblin was able to offer confirmation for both hypotheses.[34]

PARTISANSHIP-IMPARTIALITY

Should a leader be an active participant in the group's substantive deliberation, contributing his or her own opinions and factual information? Or should the leader be an impartial guide, refusing to become a partisan participant and concentrating on procedural control?

This matter is controversial. Haiman advises the leader to express his or her ideas with restraint, but feels we should not make the chairperson an "idea-eunuch," robbing the group of his or her "intellectual and emotional virility."[35] Other authorities, such as Utterback, have described the leader as a moderator who suppresses his or her own convictions in order

---

[34] Robert L. Hamblin, "Leadership and Crisis," in *Interpersonal Behavior in Small Groups,* ed. by Richard J. Ofshe (Englewood Cliffs, N.J.: Prentice-Hall, 1973), pp. 466–478.

[35] Franklyn S. Haiman, *Group Leadership and Democratic Action* (Boston: Houghton Mifflin, 1951).

to bring the will of the group to full fruition.[36] Probably the question should not be answered yes or no. A reasonable answer seems to be that the leader's partisanship or impartiality should be a matter of degree, depending on the situation.

In small, informal committee discussions, the chairperson can probably fairly and efficiently perform his or her guidance functions and still be a complete partisan or participant, expressing his or her convictions as fully and vociferously as the others do. In this situation, we would perhaps be depriving the group of its most articulate and well-informed voice if we expected the designated leader to be silent on substantive matters. He or she often is made chairperson because he or she has the most interest in and knowledge related to the group's task function. A similar position could be taken in regard to designated leaders of small conferences, study groups, and round tables.

The leaders of large committees and conferences and of public panels may find it somewhat more damaging to the group's productivity if they are active partisans. Especially if the group is faced with an extremely complex and controversial problem or if members feel strong emotional involvement, the leader may be wise to concentrate most of his or her attention on guidance and procedural functions and participate substantively only with caution. Thus the leader would contribute information only when it could not be elicited from members; withhold his or her opinions whenever possible; express his or her convictions tentatively and carefully; phrase his or her statements as "another view that could be taken into account"; avoid for the most part direct attempts to influence the group's decisions; and unless it were extremely important to him or her, avoid agreeing or disagreeing aggressively with some members in a conflict with others.

When a leader must strive to promote direct interaction in a large discussion, say, a committee or conference of twenty persons or in the forum period of public discussion, he or she has little choice about partisanship. The leader is so busy guiding, channeling contributions, clarifying, and distributing participation, that he or she has little or no opportunity to express his or her own convictions. Here the leader's function is to be an impartial guide, to help the group be maximally productive under the circumstances.

There are other situations, also, in which the leader must be an impartial guide. One is when he or she serves as arbitrator of a labor-management negotiating conference. Another arises when a sharp personal conflict occurs within the group. The leader will want to restore harmony as efficiently as possible. If he or she is to succeed, he or she must not take sides, even by subtle overtones in the voice or a facial grimace that sug-

---

[36] William E. Utterback, "The Moderator's Function in Group Thinking," *Quarterly Journal of Speech* 34 (1948): 455–458.

gests where his or her sympathies lie. To show complete impartiality requires practice because it is easy to betray feelings by signs the speaker
may not be aware of. Where the leader is an impartial guide, moderator,
or presiding chairperson in whom bias would be particularly damaging, he
or she must be especially careful not to reveal his or her opinions or evaluations. An impatient gesture or vocal inflection, an amused smile, or an
unguarded retort can suggest partisan feeling that may limit the leader's
effectiveness in performing his or her vital functions.

These differences in the extent of partisan participation are matters of
degree. The designated leader must decide whether it is appropriate under
the specific conditions to be more partisan than guide, less partisan than
guide, almost wholly an impartial guide, or completely neutral. Furthermore, what seems reasonable will vary with the attitudes, intentions, and
values of the persons involved. Perhaps the possibilities can best be represented by a continuum suggesting the relative locations of types of discussions and the extent to which leaders may wish to be partisan.

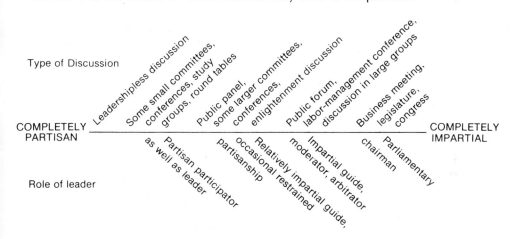

THE RISKY SHIFT PHENOMENON

Researchers have been interested in the question of group risk taking,
or the extent to which group discussion influences how bold individuals
are willing to be in agreeing to a risky outcome. One assumption is that
group decision is a composite or average of member views. Another is
that the compromises necessary in a management team lead to caution,
operating against boldness. Some studies have indicated, however, that
group interaction encourages members to shift to a more risky decision
than would have been expected from the average of the members' prediscussion positions.

Wallach, Kogan, and Bem tested individuals on a number of hypothetical situations, asking them to choose between a cautious and a risky
course of action. For example, subjects were asked whether a man with

a severe heart ailment should undergo an operation that might cure him or that also might prove fatal. Then, in groups of six, they were asked to reconsider each hypothetical situation and decide as a group what action to favor. After the discussions, each person ranked the others in terms of how much influence each had had on the group's decision. The study showed that groups moved toward bolder risk taking if they reached unanimous positions. In their control groups, no shift toward greater risk occurred in the absence of group discussion.[37]

This study is important to understanding leadership in groups because subjects in this experiment who were willing to take bold, risky positions during the discussion were perceived by more conservative members as having more influence on the group. Another interesting aspect of this study concerned the sex of participants. Wallach and his colleagues wondered whether men in group discussion might be more willing than women to shift toward greater risk taking, on the basis of the notion that "one of the expected indications of manliness in our society is a willingness to be bold and daring in decision making." [38] Such was not the case. They found that willingness to move toward greater risk after discussion held for women as well as men.

Other researchers have questioned whether the risky shift is dependent only on group discussion. Wallach and others explain the shift in terms of spreading responsibility among several persons and developing positive affective bonds during interaction. Teger and Pruitt found in a similar study that shift was greater in a risky direction after discussion, but found that a group also moved toward greater risk after simply exchanging "minimal information about their prior decisions." These experimenters also speculate that willingness to take risks is a function of the kind of subject being discussed.[39]

LEADERSHIP AND COMMUNICATION

In Chapter 12 we will examine closely the operation of leadership as it is affected by communication and the reciprocal influences of communication on leadership. Communication is the central process relating persons who cooperate in group decision making. It is the essential activity, the net tying members together. Indeed leadership can be thought of as the energizing catalyst directing the group, through communication, toward productivity.

There is little question that the leadership role is one of the most important influences in a group structure, and part of this influence stems from

[37] Michael A. Wallach, Nathan Kogan, and Daryl J. Bem, "Group Influence on Individual Risk Taking," in *Interpersonal Behavior in Small Groups,* pp. 524–541.

[38] Ibid., p. 526.

[39] Allan I. Teger and Dean G. Pruitt, "Components of Group Risk Taking," in *Interpersonal Behavior in Small Groups,* p. 553.

the communication of those contributing leadership. We must consider how communication contributes to leadership effectiveness and how leadership styles affect group outcomes.

SUPPLEMENTARY READING

Bormann, Ernest G. *Discussion and Group Methods*. Second Edition. New York: Harper and Row, 1975. Chapter 11.

Cartwright, Dorwin and Zander, Alvin, eds. *Group Dynamics: Research and Theory*. Third Edition. New York: Harper and Row, 1968. Pp. 351–388.

Cathcart, Robert S., and Samovar, Larry, eds. *Small Group Communication: A Reader*. Second Edition. Dubuque, Iowa: William C. Brown, 1974. Section IV.

Fiedler, Fred E. "The Contingency Model: A Theory of Leadership Effectiveness." In *Group Processes*, ed. by Peter B. Smith. Baltimore: Penguin Books, 1970.

Gouran, Dennis S. "Perspectives on the Study of Leadership: Its Present and Its Future." *Quarterly Journal of Speech* 60 (October 1974): 376–381.

Halal, W. E. "Toward a General Theory of Leadership." *Human Relations* 27 (1974): 401–416.

Ofshe, Richard R., ed. *Interpersonal Behavior in Small Groups*. Englewood Cliffs, N.J.: Prentice-Hall, 1973. Part IV.

Rosenfeld, Lawrence B. *Human Interaction in the Small Group Setting*. Columbus, Ohio: Charles E. Merrill, 1973. Chapter 6.

Stogdill, Ralph M. *Handbook of Leadership: A Survey of Theory and Research*. New York: The Free Press, 1974.

QUESTIONS AND EXERCISES

1. Make a list of the leadership functions that you believe necessary for a successful group. How many of these functions were performed in your group?
2. Identify three of the major types of leadership functions. Which type is most important? Why?
3. How many members of your group will now admit that they wanted to be the leader when the group first met? If they concealed their desire to be leader, why did they conceal it?
4. What leadership style did your group use? Was it effective? Why or why not?
5. Each member of your group should now rank order all members as to leadership ability. Tabulate results and discuss as a group.
6. Prepare a paper describing the leadership behaviors in your group. Identify both functional and dysfunctional leadership behaviors. Indicate how leadership effectiveness might have been improved.

12 The Quality of Leadership Communication as a Determinant of Quality of Group Outcomes

This book has been geared to the proposition that quality of small-group communication is a major determinant of the quality of group outcomes. This chapter is geared to the closely related proposition that quality of leadership communication is a major determinant of the quality of group outcomes. These propositions no longer feature the speculative assertion of relationships. We now have impressive empirical support for the relationship between quality of communication and group outcomes.

In many groups, we believe, the *quality of leadership communication is the most important determinant of the quality of group outcomes.* By *leadership communication,* we refer to all those *communication behaviors in the group that exert significant influence on one or more members of the group and in exerting such influence have a measurable impact on the quality of group outcomes.*

The last chapter identified and analyzed the major types of functions a leader must perform. Performing those functions individually or collectively requires communication. As we might expect, the effectiveness with which leaders perform these functions depends to a large extent on the quality of their communication.

As a communicator, a leader must march to the beat of many different drummers. At minimum, he or she is faced with two sets of demands: (1) the demands of the group as a social system and (2) the demands of group members as individuals. The first set of demands focuses on "group desires" when the members are thinking and acting as a unit. When "system" demands are dominant, it is particularly important that the leader emphasize productivity, clearly define role relationships, and communicate assertively. When the "personal" demands of the individual members are dominant, it is important that the leader allow group members to take the initiative, tolerate uncertainty and postponement of decision, exhibit proper sensitivity to status differences among members, reconcile conflicting demands, and be able to anticipate and predict the outcomes that will result from group interaction.[1]

Beyond the system and personal demands he or she faces, the leader must confront other challenges to his or her communication skills. If a leader wishes to gain and retain a leadership position he or she must avoid certain leadership communication behaviors. More specifically, the group member with leadership aspirations must avoid the following types of behavior: (1) being untrustworthy, (2) being manipulative, (3) being uncommunicative, (4) being self-deprecating, (5) being dogmatic, (6) being authoritarian, (7) being withdrawn, and (8) being verbose.[2]

Even if the leader performs his or her basic functions successfully and avoids the threat of being eliminated, he or she must be prepared to face a series of serious communication problems. Leaders must have answers for a variety of persistent questions: how to maintain a high level of interest and involvement among group members, how to determine whether the conceptual level of the discussion is consistent with the knowledge and intellectual ability of the discussants, how to overcome the principal barriers to effective listening, how to discriminate accurately between the discussants' stated and actual intentions, how to deal with the nonpropositional and discontinuous use of the language of discussion that has the effect of obscuring meaning, how to deal with manipulative discussants who are moving to take over leadership, how to deal with discussants who are using techniques of facial management to mislead and deceive others, and so on.[3]

When one considers the demands placed on a leader's communication skills, it is not surprising that many groups experience a leadership vacuum. When one realizes how little attention has been given to leadership com-

[1] A. F. Brown, "Reactions to Leadership," *Educational Administration Quarterly* 3 (1967): 64–69.

[2] J. Geier, "A Descriptive Analysis of an Interaction Pattern Resulting in Leadership Emergence in Leaderless Group Discussion," Ph.D. dissertation, University of Minnesota, 1963, and idem, "A Trait Approach in the Study of Leadership in Small Groups," *Journal of Communication* 17 (1967): 316–323. Geier describes his research, which was geared to identifying those negative behaviors that will eliminate a group member as a potential leader.

[3] E. D. Nathan, *Twenty Questions on Conference Leadership* (Reading, Mass.: Addison-Wesley, 1969), pp. vii–ix.

munication behavior, it is not surprising that the leader's response to communication challenge is often intuitive or even instinctive.

Meeting the communication challenges that are inherent in a leadership
position is a difficult business. We believe that leaders should not only
know which leadership communication behaviors to avoid, but also which
ones to cultivate. This chapter is designed to provide that type of knowledge. By taking the Leadership Communication Behavior Test, the reader
should enhance his or her capacity to deal effectively with the communication challenges that he or she will encounter.

The leader must, of course, make an effort to avoid communication challenges that are insurmountable. One such insurmountable challenge is the
use of a leadership style that is incompatible with the leadership attitudes
of the members of the group.

Choosing the Functional Leadership Style

Many groups have little, if any, freedom of choice as to leadership style.
The nature of their situation may be such that the high-status leader dic-
tates to the rest of the group. Those groups that can make such a choice
are faced with an important question: What leadership style will be most
functional for our group?

Traditionally, the question has been considered strictly in terms of
power relationships in the group. Some members prefer that most of
the power in the group be centralized in one individual. Others prefer that
power be shared by all members of the group. No set of preferences for
a given type of power relationship is intrinsically good or bad. A group
should strive, however, to choose a leadership style consistent with the
preferences of most of the members of the group.

Measuring an individual's attitudes toward, or preferences for, a given
style of leadership is difficult for at least two reasons. First, authorities
cannot agree on the number or kinds of leadership styles that are actually
used in the small group. For example, Halal identifies five types of leadership style: autocracy, bureaucracy, human relations, participation, and
autonomy. But in his thorough review of the leadership literature, he
notes that at least three different labels have been used for the autocratic
style, eleven labels for bureaucracy, seven for human relations, four for
participation, and six separate labels for autonomy.[4]

Secondly, authorities cannot agree on how to measure our attitudes to-

[4] W. E. Halal, "Toward a General Theory of Leadership," *Human Relations* 27 (1974):
404. In his provocative, theoretical approach to leadership effectiveness, Halal identifies
the three primary dimensions of leadership as (1) leadership style, (2) task technology, and
(3) subordinate motivation. Leadership effectiveness depends on the compatibility of leadership with the other two dimensions of leadership.

ward different types of leadership (and leadership roles). Indeed Sweney, Fiechtner, and Samores note that the staggering array of instruments used to measure preferences for a given leadership style include the following instruments: the California F Scale, role preference and role pressure measure from Sweney's Response to Power Model, Fiedler's Least Preferred Co-Worker Scale and Assumed Similarity between Opposites Scale, Costley and Downey's six scales used to measure McGregor's "Theory X" and "Theory Y" constructs, modified scales for the Block and Mouton Managerial Grid, and scales from the 16 PF.[5]

Despite the variety of leadership measures, most instruments attempt to measure an individual's attitudes toward a centralized (or decentralized) leadership style. Recent research suggests that a majority of instruments focus on and measure a person's preference for authoritarian leadership.[6] In spite of some possible methodological deficiencies, the California F Test probably remains the most practical and best measure of one's attitudes toward authoritarian leadership.

In the leadership section in our courses in small-group communication, we stress that groups should employ the leadership style that most closely matches the leadership preferences of the members of the group. To determine such preferences, we ask each group member to take the F test. If scores are high on the test, it suggests that the group should employ a centralized style of leadership.

In spite of its value in helping a group choose a functional style of leadership, the F test does have some limitations. First, some of the items may strike the reader as unrealistic. Secondly, it takes some time to administer. Therefore, we feel that the Preference Test for Leadership Style may be a more useful instrument.[7] This instrument is easy to apply and score.

Choosing a leadership style that is compatible with the leadership preferences of the group members is highly functional in one sense. It means almost by definition that members are likely to be satisfied with the power relationships in the group. For example, individuals who prefer authoritarian or autocratic leadership have a strong need for centralized leadership. Curiously, they may have a strong need to dominate other group members, but if they find they cannot dominate the group, they want another member to dominate. Thus the authoritarian style of leadership can be "considered to be the most rudimentary form of leadership characterized by the use of powerful, authoritarian methods for obtaining compliance, such as force and tradition. As a result, complete control may be exercised over all aspects of subordinate behavior."[8] In a sense, the au-

[5] A. B. Sweney, L. A. Fiechtner, and R. J. Samores, "An Integrative Factor Analysis of Leadership Measures and Theories," *Journal of Psychology* 90 (1975): 75–85.

[6] .Ibid., p. 80.

[7] J. F. Sargent and G. R. Miller, "Some Differences in Certain Communication Behaviors of Autocratic and Democratic Group Leaders," *Journal of Communication* 21 (1971): p. 239.

[8] Halal, "Toward a General Theory of Leadership," p. 404.

thoritarian leadership style in the small group represents a paradox. It is true that members with authoritarian attitudes will probably be most satisfied with an authoritarian leadership style. It is also true that members tend to be most satisfied with group outcomes that they had a major role in producing—such major roles are incompatible with authoritarian leadership.

Communication Style and Quality of Group Outcomes

In many groups, *communication style is apt to be the most important determinant of the quality of group outcomes*. In this case, a *communication style* consists of those *leadership communication behaviors in a group that are sufficiently distinctive so that we may use such behaviors to distinguish one group from another*.

From this perspective, communication style is a very important concept. Group members have little chance to control many factors that may affect the quality of group outcomes. They do have the potential to exert much control over the nature of the communication style in the small group, however. For example, group members may be appalled by a highly formalized communication style that lacks both spontaneity and critical interaction. Significantly, group members typically have opportunities to modify the communication style in their group.

In contrast, group members may have limited opportunities to modify the nature of the task or situation. These factors are often beyond the group's control because they are *external* factors and, as such, are often fixed features. Unlike these fixed external features, the group's communication style is an *internal* factor that is usually under the direct control of group members.

For the group member, this raises a question of great functional importance: What leadership communication behaviors make up the communication style that is most apt to produce high-quality group outcomes? That question is, of course, difficult to answer. Few leadership communication behaviors will be equally desirable for all tasks, situations, and leadership styles. Indeed these factors may have a major impact on the nature of leadership communication.[9] However, we now know that there is a set of leadership communication behaviors that are desirable for a great variety of tasks and situations. Although we cannot go so far as to assert that such

[9] J. F. Sargent and G. R. Miller, "Some Differences in Certain Communication Behaviors of Autocratic and Democratic Group Leaders," *Journal of Communication* 21 (1971): 245, found that style of leadership can have an identifiable impact on the quality and quantity of communication in the small group. Autocratic leaders talk more than democratic leaders and exhibit more negative social-emotional behavior whereas the democratic leader puts more emphasis on asking questions and encouraging participation.

behaviors are always desirable in all contexts or that they are universally accepted, we can confidently assert that these behaviors are consistently associated with high-quality group outcomes.

Many individuals do not have a clear-cut idea as to what leadership communication behaviors are desirable and undesirable. To test your knowledge on this important subject, we have developed the Leadership Communication Behavior Test. It is designed not only to test your knowledge, but also to provide you with a model of those leadership communication behaviors that make up the most functional communication style in the small group. It was developed by summarizing and synthesizing the findings from a variety of recent studies that have examined the relationships between quality of leadership communication behaviors and quality of group outcomes.

To take the Leadership Communication Behavior Test (Figure 12.1), simply answer "true" to those items with which you agree and "false" to those items with which you disagree.

FIGURE 12.1
LEADERSHIP COMMUNICATION BEHAVIOR TEST

_____ 1. Spontaneous expression of feelings is apt to be counterproductive.

_____ 2. One person may profitably dominate procedural, but not substantive, leadership communication.

_____ 3. Trust-building communication helps to satisfy a very important interpersonal need in a group.

_____ 4. Communication that encourages self-disclosure about the members' personal goals and values is a luxury rather than a necessity.

_____ 5. Only the leader should define the nature of the problem the group faces.

_____ 6. Limited participation by a group member is often justified because of the nature of the situation.

_____ 7. Maximum opportunity to express displeasure should be afforded to all members of the group.

_____ 8. In the interests of efficient communication, the member who makes a mistake should be blamed for it.

_____ 9. Keeping lines of communication open between all group members is a goal of secondary importance.

_____10. Dissenting views should be encouraged and protected.

_____11. Effective leaders provide tangible evidence of careful listening.

_____12. Rules for providing social rewards and punishments should be communicated clearly in the formative stages of a group.

_____13. Only the designated leader should seek clarification of vague statements.

_____14. Leaders and potential leaders should frequently initiate discussion of new ideas.

_____15. Critical appraisal of ideas is particularly important in a highly cohesive group.

_____16. The group member who exhibits patience with others is apt to be eliminated as a potential leader.

_____17. One's feedback should be carefully tailored so that it does not raise the level of tension in the group.

_____18. Because of the demonstrated ego-needs of group members, it is impossible to use too much positive reinforcement in a group.

_____19. The member who provides the greatest number of problem-solving responses is rarely perceived as the group leader.

_____20. Talking as much as possible may be a bit tiring, but it will rarely eliminate a group member as a potential leader.

_____21. To avoid inefficient and sloppy communication, the group atmosphere should be as formal as possible.

_____22. Flexible communication is more apt to be viewed as a sign of weakness than a sign of strength.

_____23. Dominant behavior is apt to be more useful than dogmatic behavior.

_____24. To decode ambiguous messages, one should rely on nonverbal rather than verbal cues.

_____25. A leader should be more concerned about the ways group members perceive interpersonal relationships in the group than about his or her own feelings.

_____26. The leader should move openly to expose the deceitful communicator in front of the group.

_____27. The effective group leader is apt to expend more energy in trying to modify the nature of the task than in improving communication.

_____28. Negative reinforcement is the best way to handle the group member who is highly ego-involved on an issue.

_____29. Frequent summaries are important to determine consensus on ideas and to maintain thought continuity.

_____30. Seeking clarification of vague messages and providing summaries are apt to create more problems than they solve.

_____31. Actively empathizing with insecure and reticent members simply reflects a lack of self-discipline.

_____32. In the interests of efficient communication, it may be wise to exert conformity pressure on group members expressing dissenting views.

_____33. Once a group has reached a decision, the leader should move to protect it from conflicting information, which may simply confuse the issue.

_____34. Risk taking is consistently associated with effective leadership.

_____35. Decreasing the size of a group often leads to more effective leadership.

_____36. The tendency negatively to stereotype those who take opposing views must be avoided.

_____37. The leader who is spontaneous tends to stimulate spontaneous communicative interaction among group members.   ·

_____38. The leader should recognize irrelevant as well as relevant suggestions.

_____39. Nominal grouping is often an effective communicative technique when the group is attempting to generate ideas.

_____40. The effective leader tailors his or her communication style so that it is congruent with the needs of group members.

The correct answers for the test in Figure 12.1 and the rationale for each answer have been provided in Figure 12.2. Check your answers against the key, and compute the number of correct answers. If you get thirty-four or more correct, your performance was excellent; thirty-four to twenty-eight is good; below twenty-eight suggests that you should reread this chapter very carefully.

FIGURE 12.2
LEADERSHIP COMMUNICATION BEHAVIOR TEST

(Answers)

1. F—Spontaneity of expression is consistently associated with effective leadership, although it may be precluded in highly directive leadership styles.
2. T—Single-person control of procedural functions often works, but group members resent and resist substantive control.
3. T—Recent leadership research gives trust a very high priority.
4. F—Groups low on self-disclosure frequently lack a sense of interdependency and are low in cohesiveness.
5. F—Contrary to popular opinion, the entire group should take an active role in defining the problem, with a single leader assuming the function only if the group cannot or will not.
6. F—Limited participation typically eliminates an individual as a potential leader.
7. T—Recent research shows that any attempt to inhibit the expression of displeasure is apt to create interpersonal problems.
8. F—The tactic of placing direct blame should clearly be avoided.
9. F—Keeping lines of communication open is vitally important in order to make effective use of the human resources in the group.
10. T—Failure to do so can lead to the groupthink phenomenon.

11. T—Listening and effective leadership are consistently related to each other.
12. T—Failure to do so is often a major source of frustration.
13. F—Any group member may do it as long as it is done.
14. T—Effective leaders frequently initiate new ideas.
15. T—Cohesive groups tend to lack critical interaction.
16. F—Patience has been identified as a quality of effective leadership.
17. F—Dishonest feedback represents a more serious communication problem than an increase in the level of tension.
18. F—Too much positive reinforcement is strongly associated with digressive communication.
19. F—The group member who provides many problem-solving responses is much more apt to be perceived as, and to emerge as, a leader.
20. F—Oververbalization often eliminates a person as a potential leader.
21. F—An overly formal atmosphere tends to be more disruptive than an overly informal atmosphere.
22. F—On the contrary, dogmatic communication typically eliminates a person as a potential leader and creates additional problems.
23. T—Dominant behavior is consistently associated with effective leadership, but dogmatic behavior rarely is.
24. T—See Chapter 8.
25. T—Group members do things more often for their reasons than for yours.
26. F—The problem should be handled by other means.
27. F—Group members can rarely manipulate the task to make it more desirable, but quality of communication can typically be improved.
28. F—See Chapter 7.
29. T—See Chapter 11.
30. F—Such activities may be a chore, but they are a necessity.
31. F—Empathy has been found to be strongly related to effective leadership.
32. F—See the consensus climate in Chapter 8.
33. F—New information may require a modification in the decision(s).
34. F—The advisability of risk taking depends on many factors.
35. T—Excessive group size can reduce leadership effectiveness.
36. T—See section on consensus climate in Chapter 8.
37. T—Recent research strongly supports this relationship.
38. T—To do otherwise would be arbitrary.
39. T—See Chapter 10.
40. T—Generally true, although there are some hazards in employing this technique.

The test in Figure 12.1 should provide you with a clear idea as to the leadership communication behaviors that make up a desirable communication style. Perhaps, more importantly, it should stimulate your thinking about such a communication style. Of course, none of these leadership communication behaviors is suitable for all tasks, interpersonal climates, or situations or for all leadership styles. In that sense, none of the keyed choices is absolutely correct—indeed the correctness of some of the more

difficult choices might legitimately be debated. However, much recent research has been devoted to the specific question of which leadership communication behaviors are associated with high-quality group outcomes. All
of the answers in this test are based directly on such empirical research.
The reader might profitably examine such research as he or she contem-
plates his or her own leadership communication behavior.[10]

Leadership Communication Behavior and Group Outcomes

This chapter has examined the relationship between the quality of communication in a group and leadership effectiveness. This relationship is difficult to examine for a number of reasons. First, the concept of quality of
communication is treated in a unique way in this book. It probably has not
been examined previously in the same ways and in such detail. Therefore,
it is difficult to find a body of empirical studies that apply directly to this
conceptual framework. In addition, leadership effectiveness has been defined in many different ways by those who are examining the subject. In
spite of these difficulties, it seems clear that, in general, the higher the
quality of leadership communication in a group, the more desirable the
group outcomes.

Maier has conducted a series of insightful studies on the relationship
between group process and group product. Although his terminology differs from ours, his results seem clearly to support our thesis. For example,
Maier notes that "it is apparent that a skilled leader can greatly improve
the quality of a group's thinking. This is shown by the fact that only with
the trained leader does the elegant solution occur with any dependable
degree of frequency." [11] Maier's leadership training would embrace many
of the qualities of leadership communication emphasized in the test you
have just taken. Indeed, at least by inference, his research suggests that
quality of leadership communication is the most important determinant of
high-quality group outcomes.

In this book we have described the interpersonal and task outcomes that
are associated with small-group communication of varying quality. Ulti-

---

[10] For a particularly useful sample of research designed to examine the relationship(s)
between leadership communication behavior and group outcomes, see N. R. F. Maier,
Problem Solving and Creativity in Individuals and Groups (Belmont, Calif.: Brooks/Cole,
1970), pp. 334–376; T. J. Long and D. Bosshart, "The Facilitator Behavior Index," *Psychological Reports* 34 (1974): 1059–1068; F. P. Scioli, J. W. Dyson, and D. W. Fleitas, "The
Relationship of Personality and Decisional Structure to Leadership," *Small Group Behavior*
5 (1974): 3–22; D. D. Van Fleet, "Toward Identifying Critical Elements in a Behavioral
Description of Leadership," *Public Personnel Management* 3 (1974): 70–82; and Stogdill,
Handbook of Leadership, pp. 142–155, 220–231, and 247–254.

[11] Maier, *Problem Solving and Creativity in Individuals and Groups,* p. 365.

mately, the outcome that has been given highest priority is the solution, decision, or product with ideational content of the best possible quality. In the leadership literature three major types of group outcomes have been examined, however: (1) group productivity, (2) follower satisfaction, and (3) group cohesiveness. Although these outcomes are not mutually exclusive (it is possible for a highly cohesive group to be highly productive even while the members are highly satisfied), it is difficult to achieve all three outcomes simultaneously in a given group.

For this reason, research examining the relationship between leadership styles and group outcomes often yields perplexing results. For example, centralized leadership styles have often been thought to lead to very productive groups but at substantial sacrifice to the level of cohesiveness and satisfaction in the group. In fact, Stogdill has done an exhaustive and illuminating review of empirical research examining these relationships in his *Handbook of Leadership: A Survey of Theory and Research.*

Stogdill finds that more centralized styles of leadership and leadership behavior (distant, directive, and structured) are more often related to productivity than one would expect by chance; however, the autocratic and restrictive styles are not related to productivity.[12] At the same time, these centralized styles of leaderships tend to depress follower satisfaction.[13]

In contrast, decentralized styles of leadership, which emphasize relationships among members, tend to increase satisfaction of followers. Moreover, such leadership styles, with the exception of the permissive style, tend to increase the level of cohesiveness.[14] Given this relationship between leadership styles and group outcomes, the aspiring leader is faced with an obvious problem. If his or her leadership effectiveness is to be based solely on the choice of leadership style, he or she is confronted with a dilemma. A given leadership style may increase the chances for a desirable outcome in terms of productivity but decrease the chances for desirable outcomes in terms of level of follower satisfaction and cohesiveness.

It is conceivable, of course, that a leader will decide to sacrifice follower satisfaction and cohesiveness because of a strong desire for maximum productivity. In the long term, however, this may be a costly sacrifice. If members' dissatisfaction exceeds a certain point and if cohesiveness drops below a certain point, the actual productivity of a group may be seriously jeopardized.

The aspiring leader is faced with an obvious question. What, if anything, can he or she do to maximize the chances that all three types of group outcomes will be desirable? Significantly, Stogdill concludes that only one set of behaviors seems positively related to high productivity, high follower satisfaction, and high cohesiveness. He labels such behaviors "initiating

---

[12] Stogdill, *Handbook of Leadership*, p. 403.

[13] Ibid., p. 404.

[14] Ibid., pp. 404–405.

structure." He notes that the behaviors associated with what we might call the "initiating structure" style of leadership are "behaviors that let followers know what is expected of them and what they can expect of the leader; the behaviors are neither autocratic, restrictive, directive, nor task pressure oriented." [15] Although Stogdill does not use the term *communication style* to describe such behaviors, they are entirely compatible with the leadership communication behaviors that we have described in the Leadership Communication Behavior Test.

In short, the central thesis of this book is that quality of communication is a major determinant of the quality of group outcomes. Moreover, we probably have greater opportunities to affect positively the quality of communication in a group than to affect those other factors that help determine quality of group outcomes. Certainly, the nature of leadership communication in a group can have a major impact on the quality of those outcomes. In broadest perspective, we would maintain that the most feasible way to lead a group effectively is to work actively to maximize the quality of our own leadership communication behavior and to maximize the quality of the communication of other group members.

SUPPLEMENTARY READING

Bormann, E. G. *Discussion and Group Methods: Theory and Practice.* New York: Harper and Row, 1975. Chapter 11.

Dubno, P. "Leadership, Group Effectiveness, and Speed of Decision." *The Journal of Social Psychology* 65 (1965): 35–60.

Eagly, A. H. "Leadership Style and Role Differentiation as Determinants of Group Effectiveness." *Journal of Personality* 38 (1970): 509–524.

Fiedler, F. *A Theory of Leadership Effectiveness.* New York: McGraw-Hill, 1967. Chapter 15.

Goldman, M., and Fraas, L. A. "The Effects of Leader Selection on Group Performance." *Sociometry* 28 (1965): 82–88.

Miller, R. D. "A Systems Concept of Training." *Training Development Journal* 23 (1969): 4–14.

Shaw, M. *Group Dynamics: The Psychology of Small Group Behavior.* New York: McGraw-Hill, 1971. Pp. 267–280.

Stogdill, R. M. *Handbook of Leadership: A Survey of Theory and Research.* New York: The Free Press, 1974. Chapters 12, 18, 31, and 39.

QUESTIONS AND EXERCISES

1. Identify the leadership problems that arose in your group. What steps should have been taken to deal with these problems?

[15] Ibid., p. 405.

2. Did any potential leader in your group eliminate himself or herself as a possible leader by his or her negative behaviors? If so, what did he or she do? Why were his or her behaviors perceived as negative?

3. Identify the "system" and "personal" demands to which the leadership in your group should have responded. Describe the responses to these demands. Were they adequate? Why or why not?

4. How did your group choose a leadership style? Was the choice a good one? At this time, each member of your group should take the Preference Test for Leadership Style and compute individual scores. Discuss the scores as a group, and decide which leadership style would be most suitable for your group.

5. As a group, prepare a one-hour discussion to be presented in class. Do the following things: (1) identify those leadership communication behaviors that helped raise and lower the quality of your group's product, (2) explain why the leadership communication behaviors were desirable or undesirable, and (3) indicate specifically what might have been done in your group to improve the quality of leadership communication behavior.

6. As a group, prepare a one-hour training session on leadership effectiveness, and present it in class. Emphasize what leadership behaviors are desirable and how members of a group may be trained to engage in desirable leadership communication behaviors.

Index